M000305834

FROM BOSS CRUMP TO KING WILLIE

Elle,
Thank you for your support.

Otis Sanford

From
BOSS CRUMP
to
KING WILLIE

HOW RACE CHANGED MEMPHIS POLITICS

7-30-17

Otis Sanford

The University of Tennessee Press / Knoxville

Copyright © 2017 by The University of Tennessee Press / Knoxville.
All Rights Reserved. Manufactured in the United States of America.
Cloth: 1st printing, 2017; 2nd printing, 2017.

Photos courtesy of the *Commercial Appeal* unless otherwise noted.

Library of Congress Cataloging-in-Publication Data

Names: Sanford, Otis, author.
Title: From Boss Crump to King Willie: how race changed Memphis politics /
    Otis Sanford.
Description: First edition. | Knoxville: The University of Tennessee Press,
    [2017] | Includes bibliographical references and index.
Identifiers: LCCN 2016049353 (print) | LCCN 2016050451 (ebook) | ISBN
    9781621903222 (pbk.) | ISBN 9781621903239 (pdf) | ISBN 9781621903246
    (Kindle)
Subjects: LCSH: Memphis (Tenn.)—Politics and government—20th century. |
    Memphis (Tenn.)—Race relations—History—20th century. | African
    Americans—Tennessee—Memphis—Politics and government—20th century. |
    Crump, Edward Hull, 1874-1954. | Herenton, W. W. (Willie W.), 1940-
Classification: LCC F444.M557 S26 2017 (print) | LCC F444.M557 (ebook) | DDC
    305.896/073076819—dc 3
LC record available at https://lccn.loc.gov/2016049353

To Bertha Sanford, who taught me the joy of writing; Freddie Sanford, who taught me the importance of newspapers; and Elaine Y. Sanford, who encouraged me to write this book.

Contents

ILLUSTRATIONS

ACKNOWLEDGMENTS

Special thanks to the staff of the *Commercial Appeal*, including Louis Graham, editor, and John Sale, assistant managing editor for visuals, for their outstanding cooperation in the research for this book. Also, a huge thanks to G. Wayne Dowdy and the staff at the Memphis and Shelby County Room at the Benjamin L. Hooks Central Library for assisting with research.

I also owe gratitude to Ben Kamin, Thelma Balfour, and Gene Dattel, three fine authors who counseled me in thinking through the process for writing this book; to Suzanne Kerr, a former colleague who also advised me, and to Dr. Matthew Haught and Teri Hayslett, my colleagues in the Department of Journalism and Strategic Media at the University of Memphis, for their assistance as well.

In addition, I must remember with gratitude my high school journalism teacher, the late Charles Ray Owens, who launched my journalism career. And thanks to my closest mentors: Robert Oakley, Angus McEachran, Dr. Will Norton, the late Flora Rathburn, and the late Robert G. McGruder.

Finally, thanks to all of the people who consented to interviews and candidly discussed their role in the political evolution of Memphis. Their stories are what helped to make this book possible.

Introduction

THE POLITICAL EVOLUTION OF MEMPHIS, Tennessee, from the rise of Edward
Hull "Boss" Crump to the eighteen-year reign of Dr. Willie W.
Herenton, the city's first elected black mayor, is one of the most com-
pelling stories in American history. Its numerous characters—primarily elected and appointed leaders and community activists, both black
and white—were complex, controversial, and, in many cases, charismatic.
Some, especially Crump, were at times conniving and ruthless. But most
were compassionate and forward thinking.

I have no doubt that each of them possessed a genuine love for Memphis.
And each contributed mightily to the city's progress as well as its racial
divisions. Crump, for example, was similar in many ways to other big-city
political bosses of the early decades of the twentieth century, including
Tom Pendergast in Kansas City and William M. "Boss" Tweed in New York
City, although Crump was never officially linked to any overt criminal
corruption.

Arrogant and paternalistic, Crump achieved enduring success as the
undisputed boss of Memphis by building an unprecedented and unrivaled
coalition of black and white voters at a time when racial segregation in
America and black disfranchisement through the South were at their zenith.
Still in his twenties when he won his first elected office in Shelby County
in 1902, Crump became convinced that Memphis sorely needed a strong
leader. It also needed political structure if the city was to grow and prosper.
And he considered himself just the man—the only man—for the job.

At the other end of this story is Herenton, a native son of Memphis and arguably the best-educated man to ever occupy the mayor's office. He is a former Golden Gloves boxing champion and, like Crump, a tall, imposing figure with a persona as big as they come. In 1991, Herenton was simply the right person in the right place at the right time to take advantage of the unified effort by black voters in Memphis to, at long last, elect one of their own as mayor.

Because he was fast with his fists, Herenton as a young man earned the nickname "Duke." His supporters and admirers later called him "Doc." But during his time as mayor, his harshest critics—mostly white conservatives from the suburbs surrounding Memphis along with conservative radio talk show host Mike Fleming—often referred to him as "King Willie." Neither Crump nor Herenton cared much for the monikers their detractors gave them. But the names stuck throughout their respective political careers. Hence the title of this book is *From Boss Crump to King Willie*.

My decades-long desire to tell this story stems from the fact that I have loved Memphis for as long as I can remember. This once-barbarous city atop the Chickasaw Bluffs overlooking the Mississippi River has had a profound and positive impact on my life as a journalist. But that's not the sole reason I love Memphis. The city has a pace, a character, and a history that I have long respected and admired. So much has changed politically and socially in Memphis over my lifetime, and the city is arguably not as prosperous as it once was. Peer cities such as Nashville, Charlotte, and Louisville have experienced greater economic growth over the last two decades primarily for two reasons—less poverty and less racial strife.

But Memphis in the early twentieth century was a boom town of sorts. It was the center of the cotton trade, which made plenty of Memphians wealthy and influential. In addition, African Americans prospered as business owners and professionals in far greater numbers than those in other major southern cities. And despite an economic decline, Memphis today remains the metropolis of the mid-South—particularly the surrounding counties in West Tennessee, northern Mississippi, and eastern Arkansas—and is the only city of any real size within a two-hundred-mile radius.

I am among those middle-of-the-pack baby boomers from a rural community not far from Memphis who craved a life beyond the two-lane gravel roads and cotton fields. Thanks to the newspapers, magazines, and television shows that came into our home, I was completely taken by the allure of the big city.

Our farm was located two miles west of tiny Como, Mississippi, and about fifty miles due south of Memphis. I am the last of seven children born to Freddie and Bertha Sanford. And our forty-acre farm was the center of my world for the first eighteen years of my life. The cotton produced on several acres of our land was my family's primary source of income. We grew our own vegetables in a large garden a stone's throw up the hill from our farmhouse. And we maintained "truck patches" that yielded sweet potatoes, Irish potatoes, watermelons, and even, for a couple of years, popcorn. We raised several head of cattle and hogs, along with scores of chickens that roosted in a tin-top hen house just steps away from our back porch. My father was not much of a hunter, but he kept a shotgun and a rifle beside his bed, mostly to ward off the foxes that occasionally preyed on Mom's prized chickens.

Before Dad could afford to buy a used John Deere tractor to till the fields, we relied on two mules to do the job. My two older brothers were primarily responsible for the plowing, but once I was old enough to help out, I gladly did my part on many spring and summer days. When I wasn't helping with the plowing, I was chopping cotton, picking peas, pulling corn, or digging potatoes with my siblings and my mom, who supervised it all.

As I worked on the farm, I constantly fantasized about a life in the city. And that city was always Memphis. Four of my uncles had long since left the farm life in Mississippi and were established Memphis citizens. Three of them had been in the military and, as a result, got good jobs after they returned home; one worked for the U.S. Post Office, a coveted job for any black person, and another uncle worked at the Memphis Defense Depot, which managed the delivery of supplies for the U.S. Army.

Every trip we made to Memphis to visit them at their homes on well-kept streets in South Memphis and the Orange Mound neighborhood was for me a special occasion. I was dazzled by Memphis' streetlights, taxi cabs, bustling traffic, and fancy stores. I particularly relished our family's annual trip to the all-black Tri-State Fair, and later the Mid-South Fair, after it was integrated in the mid-1960s. I delighted in just seeing the huge, red-cursive Kellogg's sign at the cereal plant on Airways Boulevard in route to the fairgrounds. Nothing like that existed in Como. I also loved shopping with my mother at the downtown department stores, especially Goldsmith's, Lowenstein's, and Shainberg's. It was an added bonus when we took the number 4 Walker city bus from my uncle's home on Wilson Street in South Memphis to get downtown.

Memphis is also where we got our news, through the Mississippi edition of the *Commercial Appeal* newspaper, which was mailed to us six days a week. I started reading the paper every day at the urging of my father, who had little time to spend with it but wanted to keep up mostly with news about baseball. I dutifully kept him informed, but eventually my appetite for news expanded beyond the sports pages.

By the time I was ten years old, I was genuinely interested in Memphis politics, Memphis crime, and even Memphis society news. In addition, I listened constantly to most of the Memphis AM radio stations, particularly WDIA, the first radio station in America to broadcast an all-black format, and WLOK, WMPS and WHBQ. I idolized all of the disc jockeys on WDIA and knew precisely when they went on the air each day. They included A. C. "Moohah" Williams, Nat D. Williams, Rufus Thomas, Robert "Honey Boy" Thomas, Chris "The Love Man" Turner, Herb "The K" Kneeland, Theo "Bless My Bones" Wade, and Ford Nelson. On April 4, 1968, WDIA was the medium that first told my father and me of the death of Dr. Martin Luther King Jr., who was killed by an assassin's bullet at the Lorraine Motel in downtown Memphis.

At the age of thirteen, I officially discovered journalism firsthand when as a seventh grader I wrote my first published article for the *Eagle Echo*, the student newspaper at North Panola Vocational High School. The fact that this segregated school, where students used textbooks handed down from the white county schools, actually published a newspaper was remarkable in itself. When I saw my first article in print, I knew for certain that I wanted to be a reporter. My dream job was to work for the *Commercial Appeal*, and I feel blessed to have achieved that goal. I was hired first as a summer copy clerk in 1973, before beginning my junior year as a journalism student at the University of Mississippi. Less than four years later, in January 1977, I was hired full time at the *Commercial Appeal* as a general assignment reporter, and that began my association with one of the South's preeminent newspapers—a relationship that continues to this day.

Through the years, I have grown to understand and appreciate Memphis' colorful and turbulent history, from the race riots after the Civil War through the yellow fever epidemics of the 1870s and the steady influx into Memphis of African Americans from the plantations of Mississippi, Arkansas, and West Tennessee. This book seeks to capture the one hundred–plus years of struggle by Memphis's African Americans for social acceptance and political inclusion. It also examines the role editors of the city's newspapers played in shaping the political fortunes of Memphis.

At various points over the last one hundred years, these editors were either ardent supporters or impassioned critics of the powerful men who ran Memphis—particularly Boss Crump. The most noteworthy of these editors was Charles Patrick Joseph Mooney, who was managing editor of the *Commercial Appeal* as Crump began his rise to power after his election as mayor in 1909. Mooney's attitude toward Crump and the black Memphians who supported him in subsequent elections can only be described as disdainful. I hope the fact that Mooney and I held the same position at the *Commercial Appeal*—managing editor—will go down as a worthy footnote in the history of the newspaper and of Memphis. Mooney cared deeply about good journalism and about his adopted city of Memphis—as I do. But someone with my skin color would never have been welcomed onto his newspaper staff in any capacity other than janitor or delivery boy.

Under Mooney's leadership, the *Commercial Appeal* became known as the "Old Reliable." But most black Memphians of that day said the nickname really meant "reliably racist." Mooney, Crump, and most of their contemporaries from the dawn of the twentieth century were products of their segregated world. They all wanted to make Memphis better, but they believed that black people were inferior and needed to keep to themselves because society deemed it that way. Crump, however, was at least astute enough to understand that Memphis's burgeoning black population could be a political asset, and he strongly believed that law-abiding blacks were entitled to some dignity, including the right to vote. Mooney, on the other hand, never fully recognized any real value in the black community. And that sentiment, unfortunately, remained a part of his newspaper's culture and legacy for more than forty years after his death in 1926.

Mostly, though, this book is about the citizens of Memphis and the myriad factors that led them to entrust political power to Crump for almost fifty years. This book is also about the events, some tragic, that created the massive population shift that made Memphis a majority African American city. It is about the patience and persistence of black citizens in Memphis who endured terrorism, shook off racism, and accepted the segregated climate of their day while also displaying an air of privilege because they could exercise the right to vote several decades before African Americans in most other parts of the South. A choice few in Memphis's black community even became major players in the white-dominated world of national politics.

Crump's death in 1954 effectively meant the end of the organization that had called all of the political shots in Memphis, Shelby County, and Tennessee for forty-five years. I was just a year old when Boss Crump died, and of course all of his closest allies and loudest detractors have also long since passed on. But his reign as the Man in Memphis is well documented in other books, newspaper articles, archives, and personal papers, and I have relied heavily on these sources to paint a detailed picture of Crump and his relationship with black Memphians.

Other parts of this book are a memoir of sorts, representing my experiences and perspective as a journalist in Memphis for most of my adult life. Many of the events recounted here are based on my own reporting for the *Commercial Appeal*, starting in 1977, and on interviews with numerous people who played key roles in the evolution of Memphis politics.

Finally, it is my hope that this book will give both Memphians and non-Memphians, young and old, a deeper appreciation of why this city—warts and all—is such an amazing place. When judged by the standards of today's society, the political history of Memphis is not a particularly pretty or uplifting story. It includes literally and figuratively plenty of villains, cutthroats, and cowards. But it also includes people of courage, goodwill, humility, compassion, and steadfastness. It includes people who spent their lives—and in some cases lost their lives—working to make Memphis better for all its citizens, regardless of race. Simply put, this book is my view of the political evolution of Memphis, *From Boss Crump to King Willie*.

CHAPTER 1

THE MAN FROM HOLLY SPRINGS

"**ISN'T THIS A FINE THING**," the old man grumbled, nearly inaudibly, as he lay beneath an oxygen canopy, his once-resounding voice now just barely above a whisper. "I've spent all my life in a goldfish bowl and now I'm going to end up in a tent." It would be the last quip ever to come from the lips of the man who had spent his entire adult life spewing one acid barb after another, directed mostly toward those he counted as political enemies. This time, however, the old man's sarcasm was directed inward, and it effectively summed up the public life of a boisterous, often vindictive, yet intensely private southern patriarch.

Death arrived at Edward Hull Crump's meticulously landscaped home at 1962 Peabody Avenue in his beloved and adopted hometown of Memphis, Tennessee, at 4:53 p.m. on October 16, 1954. A steadily failing heart had forced Crump to his bed for good on October 3, one day after his eightieth birthday. His deteriorating condition had been evident for weeks. But the old man remained mentally alert until the last forty-eight hours of his life, when he finally lost his keenness of mind; eventually he lapsed into a semi-conscious state.

Mere weeks earlier, in August 1954, he had put all that he had into one final political campaign, the Tennessee Democratic primary election, which saw the incumbent governor, Frank Clement, defeat Crump's former ally–turned–nemesis, Gordon Browning of Huntingdon, Tennessee. Following a pattern that persisted throughout his political career, Crump had supported Browning during the lawyer's first successful run for governor in

1936. The two men previously served in the U.S. House of Representatives together, and the Crump organization produced nearly 60,000 votes in Shelby County for Browning that year, compared with just 825 for his opponent. Browning dispatched a telegram to Crump immediately after that election: "There are 60,000 reasons why I love Shelby County."[1]

But Browning and Crump soon parted ways after Browning decided he would be his own man in the governor's office and not a Crump puppet. After less than a year as governor, Browning called a special legislative session to pass a bill that in effect limited the voting power of Shelby County in the Tennessee General Assembly. Browning's action came at a huge cost. He was soundly defeated for reelection in 1938 by Prentice Cooper, a state senator from Shelbyville. Crump spent heavily on political advertising for Cooper and delivered enough votes in Shelby County to give him the victory by a margin of seventy-three thousand votes across the state. Speaking to the *Commercial Appeal* about Browning fourteen years later, Boss Crump said, "I served with him in Congress, but didn't realize he was so unworthy."[2]

Browning, however, recaptured the governor's office in 1948, the year the Crump machine suffered its most embarrassing election losses ever, both nationally and at the state level. But with the emergence of Clement in 1952, Browning's grip on the office was again short lived. During the 1954 campaign, Crump insisted on coordinating the local effort for Clement, working mostly by telephone from his home since he was physically unable to get to his downtown office at Main Street and Adams Avenue. As the August primary approached, Crump frequently rousted his top lieutenants, including Shelby County District Attorney General John Heiskell and City Commissioner Joe Boyle, from bed late at night or early in the morning to attend to campaign duties. Crump was so immersed in running the campaign that he failed to cast a vote himself on election day, the first time ever he missed voting.[3]

Clement's victory over Browning in the August 1954 Democratic primary meant that Crump's political career ended the same way it had started more than fifty years earlier, as a winner. But his dogged determination to personally keep Browning from reclaiming the governor's office exacted a final toll on the old man's health. Two weeks after the election, on August 23, Crump was admitted to Baptist Hospital, ostensibly for a routine physical checkup, and remained there until September 6. All that members of Crump's political inner circle could do was wonder and worry, since no visitors were allowed and the old man's room number was kept private.

That didn't stop Commissioner Boyle, a trusted Crump soldier who had previously served the Boss as police chief. Boyle somehow discovered the location of Crump's room and went to check on his longtime friend and mentor. Boyle waited just outside the room until a Crump family member stepped into the corridor. The ailing old man overheard their conversation outside his room and immediately recognized Boyle's voice.

Seconds later, Crump was standing in the doorway in his pajamas, greeting Boyle with a handshake. "How are you, Mr. Crump?" Boyle asked. "Fine," the old man replied. "I will be out of here in a few days."[4] Not wanting to bother the Boss further, Boyle turned and walked out of the hospital with mixed feelings of relief and uneasiness. It was the last time Boyle or any of Crump's other political minions saw him alive.

As word of Crump's death made its way around town during the early evening hours of October 16, associates and underlings flocked to the house on Peabody while city residents by the hundreds began to drive slowly past the home to pay their respects or to simply confirm that the Boss really was gone. The first person to arrive at the home was Logan Hipp, who was summoned immediately after Crump's death by a member of the family.

Known to most Memphians as "Shifty" Logan, Hipp was a familiar and colorful character around town. He had earned his nickname not so much because of any illegal dealings, although it wouldn't have been surprising for him to pull a few con jobs on unsuspecting pigeons. Rather, Shifty earned the name because of his crafty moves in the boxing ring. A 2009 article in *Memphis Magazine* noted that a local sportswriter once described Shifty's boxing style this way: "There was never anything else in heaven or earth quite like this crazy gyration, but if you could picture the frantic antics of a kangaroo which had just experienced the misfortune of sitting on an anthill, you will get a faint idea."

According to the magazine, a thirty-year-old Shifty in 1933 convinced former heavyweight champion Jack Dempsey to take him on in an exhibition match at a downtown Memphis theater: "The 'Manassa Mauler' (Dempsey's nickname) toyed with his challenger for a round or two, as Shifty jumped this way and that, even landing a few punches on Dempsey's noggin. That was enough. A reporter at the match wrote, 'Dempsey's incomparable right then flicked out, and this time Shifty was carried away literally and figuratively.'"[5] Despite having been coldcocked by Dempsey, Shifty and the former champ remained friends and the two staged some thirty other exhibition matches in later years.

After his boxing days, Shifty worked for the Memphis Fire Department and then for the city's sanitation division. The 2009 magazine article recounts, in Shifty's own words, one incident that occurred while he was steering the back end of a hook-and-ladder truck during his relatively brief tenure as a fireman: "We were going to some little punk two-dollar fire somewhere, and we turn a corner, and I get the back wheels stuck in a wet street-car track." Shifty was thrown from the truck and knocked unconscious. When he came to, the magazine said, he apparently thought he was back in the ring and starting thrashing around and yelling, "I ain't out yet." Later, while explaining the accident, he told fire department officials, "Just because your front end gets around the corner, ain't no sign your back end is going to make it."[6]

As a city employee, Shifty was obligated to work in political campaigns, and he eagerly obliged. He was frequently seen canvassing the polls on election day, helping any and all candidates whom Crump supported. If there was any trouble at the precinct, as there often was during Crump's reign as political boss, Shifty Logan, the burly, pug-faced ex-boxer, could easily settle the dispute by knocking a few heads, if need be.

How and why Shifty became one of the first Memphians to reach Crump's home mere minutes after his death remains a mystery to this day. More than likely, it was for security reasons. Crump had enemies, and he trusted Shifty because he always had the Boss's back. The grieving family obviously felt a small bit of comfort just having Shifty there. And Shifty's loyalty was evident by his mad rush to Peabody Avenue that brisk Saturday afternoon in October 1954. In a sense, it represented a microcosm of Memphis. Everyone in the Bluff City—whites and blacks, people who loved him and people who loathed him—stopped what they were doing that day to pay respect to the incomparable political boss whose notoriety also made headlines nationally and internationally. At work or at play, they paused to honor the leader who had singlehandedly transformed Memphis from a dysfunctional, bawdy, and corrupt Mississippi River town to a growing, progressive, and clean city.

His methods were not always scrupulous. Some were at best shady and underhanded, and at worst shamefully vindictive. But the man who had cultivated innumerable friends in high places and who ran Memphis with an iron fist was, at his core, compassionate and kindhearted. He also was overly defensive, paternalistic, and egotistical. If you crossed him, even over a minor issue, you paid dearly for it. He wasn't just content with belittling his opponents. He wanted to crush them.

Memphians, black and white, rich and poor, acquiesced to the Crump way. He fostered allies not just in the halls of Memphis and Shelby County government, but in virtually every civic, social, garden, and country club in the city. His greatest strength eventually came from the black churches and black community leaders who fueled the Crump political machine. Crump had been in their midst for so long that they all felt they knew him personally. Memphians, black and white, handed him unfettered power for nearly half a century, accepting his machine politics because through it, he served Memphis even as he empowered himself. And he brought order to the disorder—by any means necessary.

Edward Hull Crump Jr. was born October 2, 1874, near Holly Springs, Mississippi, a bucolic town less than fifty miles southeast of today's Memphis city limits. His father was a Confederate soldier who was wounded in battle during the Civil War and died of yellow fever in 1878, when Crump was four years old.[7] Young Crump grew up poor by white society standards on his family's modest plantation just outside Holly Springs and later in town after his mother gave up plantation living. As a child, Crump was comfortable around the black sharecroppers and day laborers, only a few years removed from slavery, who populated rural Mississippi.[8]

Young Crump became a better-than-average baseball player for the teams in and around Holly Springs. Known as Skinny, he played first base, and even then he had no trouble cultivating fans. During games, Crump's supporters would shout, "Throw it to Skinny at first base. He'll get it out of the sky."[9] The experience on the baseball diamond left him with a strong love of sports, and the competition it fostered, that lasted the rest of his life.

He also had an industrious side. One of his first jobs was selling fruit to passengers aboard trains that stopped in Holly Springs. He also worked setting type for the *Holly Springs South Reporter*, the local newspaper owned by a second cousin.[10] In his late teens, however, Crump realized that rural Mississippi had little to offer a young man with his lofty ambitions, and he developed a hankering for city life. At eighteen, he packed a bag and boarded a train bound for Memphis. He had no job waiting for him. But he was sure that Memphis offered the promise of success that country living could never provide.

The first person he met when he set foot in downtown Memphis was Richard Borner, who worked at a firehouse just down the street from the train station. After introducing himself, young Crump asked Borner to direct him "to the middle of town," where he might find a room and board.[11] Crump struggled at first to find meaningful employment, but he eventually landed a job as a bookkeeper for a saddle, buggy, and harness company. Crump's work ethic was quickly noticed, as were his good looks and southern charm. On January 22, 1902, the twenty-seven-year-old Crump married twenty-four-year-old socialite Bessie Byrd McLean, the only child of wealthy business executive Robert McLean and his wife, Carrie.

Because of the McLean family's social standing, the midweek evening wedding at Calvary Episcopal Church was the talk of Memphis and was covered extensively in all the local newspapers. The *Commercial Appeal* described the nuptials this way: "A lovelier bride and a more popular bridegroom than those of last evening when Miss Bessie McLean and Edward H. Crump were united in marriage have never given interest to a wedding in Memphis. The edifice was elaborately and artistically decked with palms, ferns, bride roses and white satin ribbons. . . . The chandeliers throughout the church were wreathed in Southern smilax."[12]

The newspaper said the bride "has won in the few years of her young ladyhood an unsurpassed popularity by reason of her beauty and charming personality. Mr. Crump is one of the most able and energetic young businessmen of the city and is possessed of a character of sterling worth that places him high in the estimate of all who know him."[13]

The following year, Crump moved from employee to owner of the saddle and harness company. He purchased the business with credit from his well-to-do father-in-law, a onetime vice president of the highly successful William R. Moore Dry Good Company. Borner, the first man Crump met in Memphis, was among the many who bought buggies from Crump's company simply because they admired the new owner. In later years, Borner was chief operator of a fire wagon named for Crump, which to this day remains on display at the Fire Museum of Memphis downtown. Crump never forgot the old firefighter. And Borner, like most Memphians, idolized Crump. "There'll never be another friend like him," Borner told a reporter after Crump's death.[14]

Crump's penchant for business soon gave way to a deeper passion—politics. He had fallen in love with his adopted hometown and married into one of the city's most prominent families. But he grew more and more disheartened with the leadership of local government. The potential for Memphis to become a great city was there. Commerce on the Mississippi River, along with the bustling cotton business centered along the riverfront, had transformed Memphis from a rough-and-tumble backwater hamlet teeming with cutthroats and con artists to a growing metropolis.

Yet racial strife was ever present. When Crump arrived in town in 1892, Memphis was only twenty-six years removed from one of the most horrific race riots in American history, in early May 1866. A detailed report prepared two months later by a special investigative committee appointed by the U.S. House of Representatives concluded that the riot was in reality a massacre of scores of black men, women, and children by angry mobs of whites. The investigators interviewed 170 people, including black citizens who escaped the horrors and were willing to explain the carnage they had witnessed.

The report stated: "Most of the newspapers in the city had grossly misrepresented nearly everything connected with (the disturbance) while great efforts had been made by the citizens to belittle it into a simple row between some discharged Negro soldiers and the Irish police. It was called in derision the 'nigger riots,' while in fact . . . the Negroes had nothing to do with it after the first day except to be killed and abused."[15]

The report further stated: "The outbreak of the disturbance, resulting from collision between some policemen and discharged colored soldiers, was seized upon as a pretext for an organized and bloody massacre of the colored people of Memphis, regardless of age, sex or condition, inspired by the teachings of the press, and led on by sworn officers of the law composing the city government, and others."[16] The committee concluded that white Memphians strongly resented the Union army's presence in the city during the Civil War and were especially hostile to the black soldiers who wore the Union uniforms.

After the war ended in 1865, some of the discharged black soldiers who chose to remain in Memphis brought their families and other blacks to settle there as well, exacerbating the hostility. In all, forty-six black men, women, and children and two whites—a policeman and a fireman—were killed in the disturbance. Seventy-five people were wounded, and the violence resulted in property damage totaling $130,981, mostly to Freedman

Bureau schools and black-owned houses, cabins, and churches.[17] The congressional investigators also pointed out that white Memphians had developed "intensified hatred against Negroes" after slavery was abolished, and that "it was impossible for a colored man in Memphis to get justice against a white man."[18]

Despite the atrocities of May 1866, African Americans continued to flow into Memphis in the decades that followed. They, like Crump, were drawn by the promise of a better life away from the cotton fields and plantation shacks. The influx became part of the Great Migration in which African Americans fled the rural South by the hundreds of thousands. Those who could afford it traveled farther north to Chicago, Detroit, Milwaukee, and Cleveland, while others settled in St. Louis or went to the Northeast to New York City, Washington, D.C., Baltimore, and Philadelphia.[19]

This mass movement of black Americans can be directly attributed to the end of Reconstruction, during which blacks held numerous elected offices throughout the South, including the governorship of Louisiana.[20] After Reconstruction, African Americans were systemically excluded from public office through state laws and—more often—violent intimidation. As a result, most African Americans who flocked to Memphis had no illusions of ever gaining equality with whites, although blacks could vote in Memphis, a practice strictly forbidden elsewhere in the Deep South after Reconstruction.

These new settlers were simply looking to be far removed—not so much by distance, but mentally—from a sharecropper's existence. Some, however, were influenced by the fact that, if nothing else, they could at least have a good time after hours in Memphis, with its plethora of segregated saloons, houses of prostitution, and gambling joints, mostly on Beale Street. They also had heard about the prosperous blacks who called Memphis home, including Robert R. Church, who opened his first saloon on Beale in 1865 and went on to become arguably the wealthiest black man in America.

Church, the son of a white steamboat captain and a black seamstress, can accurately be described as the father of black capitalism in Memphis, and for a time he was extremely active in local political affairs. He even ran for a Memphis City Council seat in 1882, but he lost.[21] Church used his considerable earnings from the saloons to become a legitimate Beale Street banker, opening the Solvent Savings Bank and Trust in 1906.[22] He also made a fortune in real estate and was later joined by others who saw Memphis as a budding mecca for black business prosperity. Soon Memphis was flourishing with black doctors, dentists, and lawyers who genuinely cared about the welfare of all black Memphians but also considered themselves several notches above the mostly poor and uneducated blacks in the city.

Although many of these aristocratic blacks could get an audience with the city's white elected leaders if they wished, Church, the most influential among the black upper crust, eventually lost interest in local politics, as did most of the white cotton barons who were busy earning their wealth on Front Street. This relative lack of accountability from the business sector contributed to the inefficiency and disorder in government that Crump noticed soon after his quiet arrival on the Memphis scene. He was determined to change it. And he did, with help from thousands of unlikely allies—the growing number of black citizens in Memphis.

CHAPTER 2

COURTING THE BLACK VOTE

NINE YEARS BEFORE E. H. Crump was born, Robert R. Church—also a native of Holly Springs, Mississippi—opened a bustling saloon on Beale Street and started raking in the money. But by the time his well-educated son, Robert Jr., took over the family banking business after his father's death in 1912, Crump had become ensconced in the high society of Memphis and was well on his way to building his enduring political machine.

Unlike the elder Church, Robert Jr. had a much more enduring passion for politics, knowing full well that—because he was black and Reconstruction was over—he would likely never hold elected office himself. Instead, he used his standing as inheritor of his father's business to establish the all-black Lincoln League, an organization devoted to Republican politics and the legacy of the sixteenth president of the United States, the man responsible for freeing the slaves through the Emancipation Proclamation. Young Church became the most influential Republican in Memphis and, for a time, Crump tolerated his lofty political standing. But eventually Church's sway with national Republicans would put him on a collision course with the ascending boss of Memphis.

Crump formally entered politics on October 21, 1902, when he was elected as a delegate to the Shelby County Democratic Legislative Convention. He next got elected to the Board of Public Works, part of Memphis' convoluted bicameral legislative system. It was there that he saw firsthand the gross inefficiency and sheer lack of accountability under which the city operated.

When he pushed for changes, he was shot down every time. For example, when he sought in 1906 to raise the license fee for the city's 599 saloons from $60.00 to $250.00, the plan was roundly rejected.

When Crump introduced another ordinance that same year to set a speed limit of six miles an hour for the cars that were beginning to appear on unpaved Memphis streets, that proposal was voted down as well.[1] With each setback, Crump grew increasingly frustrated, and he resigned the Board of Public Works seat in September 1907. But he wasn't through with public office; he was merely regrouping. Three months later, Crump announced his candidacy for a vacancy on the more powerful city Board of Fire and Police Commissioners. He won easily, but it was clear Crump had set his sights on becoming mayor and changing local governance for good.

When the Tennessee General Assembly gathered in Nashville for the start of its 1909 legislative session, Crump traveled to the state capital to lobby for passage of a bill allowing Memphis to convert to a commission form of government. The stated intent was to create a more efficient government by giving a few commissioners—elected citywide—the authority over all legislative and administrative affairs in the city. The bill easily passed and became law in February 1909.[2]

Crump then turned his attention to the mayoral election later that year. His opponent was former mayor Joe Williams, whom Crump painted as the poster child for city inefficiency and stagnation. He blamed Williams for failing to get streets paved and failing to deal effectively with the city's crime problem. But Williams had one important asset that Crump didn't have—the support of African Americans, saloon owners, and the white working class. In an omen of the many racially polarizing elections to follow, Crump's supporters appealed exclusively to business leaders and the white middle class.

Newspaper advertisements bought by the Crump campaign trumpeted the charge that Williams was supported by low-life whites and unscrupulous blacks. In one ad, Crump accused Williams of organizing "crap-shooting negroes, who will sell their vote for a few cents or a drink of mean whiskey."[3] The allegation was laced with irony, since that is exactly how the Crump machine is said to have secured black votes in subsequent elections.

On election day, November 4, 1909, Crump took no chances. He was determined to win at all costs. He personally showed up at a black polling precinct and spotted a man carrying a ballot that had already been marked

Courting the Black Vote

into the voting booth. He and the voter argued. When the voter tried to get past Crump, the candidate punched him in the face and then "threatened further violence if he saw any more marked ballots."[4] That evening, as the votes were being counted at the old Shelby County Courthouse—where Ellis Auditorium was later built—Crump waited anxiously for the last ballot box to arrive from a polling site set up in a tent near the corner of Peabody and McLean.

Sam Kahn, a *Commercial Appeal* reporter who later became the paper's city editor, was there surveying the results. Years later, Kahn recounted the tense scene: "The hour was getting late and still the deciding box had not come in. Mr. Crump, whom I had known when he was in the harness and buggy business with the firm of Crump & Rehkopf, . . . said, 'Sam, let's go out and get that box.' Mr. Crump got a pistol from a friend in the crowded room. He handed it to W. J. Hayes, later police chief, with this injunction: 'Bill, don't let anyone touch those ballots or sheets until I get back.' No one did. Mr. Crump, with the owner of a car and I, went to the voting tent, picked up the box and tally sheet and brought them back to the courthouse. When the figures from the retrieved box had been tallied, Mr. Crump was in politics to stay."[5]

Crump defeated Williams by a scant seventy-nine votes. It was the closest and most thrilling victory of his long political career, he said years later. A recount confirmed Crump's victory, but Williams contested the outcome in court. Eventually, a chastened Williams stated in open court that the election had been "painfully honest." Williams's own attorney, F. T. Fitzhugh, in apologetic fashion, asked the court to dismiss the charge of election fraud against Crump. And Williams penned a letter to the mayor-elect saying there had indeed been "an honest recount. . . . The boxes have only disclosed the greatest ignorance and carelessness on the part of many voters, and the exposure of fraud has failed most utterly. . . . I want the dead past to bury its dead, and in withdrawing my suit, I wish to say I hope your administration will be a credit to yourself and friends, and of great benefit to the community. And I further wish to assure you that I leave this contest without animosity."[6]

The victorious Crump learned a valuable lesson in the 1909 mayoral election. If he planned to be successful in politics over the long haul, he couldn't rely only on the business establishment, the white middle class, and upper-crust voters. He also needed the common people. More specifically, he needed African Americans, and he immediately devised plans to get them, by hook or by crook. Interestingly enough, the same year that Crump was elected mayor, the National Association for the Advancement of Colored People (NAACP) was formed to address escalating violence—mainly lynchings—against black Americans and to secure black voting rights, which had been systematically stripped away in other parts of the country.

With Crump's election also came a change in the structure of city government. The unwieldy bicameral city council was replaced by a smaller board of commissioners, with the mayor as its head. The group would be elected at-large and would act as both legislators and heads of city departments. Crump also was successful in giving himself and all future mayors four-year terms instead of two, starting in 1911. The dapper, six-foot-tall mayor also set about dealing with the city's out-of-control crime problem. Immediately after taking office, Crump told the Memphis newspapers his administration would deal with crime in three ways: "Rid the city of thieves and thugs, break up the practice of carrying pistols, and clean up the dives which have flourished so long in this city."[7]

The police response to Crump's declaration was swift. Blacks were ordered off the streets at midnight. Those who languished were taken to jail. Open gambling was curtailed, some dance halls were shut down, and prostitution was confined to a certain area of town.[8] But these efforts were not sustained. In fact, by 1916, Memphis had become the "murder capital" of the nation, owing to its reputation for hand-to-hand street brawls, knife fights, and shootouts.[9] Crump himself relied on payoff money from the city's purveyors of vice to operate his political organization, although he took great pains not to personally accept money or bribes from such businesses. He also insisted that members of his administration take no money or gifts. If they did, they were summarily dismissed.[10]

During his reelection bid in 1911, Crump set his sights on wooing black voters. The idea, he said years later, came from one of his lieutenants— most likely Frank Rice, his longtime campaign manager and most trusted adviser. Rice reminded him that "the Episcopal Bishop's vote in the ballot box counted for no more than that of the humblest Negro. All votes look alike in the ballot box."[11]

The first opportunity to court the black vote came early in Crump's first term, when he nudged the Memphis Park Commission to establish a segregated park for black residents. Mostly because of his rural upbringing, Crump was a nature lover. He frequently took long Sunday afternoon rides to the countryside and he loved to throw outdoor parties and picnics. He was an outspoken advocate for fine recreational parks for the citizens of Memphis, and he came to believe that black citizens shouldn't be left out.

Surprisingly, the *Commercial Appeal*, which had been reliably indifferent—even hostile—to the concerns of black Memphians, endorsed the idea of a "Negro park." In an April 20, 1910, editorial, the newspaper wrote, "The decent negroes of Memphis want a park. By a common consent they have withdrawn from the public parks now used by white people. We believe it would be a good thing for Memphis and a good thing for Negroes."[12]

But the racism that had so defined Memphis for decades flared once more with the volatile issue of a city-owned park for black citizens. Col. Robert Galloway, chairman of the Memphis Park Commission, was vehemently opposed to the idea. After months of debate, another Galloway chimed in, rather mockingly, with a suggestion that a tiny island in the middle of the Mississippi River would be a good spot for the Negro park.

In a statement published in the *Commercial Appeal* on February 14, 1911, probate court judge Jacob S. Galloway, who was no relation to the parks chairman, noted that the island was covered by water in the spring, and when the water subsided it left "a rich alluvial deposit . . . which accounts for the rich luxuriant growth that covers the island. The Negro ought to be in his glory among all that tropical growth." The judge added that Negroes are not banned by law from city parks, but "they do not visit these places because they know they are not wanted."[13]

Crump was not amused. He drafted a letter on February 22, 1911, stating, "I desire to say that I am in favor of a Negro park if a suitable location can be had. Otherwise I am opposed to it, and you can be assured that the commissioners of the city will give the Negro park question every consideration before it is finally acted upon."[14] The belief among many white Memphians was that if too many blacks congregated at one time in their own park away from Beale Street, the frolicking would get out of hand. Black millionaire businessman Robert R. Church had built his own park for African Americans on Beale Street in 1899, and city parks chairman Robert Galloway didn't want another one.

The contentious debate continued for two more years before the issue was settled. When it was, Crump got his way. In April 1913 the city purchased fifty acres of remote land east of the city limits and created Douglass Park. Robert Galloway immediately resigned as park commission chairman in protest. Black Memphians, however, rejoiced. And on July 11, 1914, hundreds of black citizens gathered at the park for the official dedication. The *Commercial Appeal* noted in its coverage that the park was "inaccessible for the most part." Most visitors had to take the Raleigh Springs streetcar line and then ride in wagons to get to the secluded site. Those who could not hop aboard the wagons were forced to walk.

Black speakers at the park dedication included Rev. T. J. Searcy and Rev. T. O. Fuller. Addressing the concerns of white residents, Searcy said he hoped the Negroes of Memphis would make Douglass Park "a place for high-class recreation and not one for idle frolicking." The keynote address was delivered by Judge J. M. Greer, who represented Crump and the white citizenry. Greer gave a lengthy speech reminding his black audience how far they had progressed since slavery was officially abolished just forty-nine years earlier.

Greer also acknowledged being "born a slaveholder" and spoke fondly about a slave boy two years older than him who personally tended to his needs. "Out of this irresponsible, menial condition, the Negro came into freedom with no property, no education and with limited intelligence." Despite what he called progress, Greer still dismissed the notion that blacks were the equals of whites, and he said his audience should "always demand separation socially" from the white race. The white man, he said, had endured a thousand years of struggle in preparation for self-government. Blacks, he implied, were incapable of governing themselves.[15]

No one in the crowd appeared offended by Judge Greer's racist remarks. They looked beyond his words and saw the seeds of a brighter day for them in rough and rowdy Memphis. The Douglass Park dedication became a defining moment in the relationship between Crump and the burgeoning black citizenry of Memphis. Make no mistake, Crump's support for the black park was more about politics and power than altruism. He was clearly running all areas of government in Memphis now and was not about to let Robert Galloway, Jacob Galloway, or anyone else dictate public policy or tell him what he couldn't do.

For black Memphians, the creation of Douglass Park was validation that their votes for Crump were starting to pay off. In the 1911 mayoral election, blacks had abandoned Joe Williams, who sought a second time to win back the seat, and voted overwhelmingly for Crump. They had grown weary of being tormented by white racists. They were content, for the moment at least, with receiving crumbs from Crump. And they became convinced that the new boss in town would listen to more of their concerns, and perhaps finally put an end to the reign of terror against black citizens that had existed for decades.

Lingering in the minds of some African Americans was the brutality that occurred less than a year before Crump arrived in Memphis. In early 1892, the city had witnessed its worst acts of racial unrest since the deadly riots pitting white city policemen against black Union soldiers in 1866. Only this time, the violence was quickly exposed to the world by famed black journalist Ida B. Wells. Born in Holly Springs, the same town as Crump but twelve years earlier, Wells was the daughter of house servants. But she became a prolific writer and co-owner of the *Free Speech and Headlight*, a black newspaper in Memphis. Through her editorials, Wells, a former schoolteacher, condemned the lynching of black people that was so common in Memphis and other areas of the South, notably Mississippi, Alabama, and Georgia—a reign of terror that helped lead to the formation of the NAACP.

The 1892 incident began after a small group of black citizens partnered to open a grocery store at Walker Avenue and Mississippi Boulevard. The store was in direct competition with a nearby white grocer, who did not take kindly to the new establishment. Hostilities ensued and three black men associated with the new store were thrown in jail following a gun battle with police. A mob later removed the men from their cells, took them to a remote area of Memphis, and shot them to death. The killings created outrage among black Memphians, many of whom left the city bound for Oklahoma.[16]

Wells wrote extensively about the incident. But what infuriated whites in Memphis more was a later editorial in which she insinuated that southern white women were sexually attracted to black men. "Nobody in this section of the country believes the old thread-bare lies that Negro men rape white women," Wells wrote. "If Southern white men are not careful they will over-reach themselves and public sentiment will have a reaction, or a conclusion will be reached which will be very damaging to the moral reputation of their women."[17] Memphis newspapers strongly condemned Wells's editorial, with the *Memphis Commercial* stating, "There are some things the Southern white man will not tolerate, and the obscene intimations of the foregoing have brought the writer to the outermost limit of public patience."[18] The *Memphis Scimitar* was even harsher. Unaware that Wells wrote the editorial, the paper demanded that the writer be tied to a stake, branded, and castrated "with a pair of shears."[19] Wells was forced to flee to the North for her safety and never returned to Memphis.

Under Crump, such blatant racial lawlessness subsided somewhat as he attempted to forge a relationship with blacks that would further his political goals. Lynchings and beatings of black citizens continued, to be sure. But for the most part, racial harmony prevailed in Memphis—at least on the surface. Crump found it politically expedient to bring black community leader Robert Church Jr. into the fold. After inheriting his father's money and business, Church threw himself into Republican politics and became one of the most influential members of the Grand Old Party—known as the Black and Tan faction—in the city.

When a Republican occupied the White House, Church controlled the distribution of federal patronage jobs in Memphis, including those at the post office, which had a majority African American work force. He also had a say in appointments to the positions of U.S. marshal, U.S. attorney, and federal court judge, although those posts were reserved exclusively for whites. Crump accepted Church's status with the national Republicans so long as it didn't interfere with his local political organization. But once Democrat Franklin Roosevelt took office, Crump had a direct line to the White House and no longer needed Church's influence. As a result, the Boss ordered the foreclosure and sale of Church's real estate properties for failing to pay city taxes, and Church eventually left Memphis.[20]

Crump's organization also used money collected from illicit businesses in Memphis to pay the two-dollar poll tax for blacks, who in turn flocked to the polls by the thousands on election day to vote the Crump ticket. After voting, Negroes were rewarded with watermelons and other goodies. Crump's critics, including local and out-of-town newspapers, alleged that the organization also "voted" blacks, many of whom never even appeared at the voting precincts; they were merely recorded as casting ballots for Crump's slate of candidates because the Boss's organization held their poll-tax receipts. There is little doubt that this nefarious "absentee" voting on behalf of blacks did occur, although Crump dismissed the allegations as nothing more than "over-zealousness" by the press and his political opponents.[21]

Perhaps the greatest example of Crump's sway with black voters came in 1914 during a legendary campaign for Shelby County sheriff. Crump, who was in the third year of his second term as mayor, toyed with the idea of running himself for sheriff. He simply did not like, nor trust, the incumbent sheriff or the county attorney general, Z. Newton Estes. And if you were on Crump's hit list, he came gunning for you. But the Boss opted not to run after City Attorney Charles Bryan researched the city charter and discovered that city officials were prohibited from holding any other elected city or county office.[22] However, Crump shrewdly recruited a close friend, John A. Riechman, to run for sheriff instead. Riechman was president of the Memphis Associated Charities and had done an admirable job providing relief for victims of a devastating 1913 flood—many of them black—who took refuge in tents at the fairgrounds.

Partly because of a filing snafu and partly because election officials didn't appreciate Crump's heavy-handed approach, Riechman's name was not allowed on the August 1914 county ballot. But Crump would not be deterred. He launched a massive write-in campaign and set up blackboards on street corners, including along Beale Street, to teach black voters how to correctly spell Riechman's name—a requirement for the vote to count. The campaign was dubbed "Write it Riech. Place the I Before the E." Trucks carrying large signs with Riechman's name also moved slowly through mostly black neighborhoods, encouraging voters to join the write-in campaign.

Riechman's opponent, Sheriff T. G. Tate, and the *Commercial Appeal* were incensed. The write-in campaign also targeted thousands of white voters, but the *Commercial Appeal* made it appear as though only black citizens were being used by the Crump machine. In a highly inflammatory editorial on August 5, 1914, the day before the election, the newspaper said Crump was "conducting schools on Beale Street . . . seeking to teach a gin-drinking nigger enough to make a mark and write a name."[23] The *Memphis News-Scimitar*, however, took a polar opposite editorial stance. In a front page editorial also on August 5, the afternoon newspaper encouraged the write-in campaign while endorsing Riechman and the entire Crump Democratic ticket. The editorial and a political ad inside the paper also reminded voters who could not write that they could ask poll workers for a sticker bearing Riechman's name and place it on the paper ballot, then mark an X beside it.[24]

Tate, meanwhile, sought support from middle-class and well-to-do white voters. Two days before the election, he and his deputies carried out a raucous late-night raid at a gambling house called Kinnane and Honan's Place at Front Street and Winchester Avenue, which catered to black customers. The *Commercial Appeal* described it as "one of the most spectacular raids ever made on a Memphis saloon and gambling house." During the raid, twenty-one black patrons were arrested along with the two owners, who were white, for allegedly violating the city's gambling laws. Although twenty-one blacks were detained, the *Commercial Appeal*'s account of the incident said scores of others fled through windows and side doors while hundreds more African American spectators stood on the streets outside gawking at the roundup. J. M. Maher, a justice of the peace, was called to the scene that night and he "released all of the Negroes on a statutory appearance bond of $250 each." The white owners were released on their own recognizance.[25]

But neither the *Commercial Appeal*'s harsh criticism nor Tate's eleventh-hour gambling raid could hamper Crump's well-organized write-in effort for Riechman. Black and white voters alike supported the entire Crump ticket and Riechman received 13,466 votes to just 4,480 for Tate. After the election, the *Commercial Appeal* noted that the outcome was "a thorough exhibition of the power and evils of machine politics in Memphis."[26] To Crump, however, the paper's criticism was nothing more than sour grapes—and validation that his political strength had become entrenched in both city and county government, which infuriated his critics even more.

The quest to take down Crump and his ever-growing political machine got new life after two Tennessee governors—Democrat Ben Hooper and his Republican successor, Thomas C. Rye—signed legislation to force local municipalities to abide by the state prohibition laws. Crump derived most of his political strength by allowing saloons and dives that sold illegal liquor to flourish in exchange for payoffs that were then used to pay the poll taxes for black voters.

After Rye's election in the fall of 1914—with support from Crump—he pushed through an ouster law that provided a way to remove local elected officials who "neglected their duties" by not enforcing the prohibition law.[27] Attorney General Estes finally saw his chance to get rid of the Boss. In response, Crump shut down the saloons the day after Rye signed the ouster legislation into law. But before long, the joints were back in business. Crump's opponents—supported by the *Commercial Appeal*—filed an ouster petition against the mayor and his police department henchmen in September 1915 accusing them of graft and dereliction of duty. Crump initially proclaimed his innocence, but on November 3, he and the others pled guilty in chancery court and were removed from office.[28]

Courting the Black Vote

Crump earlier that year was resoundingly reelected to a third term, and he tried to make the case in court that this ouster should only apply to his second term. But the Tennessee Supreme Court ruled that his removal applied to both his second and third terms as mayor. Although he pled guilty, Crump insisted that his ouster from office was orchestrated by corrupt Wall Street tycoons who controlled the privately owned power company in Memphis. Almost from the moment he got into city government, Crump had begun pushing for a publicly owned utility, arguing that it was more cost effective for the city and Memphis utility customers. It was a fight he eventually won with the creation of the Memphis Light, Gas and Water Division (LG&W) in 1939.

But rather than continue the legal fight, the savvy boss devised a new strategy. He was sworn in for a third term on February 22, 1916, collected $879.31 in back salary, and promptly resigned—a process that took all of two minutes.[29] The newspapers trumpeted the end of the Crump machine, but they couldn't have been more wrong. Less than six months after leaving the mayor's office, Crump was easily elected as Shelby County trustee, the most profitable office in county government thanks to a fee system that allowed the office holder to keep some of the proceeds he collected. He was reelected to that office three times, all while still calling the shots in city government. And the African American vote helped make it all possible.

Crump's alliance with black leaders in Memphis paid huge dividends for his organization. During the 1911 mayoral campaign, for example, Crump courted the black vote through Harry H. Pace, a business partner of famed jazz musician W. C. Handy. Pace organized a group known as the Colored Citizens Association of Memphis and interviewed both Crump and his opponent, Joe Williams, the former mayor who had previously enjoyed black support. After the process was done, Pace recommended that the group endorse Crump: "The other candidate promises everything and I fear he will do nothing; but this redheaded fellow frankly declines to promise some of the things we want, but convinced me that he will fulfill the promises that he did make."[30]

Crump also built an enduring base of support with black pastors and other community leaders in Memphis, most notably Blair T. Hunt, longtime principal of Booker T. Washington High School and pastor of Mississippi Boulevard Christian Church. Hunt became Crump's staunchest ally in the black community and a chief defender of his political machine. After Crump's death, Hunt told the *Commercial Appeal* that the longtime boss had been a "positive" friend of the black community who through the years always asked, "All right, we've done such-and-such for the white people. What are we doing comparable for the colored?" Hunt dismissed black critics of Crump, telling the newspaper that they are "those who had interests in profitable crime and those who wanted to move too rapidly toward desegregation."[31]

Years later, in another newspaper interview, Hunt described Crump as "an ardent segregationist, as most whites were then. He was wrong, as later events showed. But he shouldn't be ridiculed for it. He was a product of his time. We oldsters have been criticized for supporting Mr. Crump. But we didn't have the 1954 (Brown versus Board of Education) decision or the Civil Rights Act. We had to accept certain things to survive. A lot of times we had to smile to keep from crying. But we had good schools. Memphis came closer to fulfilling the separate-but-equal doctrine as anywhere I know."[32]

Hunt's support and admiration for Crump never wavered. In a letter to Mayor Walter Chandler, a loyal Crump lieutenant, in 1940, Hunt wrote, "Mr. Crump is almost a human idol to us." He assured Chandler that most members of the black community also supported his administration and the efforts by city police to rid the city of crime. "Bank on my people, they will not fail you."[33] A similar letter came to Chandler from Minister Arthur W. Womack, pastor of Collins Chapel CME Church. "You and Mr. Crump are loved and honored by my congregation and I want you to speak to them some Sunday in the near future."[34]

In July 1940, Hunt and other black leaders even urged the nomination of Crump for vice president on the ticket with Franklin D. Roosevelt at the Democratic National Convention. In a handwritten letter to Chandler on July 17 of that year, Hunt wrote, "Thousands of Memphis Negroes will be happy if you will use your influence in having Mr. E. H. Crump's name presented to be vice-president."[35] Crump acknowledged the sentiments but never entertained the notion of seeking such a high office.

Throughout his life, Hunt advocated a slower, more deliberate trek toward desegregation and full racial equality. In speeches, interviews, and writings, he continually admonished younger African Americans to be patient and not push too aggressively for expanded civil rights. In a poignant letter published in the *Memphis Press-Scimitar* on February 4, 1956, Hunt likened the plight of "Old Man Race Relations" in Memphis to that of a bedridden patient suffering shock and pain after being operated on by the

U.S. Supreme Court. Blacks and whites in Memphis were now the nurses and attending physicians: "It is ours to attend the 'patient,' to administer the needed opiates and help during the period of convalescence.

"As an interested observer of the social scene, I am a gradualist. Experience and observation have taught me that you cannot cure a disease in a day. . . . So come let us reason together. Our job is clear-cut. We know something of the ailment of our patient. 'Old Man Race Relations' has suffered from a complication of phobias and manias, of fears and frustration and frenzies, of misunderstandings and misquotes, of resentments and resistances, of stupidity and stubbornness, of traditions and tragedies. He has long needed treatment. He still needs careful attention. In our anxiety to effect a cure and a too-rapid recovery, let us not alienate our friends and colleagues, persons who are just as interestedly anxious to help in the work as we are. . . . There are many people who want to help in raising the status of the Negro.

"Let us not place such friends in such an embarrassing position, where they become the helpless targets of extremists in their own circles, because of intemperance of feeling and expression on our part. . . . None of us want second-class citizenship. But there is a widening gap among us regarding the methods . . . regarding the question of immediate, revolutionary change versus gradual, evolutionary change. Personally, I am a gradualist. I am an evolutionist, not a revolutionist. I know many other negroes are gradualists. I believe I voice their sentiments when I advise that agitation evokes trouble and strife begets strife. Let's toss both agitation and strife overboard. Let's substitute persuasion, reason and merit."[36]

Hunt's lifelong stance as a gradualist on racial equality endeared him greatly to Crump. The Boss appreciated men of integrity and standing in the community, black or white. He appreciated them even more if they saw things his way politically. Indeed, Crump had given more attention to the plight of blacks in Memphis than any city leader who preceded him. Starting with Douglass Park, he expanded recreational facilities and decreed that they be named for upstanding African Americans. He ordered the hiring of more black teachers for the segregated schools and eventually black policemen, and he sought to end police brutality against black residents.

Crump also vigorously opposed the Ku Klux Klan when it sought to run candidates for city offices in 1923, although he eventually brought one Klan-sponsored candidate—Clifford Davis—into the Crump organization.

Davis was elected city judge on the Klan ticket in 1923, but later renounced the group. In 1940, with Crump's blessing, Davis went to Washington as a U.S. congressman representing Memphis. (The federal building in downtown Memphis bears Davis's name, along with that of Odell Horton, appointed the first black federal judge in Tennessee.) Crump also saw to it that blacks had "their day" at the Memphis Zoo. And he laid the groundwork for building a city-owned hospital for black residents, which became the E. H. Crump Hospital in the 1950s.

Like most Memphians of both races, Crump also considered Tom Lee a hero, after the African American laborer singlehandedly rescued thirty-one white people from an overturned sternwheeler, the *M. E. Norman*, on the Mississippi River on May 8, 1925. At Crump's direction, Lee was given a city job in the "East Garbage Division" and Crump received periodic updates on his welfare. In a December 7, 1940, letter to Crump, Mayor Walter Chandler reported that Lee was living in a debt-free house at 923 Mansfield, which had been given to him by members of the Engineers Club, who were among those Lee had saved.

Lee's "record of work started with the city of Memphis Department of Public Works in the spring of 1927 and during the time that he has served the City of Memphis . . . there has been no record of this Department having any trouble with the services he has rendered during his work hours."[37] It was also Crump who orchestrated the creation of the park on the banks of the Mississippi River in downtown Memphis that is named in honor of Tom Lee. Crump even suggested construction of the obelisk monument recognizing Lee's heroic act and organized a committee to help pay for it.

Historians have debated whether Crump ever used the term "nigger" as a direct racial slur. His biographer, William Miller, wrote that Crump "never used the word 'nigger,' and he did not permit his sons to use it." Miller, quoting Crump's son Edward during an April 1962 interview, wrote, "Father never let us use any term that would be offensive to the dignity of a person."[38]

But it seems totally implausible that Crump, given his upbringing and the times in which he lived, never uttered the slur, which was used so commonly by whites during that era. David M. Tucker, in his book *Memphis Since Crump*, recounted an incident around 1939 when Crump personally telephoned the black editor of the *Memphis World* newspaper and issued this warning: "You have a bunch of niggers teaching social equality, stirring up social hatred.

I am not going to stand for it. I've dealt with niggers all my life and I know how to treat them. That darn paper is using Communist propaganda—we are not going to put up with Pittsburgh stuff here. This is Memphis. We will deal with them in no uncertain terms and it won't be in the dark—it will be broad daylight. You be sure to tell them I said so. We are not going to tolerate a bunch of niggers spreading racial hatred and running things their way. Tell them Mr. Crump said so. You understand me?"[39]

There was also a far less heated incident in the early 1940s, when Crump agreed to a brief meeting in his office with Luke Weathers, a young black Memphian who aspired to join the Tuskegee Airmen and become a pilot. Weathers knew that the only way to fulfill his dream was with help from the boss of Memphis. But Crump dismissed the idea, telling Weathers, in essence, there are no "nigger pilots." Weathers then showed Crump a clipping from the *Pittsburgh Courier* newspaper about the Tuskegee Airmen. Crump immediately picked up the phone and called his friend in the White House, President Franklin Roosevelt. Two weeks later, Weathers had his appointment to the cadet corps in Tuskegee.[40]

No one can deny that Crump made life better for black Memphians and even welcomed the counsel of a few black community leaders. But his personal and political history clearly shows that he harbored racist feelings. He went to his grave opposing full integration of schools, parks, and other public accommodations. Granted, he abhorred the vicious treatment of blacks, particularly by the police, and he publicly spoke out against such treatment. Miller, his biographer, wrote that Crump in his later years "took the leading Negro newspapers and Ebony (magazine) so as to keep abreast of Negro thinking."[41]

With his paternalistic mindset, however, Crump always felt he knew what was best for everyone, especially the blacks who lived under his political system. His was a plantation mentality. He was simply unwilling to give the black citizens of Memphis too much too soon. He never for a moment entertained the thought of running a black candidate for public office. And for most of the years that the Crump machine was in control, few wanna-be black candidates dared to seek an elected seat. One exception was Dr. Joseph E. Walker, a well-known African American business leader who sought a seat on the Memphis City Schools Board of Education in 1951. Walker ran without the blessing of Boss Crump, who, along with Mayor Watkins Overton, had no interest in accepting a black voice in the governance of local schools. Walker ran a credible race, receiving more than seventy-four hundred votes, but lost to the Crump slate.[42]

Years earlier, in 1912, black businessman H. C. Purnell sought election to the county commission. Purnell's supporters assured then-mayor Crump that Purnell posed no challenge to the Boss's authority. They were merely seeking a modicum of black representation in local government. As with Walker in 1951, Crump was largely dismissive of Purnell's campaign, and he lost the election.[43]

Crump's standing with national Democrats and his African American constituency took an even greater hit during the 1948 national elections. President Roosevelt, Crump's close friend and fellow Democrat, had died in office of a massive stroke on April 12, 1945. And Crump was never fond of Vice President Harry S Truman, who ascended to the presidency on Roosevelt's death. Crump strongly opposed Truman's nomination for a full term at the 1948 Democratic Convention because Truman had integrated the U.S. Army and was generally a proponent of civil rights. Crump split with the national Democratic Party and supported the candidacy of Dixiecrat Strom Thurmond, an avowed segregationist from South Carolina. "I would be willing to go to jail and stay there the balance of life rather than abide by it (civil rights)," Crump proclaimed. ". . . In his (Truman's) scheming, cold-blooded effort to outdo Henry Wallace and Governor (Thomas) Dewey of New York for the Negro vote, he has endeavored to reduce the South to a country of crawling cowards."[44]

Crump also angered black Memphians, including many of his strongest allies, by refusing to permit the Freedom Train, which carried an exhibition of patriotic documents, to stop in Memphis because the train's sponsors insisted that visitors not be segregated by race. Once the 1948 election was over, Crump's Dixiecrat candidate, Thurmond, had been soundly defeated. The aging political boss also suffered defeats that year in races for Tennessee governor and U.S. Senate. The losses were a severe blow to the organization and marked the beginning of the end for the Crump machine.

Most African Americans in Memphis remained respectful and appreciative for what Crump had tried to do for them over the years. But as the old man's health began to wane, restlessness was developing among black people throughout much of the South. Ever so slowly, it was making its way into the Bluff City—not from the established black aristocratic class, but from a younger generation that knew Memphis's history as a place that was

Courting the Black Vote

hostile to blacks but also where blacks had held elected office during the late 1800s. And this young generation was ready for greater social change.

On May 17, 1954, five months before Crump's death, the U.S. Supreme Court issued its landmark decision in *Brown v. Board of Education* outlawing "separate but equal" schools and setting the stage for the dismantling of Jim Crow laws across the South. The civil rights movement was poised for a spectacular and volatile takeoff. But during the summer of 1954, Crump— his heart failing more by the day—was oblivious to it all. He threw himself into one last political campaign to reelect Frank Clement governor. He succeeded, then almost immediately took to his bed. And on Saturday afternoon, October 16, the boss of Memphis quietly passed away.

CHAPTER 3

CRUMP AND THE PRESS

BOSS CRUMP'S PERSONAL PHYSICIAN pronounced him dead at 4:53 on a Saturday afternoon. It was the absolute worst time of the day and worst day of the week for the *Memphis Press-Scimitar*, the city's evening newspaper, which did not have a Sunday edition. The paper's final edition had already gone to press that afternoon with just a bulletin on the front page saying Crump was in a deep and profound coma.[1] Copies of the final edition were being delivered to subscribers and to single-copy locations as Crump was taking his last breath.

As we say in the newspaper business, Crump's death did not occur on the *Press-Scimitar's* time. And he probably wanted it that way. The old man knew how newspapers worked. He was keenly aware of the power of the press and the competitive nature of reporters and editors to get the big story first. But he hated the *Press-Scimitar*, particularly its crusading editor Edward Meeman, so much that it's not inconceivable that he stubbornly clung to life until after the paper's last deadline of the day.

The Saturday morning edition of the *Commercial Appeal* also reported Crump's comatose condition, quoting his doctor as saying it was a "terminal situation." Crump, the story said, had been "unable to take nourishment since early Friday morning and he was under an oxygen tent all the time. His pulse is weak and he is getting medication by hypodermic, but is not responding." Crump's temperature was recorded at 102. The end was near.[2]

But if Crump's cantankerous side really intended from his deathbed to ruin the *Press-Scimitar's* breaking news scoop, it didn't work. On this

Saturday, both papers were fully staffed and were on death watch for the most famous and most talked-about Memphian since Andrew Jackson, James Winchester, and John Overton, who founded the city in 1819. Reporters and editors of both papers had prepared several advance stories about Crump and his political career. They were merely waiting for confirmation of his death from his home at 1962 Peabody. When that word finally arrived at the *Press-Scimitar* newsroom at 5:00 p.m., the staff—many of whom stayed well past the end of their shift—rushed an extra edition to the presses. The banner headline read, "DEATH TAKES E. H. CRUMP." The lead story in the five-cent Extra edition quoted Frank Pidgeon Jr., Crump's son-in-law, as saying there were about ten to fifteen members of the Crump family at his bedside when he died. Bobby Crump Jr., the patriarch's grandson, told the paper Crump was unconscious when he took his last breath. "He suffered no pain. It was very easy."[3]

Press-Scimitar reporter Clark Porteous wrote the lead story, describing Crump in flattering terms that belied the paper's overall attitude about the Boss over the previous twenty-three years of Meeman's tenure as editor. "He was a familiar figure to Memphians since the 'gay 90s,' first as a tall, thin young fellow with flaming red hair, (and) in later years as a tall, erect, well-set-up man with long white hair curling out from under a huge hat, always dressed immaculately in rather unconservative garb," Porteous wrote. "When he walked down the street, it was an event."[4]

The paper's Extra-edition coverage of stories and photographs consumed virtually all of the front page and most of page 2. The staff created two additional pages, 5A and 6A, for spillover coverage. The *Press-Scimitar* noted, rather ironically, that Crump died on what had already been decreed by Mayor Frank C. Tobey as Harmony Day in Memphis.

Meeman penned a front-page analysis, obviously written in advance of the death, asking, "What will happen to Memphis city government?" Instead of focusing solely on Crump's impact on Memphis, the mid-South, and the nation, Meeman used his piece to advocate once more for a governmental structure much different from the commission form of government that Crump had instituted and fiercely protected for more than forty years. Meeman, as he had done numerous times previously, said the five-member commission was "hopelessly out of date (and) worked only because of Mr. Crump's dominating personality."[5]

The *Commercial Appeal* also produced an extra edition that evening, commonly known as a bulldog edition, for street sales only. The front-page headline screamed, "DEATH COMES TO E. H. CRUMP." Circulators for both papers quickly scrambled to find as many newsboys as they could late on a Saturday afternoon to hawk the extras on street corners downtown and at every major shopping center around the city. One of those newsboys summoned to work was Jackson Baker, currently a senior editor for the *Memphis Flyer*, who sold papers in a bustling shopping center at Lamar Avenue and Airways.[6] The shopping center borders the black community of Orange Mound, and black residents as well as white Memphians snapped up the papers until they were sold out.

The following morning, the *Commercial Appeal*'s regular Sunday edition was dominated with coverage of Crump's death. A rare three-line banner headline on the front page summarized it all:

E. H. Crump Dies At His Home At Age 80;
Services Will be Held Tomorrow Afternoon;
Political Organization Left Without Leader[7]

Crump's funeral started at 2:30 p.m. on Monday, October 18 inside his Peabody Avenue home. It was a simple, but touching service with a few invited guests. As his body was being laid to rest one hour and sixteen minutes later at Elmwood Cemetery, the *Press-Scimitar* was putting to bed its final Monday afternoon edition with full coverage of the Crump funeral. Porteous again wrote a poignant, detailed account of the service and burial. He ended the piece with the closing prayer given at the service by Dr. Donald Henning, rector of Calvary Episcopal Church: "O Lord, support us all the day long, until the shadows lengthen and the evening comes and the busy world is hushed and the fever of life is over and our work is done. Then in thy mercy grant us a safe lodging, and a holy rest and peace at last. Amen."[8]

Crump's death didn't just end a five-decade-long political dynasty. It also ended a tumultuous fifty-year relationship between the Boss and the city's newspapers. When Crump first entered Memphis politics in 1902, there were four white-owned daily newspapers operating in the city—the *Commercial Appeal*, the *Morning News*, the *Memphis Press*, and the *Memphis Scimitar*. Two years later, businessman Gilbert D. Raine bought the *Morning News* and the evening *Scimitar* and merged the two into the *News-Scimitar*, published in the afternoon. As the brash young Crump started to make a political name for himself, he quickly realized the importance of newspapers in getting his message of change to the people of Memphis. He also understood, more than most, that the one who wins over the newspapers, is the one who wins elections. Crump soon found allies among the *News-Scimitar* editors who supported his ideas for reform of city government. The paper also supported Crump's call for public ownership of utilities.[9]

The *Commercial Appeal*, the largest and most influential of the city's paper, was far less supportive of Crump and his emergence on the political scene. The paper's skepticism of the young redhead would eventually morph into outright hostility, led by Charles Patrick Joseph Mooney, managing editor. Mooney, a devout Catholic, was a brilliant editor and newsroom leader who was adored by his staff. He wrote the timeless editorial headlined "Jesus the Perfect Man," which the newspaper still publishes each year on Christmas. Mooney's journalistic credentials were without rival among the city's newspaper editors of his time. But he also possessed a sinister side. Mooney's disdain for Crump's tactics was matched only by his dismissive—and, yes, racist—attitude toward African Americans, particularly those who gave Crump his political power. By the time the Roaring Twenties began, Crump was the most powerful politician in the mid-South. Contemporaneously, Mooney was the most powerful newsman. And they didn't like each other.

Yet they had a lot in common. They both grew up as farm boys in states adjacent to Tennessee—Crump in Mississippi and Mooney in Kentucky. They both expressed a strong distaste for the Ku Klux Klan. And both grew to love Memphis enough to make it their final resting place. But Crump and Mooney had sharply different ideas about democracy and political leadership. Although his roots were in Kentucky, Mooney was never considered a bona fide southerner. At least not by Crump, who was southern through and through, from his mannerly greetings to his cornpone sayings.

Mooney was born September 15, 1865—five months after the official end of the Civil War—in the western Knobs region of Kentucky in Bullitt County. His father, a poor dirt farmer, was a native of Ireland who died when Mooney was seven. As a teenager, Mooney learned the trade of a telegraph operator. He spent three years in college and taught school for two years before landing in Pine Bluff, Arkansas, where he joined the staff of the weekly *Press Eagle*. He came to Memphis in 1890 as a reporter for the *Avalanche* but lasted only four days before moving to the *Scimitar* and eventually becoming city editor.

In 1896, Mooney left for New York to become city editor of the *American*, owned by legendary newspaper magnate William Randolph Hearst, a man Mooney considered his mentor in journalism. He later moved to Chicago to manage the *Examiner*, and with that assignment, big-city newspapering seemed to be his destiny. But in a curious move, Mooney returned to Memphis in 1908 to become managing editor of the *Commercial Appeal*. He embraced the paper's reputation as being probusiness and antiblack. In other words, his was the newspaper primarily for the white men of means in Memphis and the mid-South.

The paper was nicknamed the "Old Reliable." But to most blacks in and around the city, that meant reliably racist. Mooney made no secret of his belief that all blacks in Memphis were second-class citizens and many of them shouldn't be granted the right to vote. More than anything else, that position put Mooney on an irreparable collision course with Crump, who after winning his first election as mayor in 1909, quickly realized he needed the black vote to stay in power.

The *Commercial Appeal* repeatedly criticized Crump's so-called manipulation of black voters, including his organization's use of cash collected from dives and gambling houses to finance the poll taxes for blacks. No incident illustrated this chasm more than the 1914 election of write-in candidate John Riechman for Shelby County sheriff. Mooney detested the write-in campaign's use of so-called illiterate blacks who were taught how to spell Riechman's name so they could write it correctly on the ballot.

An editorial on the eve of the election, headlined "An orgy of machine politics" and likely written by Mooney, made one last effort to derail Crump's plan: "The affairs of the city of Memphis and the county of Shelby are merely being merchandized for the sustenance of a crowd of political leeches and the added power of their leaders. It is a notorious fact that a horde of ignorant people have been registered. It is a further notorious fact that a great number of registration receipts are in the hands of the dive keepers and hangers-on. It is difficult for these people to vote under the best conditions. They haven't the right to vote because of their ignorance and, for a second reason, they don't vote their own sentiments."[10]

The next day, election day, the *Commercial Appeal* softened its tone, but only slightly. The paper noted with displeasure that Crump was reintroducing thousands of black residents to the voting process for the first time since Reconstruction: "The most dangerous thing that has been done is to bring back into politics thousands of worthless Negroes. We have never questioned the right of an intelligent and honest Negro to vote. The Negro who is a taxpayer and a law-abiding citizen has a right to vote and should be protected in that right. But the worthless, the incompetent, the ignorant and those who would simply vote as they are told have no business voting."[11] A news story published days earlier reported that some eleven thousand Negroes, "most of whom were herded from dives, the alleys and off steamboats and led to the registration booths, had a fine political inning."[12]

The day after Riechman's stunning write-in victory, the paper's front page story read simply, "Mayor Crump's organization, well-oiled and well provisioned, won hands down in yesterday's election." An accompanying editorial kept up the harsh, racist rhetoric. It noted that white men on the city payroll had transported blacks to the polling places and helped them cast their votes: "All coons look alike to the enthusiastic and loyal supporters of the Crump crowd. Thousands of poll taxes were paid for ignorant Negroes by the Crump followers. . . . The Negro is back in politics with every foot up."[13]

Riechman's election emboldened Crump like never before. It also energized black Memphians, who realized, perhaps for the first time, that they could impact the outcome of elections in the Bluff City. With Crump's support from black voters now cemented, he was invincible. And he never mended fences with Mooney. He blamed the editor for stoking the successful court battle to oust him from the mayor's office in 1915 for failing to enforce prohibition laws against the sale of liquor. The ouster proceedings were without question Crump's lowest moment in politics. But it didn't last long. Rather than be kicked out of office, he left voluntarily after winning his third term in 1915. Just a few months later, he was easily elected county trustee, again with help from African Americans. Crump was now secure in knowing he didn't need the blessing of the *Commercial Appeal*'s editorial pages to succeed in politics. And black Memphians would remain wary and distrustful of the newspaper for decades to come.

Undaunted, Mooney continued to attack Crump's political machine whenever he could, even though several *Commercial Appeal* staffers maintained a friendly relationship with the Boss. He granted interviews whenever he was asked and even dropped by the newsroom from time to time for friendly, nonpolitical visits. On one occasion when Crump was in the building, he stuck his head inside famed cartoonist James P. Alley's office and muttered, "Jim, you're bearing down pretty heavy. You're killing me." To which Alley replied, "Well dammit, Ed, behave yourself."[14]

That kind of banter never occurred between the Boss and Mooney. But both men ended up on the same side in the early 1920s with their opposition to the Klan. Mooney and Crump believed that the KKK represented a threat to the already precarious racial harmony that existed in Memphis. Both men blamed the hate group for giving the South a bad reputation. Both also believed, rather naively, that there were no longer any volatile racial problems in Memphis, and the Klan's presence was not needed, especially in city politics.

In 1923, Crump supported Mayor Rowlett Paine's reelection despite heated differences between the two. The Boss worked vigorously to secure victory for Paine and other city candidates who were opposed by a slate organized by the Klan. The only KKK candidate to win a city office that year was Clifford Davis, who at age twenty-five was elected to a judgeship position. In later years, Davis downplayed his brief association with the Klan. He eventually became a Crump loyalist, doing the Boss's bidding whenever needed. Davis, an eloquent orator, was Crump's handpicked choice to be Memphis's representative in Congress in 1940, and black voters at Crump's behest supported Davis at the ballot box. By then his Klan ties were well in the past, explained away as an impetuous decision by a young man full of political ambition. Davis was now a Crump disciple, and all was forgiven.

As for Mooney, his crusade against Klan activities throughout the South was incessant. The *Commercial Appeal*'s anti-Klan editorials condemned the group "for its secrecy, intolerance and use of violence." That the paper would condemn the Klan for intolerance was a bit ironic considering its many demeaning editorials over the years against black citizens, particularly during the Riechman write-in campaign for sheriff. But in Mooney's view, which was shared by Crump, there was a stark difference between racial separation and racial violence. The former was the acceptable societal practice of the time. The latter was barbaric. In 1923, the *Commercial Appeal*'s reporting and editorial cartoons on the Klan garnered a Pulitzer Prize for "the most distinguished and meritorious public service rendered by a newspaper." The Pulitzer judges noted that the paper displayed a "courageous attitude in the publication of cartoons and the handling of news in reference to the operations of the Ku Klux Klan."[15] The award was the brightest moment of Mooney's brilliant journalism career. It established him as one of the nation's premiere newspaper editors of his time. But he had more to do.

He continued to oppose Crump and battle the Klan. But Mooney's main goal was making sure the *Commercial Appeal* remained the South's top newspaper. He held dual titles of managing editor and president of the Commercial Publishing Company, and he was determined to outshine his rivals at both jobs. In 1926, the two evening newspapers in Memphis, the *News-Scimitar* and the *Press*, merged to become in *Memphis Press-Scimitar*. The combined publication dropped its affiliation with the Associated Press news service in favor of United Press International, which was owned by what later became Scripps-Howard Newspapers. The merger fueled Mooney's competitive juices even more, and he immediately set about to launch his own evening paper to go head-on against the *Press-Scimitar*. The paper would be called the *Evening Appeal* and would feature national and international news from the Associated Press as well as late-breaking local news. Mooney put in long hours planning for the launch. In doing so, he ignored some serious health issues.

The *Evening Appeal*'s debut was set for December 1, 1926. But Mooney would never see the first edition roll off the presses. On Monday morning, November 22, 1926, at the age of sixty-one, he died of apoplexy on a couch in his newspaper office. The front-page story in the *Commercial Appeal* the following morning recounted his final moments:

"The captain of the watch is dead.

"C. P. J. Mooney, managing editor of the *Commercial Appeal* and president of the Commercial Publishing Company, went on his great last assignment from his office yesterday. The call was sudden. It found him as he wished it to find him—in harness. The time was 11:40 a.m. There was little warning. Shortly before noon, he complained of feeling ill. His secretary made a desperate effort to get medical aid, but when it came it was too late. In the little office he had made his headquarters, his soul took flight while linotypes above and the busy whirl of a newspaper shop played a requiem."[16]

Mooney had suffered from a mild bout of influenza the weekend before his death, and his wife had urged him to stay home on Monday. But Mooney wouldn't hear of it. He was a stickler for deadlines and he had too much to do preparing for the launch of the *Evening Appeal*. On that fateful morning, Mooney, after arriving at his office, started to feel worse. He alerted his secretary, Emma Haskins, that he was having major discomfort. But he tried to shake it off by retreating to his office couch. Surely the spell would pass, he assured her. But it didn't.

Mooney's death was reported in every national newspaper and elicited hundreds of telegrams and letters expressing condolences. The messages filled newspaper pages for days. Boss Crump's statement was published on Wednesday, November 24, and was strikingly terse: "Shocked to hear of your distinguished editor's death. You have my deepest sympathy.— E. H. Crump."[17]

Crump and the Press

Mooney's funeral was held at the Church of the Immaculate Conception. Twelve of "Mooney's boys" served as pallbearers and solemnly carried his body to his grave in Calvary Cemetery. They were Paul Morris, who had just been named editor of the *Evening Appeal*; Bill Adler and J. C. Caruthers, editorial writers; George McCormick and Thomas Fauntleroy, both assistant managing editors; J. P. Alley, editorial cartoonist; Sam Kahn, city editor; A. D. Mynders, telegraph editor; Herbert Caldwell, sports editor; Sam Bledsoe, tri-state editor; and former *Commercial Appeal* staffers George Fossick and Fred Benecke.[18]

Mooney's sudden demise created a huge leadership void at the *Commercial Appeal*. The *Evening Appeal* launched as planned on December 1, 1926. But without Mooney around to guide it and be its public face, the paper floundered. Circulation gradually increased, but it could never overtake the newly merged *Press-Scimitar* for evening readers. The *Commercial Appeal* and *Evening Appeal*, hampered by financial problems, changed ownership twice, and new owners closed the *Evening Appeal* on July 1, 1933. Three years later, the *Commercial Appeal* was sold to Scripps-Howard, which now owned both Memphis daily newspapers.

The turmoil at the *Commercial Appeal* following Mooney's death also meant that Boss Crump's political exploits received less scrutiny from the local press. Mooney's successors, including Frank Ahlgren, who became editor in 1936, were generally supportive of Crump and his businesslike approach to running government. The post-Mooney *Commercial Appeal* also was less bothered by any manipulation of black voters by the Crump machine.

But harmony between Crump and the local press ended with Edward Meeman's arrival in Memphis as editor of the *Press-Scimitar*. Where Mooney had been a splinter in Crump's side, Meeman became a Texas-sized spur. Like Mooney, Meeman loathed machine politics. And like Mooney, Meeman had to acknowledge that Crump and most of his handpicked leaders ran an efficient, clean, progressive city. But unlike Mooney, Meeman was far more progressive on racial issues. He never used his editorial pages to demean and discredit black Memphians, as Mooney routinely did.

Born in Evansville, Indiana, in 1889, Edward John Meeman started his journalism career on the staff of his hometown paper, the *Evansville Press*. He quickly caught the eye of Scripps-Howard executives and rose through the ranks at the *Press* to become managing editor. At the time, Scripps-Howard was in expansion mode, and Meeman was tapped to launch a new paper in Knoxville, Tennessee, called the *Knoxville News*. The Knoxville offer came directly from Robert P. Scripps, son of E. W. Scripps, founder of the flourishing newspaper chain. In his posthumous autobiography, *The Editorial We*, Meeman said the assignment also came with one piece of advice from Robert Scripps: "Some Northern-born men who go South think they can solve the Negro problem. They can't. You can't. The best you can do it not to do anything against the Negroes."[19]

With that, Meeman was off to the hills of East Tennessee, where he built a successful newspaper from scratch. It was so successful, in fact, that the paper ended up buying its competitor, the *Knoxville Journal*. And Meeman was rewarded with another assignment, editor of the *Press-Scimitar* in the much larger city of Memphis. He balked at first, preferring to stay close to the Great Smoky Mountains, a place he had come to love. But Bob Scripps caustically asked him, "What do you want to do, stay here and get fat?"[20] Meeman had no quick answer and reluctantly accepted the Memphis job. His name first appeared on the *Press-Scimitar* masthead on November 23, 1931, when he succeeded Tom Sharp, who was promoted to editor of the Scripps-owned *Buffalo Times*. It didn't take long for Meeman to immerse himself into the Memphis culture and its rich—albeit segregated—social life. And it took even less time for him to start incurring the ire of Boss Crump, who was serving his first term in Congress when Meeman arrived in town.

Crump's election to Congress was another testament to his tremendous political power in Shelby County. He had grown disenchanted with incumbent Hubert Fisher, who had represented what was then the Tenth Congressional District since 1916. Crump also was eager to take his political know-how to a national level, although he insisted that self-aggrandizement was not his motivation. On June 10, 1930, he officially announced for the office just in time to capture front-page news in the *Evening Appeal*: "Having in mind only a desire to give Shelby County some constructive legislation which I consider long since overdue and without any way attempting to gratify selfish ambitions, I have announced myself as a candidate for the Tenth Congressional District."[21]

Earlier that day, Fisher announced that he would not seek another term. He accepted the fact that challenging Crump would be futile—despite holding the seat for fourteen years. Crump said one his endeavors in Congress would be to push for eradication of malaria, which included an education campaign among Shelby County blacks about the dangers of the disease in their community. When no one else stepped up to challenge the Boss in the

August Democratic primary, Crump automatically became the Democratic nominee and no votes were cast in that race. In the general election on November 9, 1930, Crump received 23,756 votes, while 1,583 votes were split between two insignificant opponents.[22] Mr. Crump was now off to Washington.

Meeman had railed against Crump's political organization while in Knoxville. But in Memphis, he got a much more intimate look at the Crump way of winning elections and running government. The more he learned about the organization and its cunning leader, the more he criticized it. In his autobiography, Meeman said he opposed the Crump machine "as a crusader committed not only to upholding democracy, but to improving it."[23] In Memphis, he became associated with the Voters' League, "which consisted mostly of followers of former Governor Malcolm Patterson, Southerners of the old school. They opposed the Crump machine for the reasons I did, and for one that I did not share with them, that he made voters of Negroes, though we agreed in hating the Crump method of voting them in truckloads, as mere pawns."[24]

In an editorial a few months after Meeman became editor, the *Press-Scimitar* extolled the efforts of the Voters' League, adding, "If Memphis had always had a strong non-partisan Voters' League, Crumpism would never have been able to fasten its ugly grip on this city. . . . If (the Voters' League) practices fundamental principles of modern popular government, it will have built a structure of democracy in which the present bossism, coercion and corruption will have no place."

Meeman also spoke out against Crump and in favor of the Voters' League at civic lunches and other community gatherings. A *Press-Scimitar* news story on one Meeman speech in 1932 carried this lead paragraph: "The aim of the political machine is not to make democracy work, but to work democracy, Edward J. Meeman, editor of The Press-Scimitar, told the Voters' League at their regular luncheon at Lowenstein's Friday."[25] Despite Meeman's efforts to prop up the Voters' League, it failed to stall the Crump machine. Meeman later lamented the fact that he was "operating a free press under a totalitarian dictatorship, which controlled nearly everything in town—not only the politics and government, but the Bar Association, the Parent-Teacher Association, the Council of Civic Clubs, the American Legion, the labor unions, the business community."[26]

As with anyone who dared to challenge him, Crump did not take the harsh criticism lightly. He fired back at Meeman with toxic rhetoric of his own, often using letters that were published in the *Press-Scimitar* to do it. In one letter to Meeman written on E. H. Crump and Company stationery and dated December 10, 1943, Crump called the *Press-Scimitar* editor crazy. He added, "Your whole mental process needs reforming. If you could only rise above your hate, you would be a happier man. You should have a first-class funeral inside yourself for your hates, jealousies, grudges, griefs and selfishness."[27]

Crump's counterattacks against Meeman also involved more than mere words in a private letter. In 1947, Crump allegedly ordered Mayor James J. Pleasants to read into the minutes of a city commission meeting a claim that Meeman was gay, or as the mayor put it, "one of those things."[28] The mayor went even further, saying, "(Meeman) has been branded as a low, contemptible liar time and time again by any number of men who are highly respected. Only a man with a perverted and degenerate mind stoops to lie about anyone. It's the mark of a coward who feels he can lie through the columns of his newspaper with impunity."[29]

Author David Tucker, in his book *Memphis Since Crump*, wrote that Pleasants later tried to apologize for the statements. Tucker quotes *Press-Scimitar* reporter Clark Porteous as saying, "Pleasants never did get over doing this terrible thing he had not wanted to do. He used to ask me if there was some way he could make amends."[30] Crump, however, had no regrets. To him, Meeman—like Mooney before him—was an outsider needlessly interfering with the orderly operation of a prospering city. Crump knew with surety that far more Memphians were loyal to him than to someone he considered a carpetbagging muckraker.

Indeed, Meeman's crusade against the machine had no effect on the outcome of elections throughout the 1930s and into the 1940s. Anyone Crump put on the ballot—including himself—emerged victorious. The election that perhaps galled Meeman the most was Crump's victory in 1939 for Memphis mayor. Crump had left Congress in 1934, preferring to devote more time to helping his sons run the family business. Crump loyalist Walter Chandler succeeded him as Shelby's representative in Washington. Before long, Crump grew disenchanted with Mayor Watkins Overton, a longtime ally. The rift started in the wake of rising flood waters that swept over the Mississippi River valley in January 1937. The flooding forced tens of thousands of residents in surrounding counties to abandon their homes and pour into Memphis. Mayor Overton quickly responded to the crisis and set up emergency shelters, the largest of which was at the fairgrounds. But the site was inundated by more than fifty thousand flood refugees, creating horrible sanitary conditions.[31]

By all accounts, Overton handed the crisis admirably. But Boss Crump, who had been ill with the flu, was outraged when he later toured the fairgrounds and discovered the crowded and unsanitary conditions. Without talking the Overton first, Crump sent a harshly critical letter to the mayor. "It is criminal on our part to pack all of these people—men, women and children—like sardines in a box at the Fairgrounds," he wrote.[32] Overton took strong offense to Crump's criticism: "I do not think it was criminal to put the people in the Fairgrounds because there was no other place to put them. It would have been criminal to have kept them there. We didn't."[33]

The Boss also was highly critical of Overton's handling of the purchases of electric properties of the Memphis Power and Light Company in 1938. The mayor and the newly formed light and power commission successfully negotiated the $13.5 million deal with Memphis Power and Light, which was hailed as "the greatest progressive step" in the city's history.[34] Bringing public power to the city had long been Boss Crump's goal. But once the deal was reached, his name was not included in the accolades and he was offended—so much so that he convinced his lieutenants on the city commission to kill the deal.

Instead, Crump stepped in and personally renegotiated the arrangement to also include the purchase of gas properties.[35] Through it all, Overton tried to remain a team player in the organization, but he finally had enough of Crump's ego, his whims, and his meddling. Overton had been mayor for twelve years, longer than anyone else in the city's history. He had guided the city through the Great Depression and frequently did Crump's bidding. But he suddenly found himself at total odds with the Boss and a majority of the city commission, who were all Crump men.

Rather than remain a puppet mayor, Overton announced he would not seek another term in the 1939 city election. And Crump swooped in once more, tapping Congressman Chandler for the job. But a quirky city law meant that Chandler would have to resign his congressional seat before running in the November 9 mayoral election. Chandler's vote was badly needed on a crucial arms-embargo repeal bill that would be taken up at year's end, so he could not resign from Congress. Crump, however, was not one to give up so easily. He developed the perfect solution and revealed it on October 23, less than three weeks before the election. He would run for the mayor's seat basically as an "elector" for Chandler. Once sworn in, Crump would resign immediately, allowing the city commission to appoint Chandler mayor.

The Boss publicly disclosed every detail of his plan from the beginning: "I am announcing my candidacy for mayor as a pinch bitter for Congressman Walter Chandler, whom we want as our permanent mayor." Crump praised Chandler for being "an untiring worker and worthy in every way." He ended the statement with a rare touch of Crump humility: "I hope I have made a clear and satisfactory statement to the people of Memphis who have shown me so much kindness and courtesy."[36]

Chandler had mixed feeling about Crump's plan. He was building an impressive resume in Congress and told friend he wanted to remain there. Yet he had no interest in disappointing Crump. And being mayor of Memphis with the Crump machine on his side was impossible to resist. The *Press-Scimitar* was indignant. "We now know who 'Mr. Blank' is," the paper said in an editorial the day Crump announced he would be a surrogate for Chandler. "We now know the identity of the man whom leading supporters of the Shelby County political organization underwrote, though they did not know who he was when they signed mayoralty nominating petitions in blank the other day in an act of blind faith. Technically, it is E. H. Crump, who is to run for the office, but actually it is Walter Chandler, who is to take the mayor's office after he had voted for repeal of the arms embargo in Washington. . . . Whether Mr. Chandler will make a good mayor remains to be seen. He has little if any executive experience and his qualifications in the field of administration are unknown and unproved.

"He is quite subservient to the machine. If there are limits to that subservience they have not been reached. If there is even a faint spark of independence we have not seen it. He was put in the doghouse by the machine without the slightest justification, yet he never complained. He is being removed from Congress where, from the standpoint of the machine and from the standpoint of most citizens, he has made good and where he is happy, to a mayoralty where he may not be happy, again without complaint. It is not in the nature of things that such 'yessing' makes for good government—to say nothing of democracy."[37]

But Meeman and the *Press-Scimitar* were powerless to stop Crump's plan. Even Chandler's six-year-old daughter Lucia understood that once Crump decreed something, it was a done deal. Lucia—the sister of future mayor

Wyeth Chandler, then nine—was so thrilled by the news that she scribble out a letter that was airmailed to her father. He received it in Washington the following morning. "I am so glad you are to be mayor," it read. "Come home soon. I love you.—Lucia."[38] Tennessee senator Kenneth McKellar, a Memphian, was equally pleased. "I'm delighted with the way Mr. Crump worked it out," he told a *Press-Scimitar* reporter.

No one bothered, or dared, to oppose Crump. And on election morning, the *Commercial Appeal*'s front-page headline left no room for suspense: "Memphis will elect Crump mayor today in 'confidence' vote."[39] Confidence was an understatement. Crump received 31,825 votes, one of the highest totals in a mayoral election ever. There were a handful of write-in votes for Overton, but they were ignored by the election commission. *Commercial Appeal* reporter Paul Coppock, who covered the election, compared the results to Crump's first mayoral victory thirty years earlier. Crump, he wrote, "was a tall red-haired dealer in buggies and harnesses when he was first elected in 1909 as a reformist with a 79-vote margin. Now he is a tall, white-haired dealer in real estate, mortgages and insurance who won his fourth mayoral election with no opposition."[40]

As Crump prepared to take the oath and immediately hand the mayor's office over to Chandler, his verbal feud with Overton took a nasty turn. On December 15, 1939, Overton, now a lame-duck mayor, issued a statement saying the city's Light, Gas and Water Division should be taken out of politics through civil service protection for LG&W employees. He also called for a reduction in water rates and said the utility should take part in a national promotion of Memphis along with supporting the Memphis community fund and the chamber of commerce. The statement made no reference to Crump, but the Boss fired back the next day with a statement of his own: "Watkins Overton's mind is as warped and out of shape with his peevishness and insincerity as a bale of cotton is with three hoops off." Overton, Crump added, was "playing the role of a perfect hypocrite."[41]

The outgoing mayor was irate. On Monday, December 18, he got deeply personal in criticizing the Boss, and the *Press-Scimitar* was more than happy to report it. It was almost as if Overton's words were co-written by Meeman. "The poison pen writes on," Overton said, referring to Crump. "The (boss') path to eternity is strewn with the wreckage of men who have dared to stand up for what they believed to be right. No one dared challenge his omnipotence, lest they be blasted.

"For 12 years I worked for Memphis, to give Memphis good government. Memphis had good government. So good that the great author (Crump) boasted of it and used it as his chief argument as he gradually extended his political and personal empire. Memphis' good government was used as a front to cover all sins. Thus the empire grew. . . . Meanwhile, I dared to do what I thought was best for the people of Memphis. I did it. Some had the temerity to say publicly that I was the best mayor Memphis ever had. That was treason. So I became next on the list of those to be destroyed. . . .

"I am aware that every means in his political and financial power, or available thru those who bow before him, will be used in an attempt to ruin me, to distort the truth, to destroy my record of good government. Can this poison pen deceive the public always? The dictator and his army await greedily the first of the year when I go out of office. I say now to the author and his poison pen: I will never bow my knee to any tyrant. I will never raise my hand in the Nazi salute to a dictator. I still believe in democracy."[42]

Overton's statement was the most stinging rebuke Crump had received in his public life. But it too had no lasting effect. Shortly after midnight on January 1, 1940, Crump, his wife, his closest allies, scores of New Year's Eve partygoers dressed in their finery, and members of the press gathered in a fresh snowfall at the downtown train station. There the Boss was sworn in as mayor. After taking the oath, he immediately reached into his suit pocket and pulled out a written statement announcing his resignation. In the statement, Crump said his only act as mayor would be to send a letter rescinding an invitation for the American Newspaper Guild to hold its 1940 convention in Memphis. Crump said the guild was not welcome in Memphis because of its affiliation with the Congress of Industrial Organizations.

Then Crump and his entourage boarded a train for New Orleans to attend the Sugar Bowl game between Texas A&M and Tulane. His ingenious maneuver meant that Memphis had four mayors during the course of a day and a half: Overton, until Crump's swearing in at fifteen minutes past midnight; Crump, until the commission could meet the following afternoon, January 2, to formally accept his resignation; Clifford Davis, acting mayor for about five minutes until the commission could approve Chandler with a standing vote; and Chandler, who was immediately sworn in. Nothing has come close to rivaling this escapade in the annals of Memphis city government before or since.

Meeman, however, continued to criticize the machine as Crump—who never again ran for office himself—continued to support winners. The crusading editor realized he could not topple the powerful boss alone. He needed allies outside of journalism, and he found them in Lucius Burch Jr. and Edmund Orgill. Burch grew up wealthy on a stylish plantation near Nashville. He attended Vanderbilt University Law School and came to Memphis in 1935 as an idealistic young lawyer determined to use his legal skills to help society.

In Memphis, Burch was not beholden to the political power structure for his livelihood. Because he grew up with privilege, he was not afraid to tangle with the Crump machine. And they tangled often. Crump more than once tried to get Burch's clients, including the railroads and Standard Oil Company, to fire him.[43] But Burch was unfazed. Fearlessness ran his family. His grandfather, Col. Duncan Cooper, and uncle, Robin Cooper, became legends of sort in Middle Tennessee after they engaged newspaper editor and former senator Edward Carmack in a duel on a Nashville street in November 1908. Carmack, who was once editor of the *Commercial Appeal*, was killed by a bullet supposedly from Robin Cooper's pistol.[44]

Burch even kept a gun tucked away in the desk drawer in his downtown Memphis law office. When a young lawyer named W. J. Michael "Mike" Cody starting practicing in the Burch, Porter and Johnson firm in 1961, Burch pulled out the Webley revolver and handed it Cody. "Young man, you're going to be here a long time," Burch said. "I don't need this pistol anymore. Mr. Crump's dead."[45]

Like Burch, Orgill also came from means. His family started Orgill Brothers, a wholesale hardware business based in Memphis in 1847, and Edmund, at forty-one, became company president in 1940 after his father's death. It was then that he also became active in civic affairs, serving as president of the Rotary Club and the Memphis Chamber of Commerce and a director of Union Planters Bank. His alliance with Burch and Meeman started with their mutual interest in the federal unionist movement of the early 1940s, influenced by the writing of *New York Times* reporter Clarence Streit. Eventually, Burch, Meeman, and Orgill became the leading advocates for government reform in Memphis. They proposed a switch to a council-manager form of government in which a part-time city council would establish policy and a full-time manager would run the day-to-day operations of city government.

Naturally, Crump vehemently opposed the change. The mayor-commission structure, which he helped orchestrate after his first mayoral victory in 1909, was working just fine to him—and for him. In newspaper ads, speeches, and letters to the editor, Crump continued to tout the fact that Memphians enjoyed lower taxes and a good, honest government that was free of graft. Memphis, Crump argued, had no red-light district, no street walkers, and no white slavery. There was also no narcotics trafficking and no organized gangs, Crump insisted. And it was all thanks to the effectiveness of the Crump machine and the commission form of government.

Once, when Crump was asked about Burch's criticism of the Crump organization, the Boss responded, "I want to tell you about Lucius Burch. If you ordered a railroad box car full of sons of bitches, and you walked down the side and you opened the car, and only Lucius Burch walked out, you wouldn't file a claim for shortage."[46]

As long as Crump was alive, the push to change city government went nowhere. But the Burch-Meeman-Orgill alliance enjoyed it most significant victory over the Crump machine in 1948 with the election of Estes Kefauver to the U.S. Senate. Crump supported John Mitchell for the seat and labeled Kefauver, a Chattanooga liberal, as a communist and a "pet coon." Kefauver turned the slur to his advantage by donning a coonskin cap and campaigning around Tennessee saying he would not be a pet coon for Crump.[47]

The alliance worked hard for Kefauver in Shelby County, carefully assembling a few other like-minded business leaders who were tacitly willing to oppose Crump. But credit for Kefauver's success must be given to African American businessman Joseph E. Walker, owner of Universal Life Insurance Company based in Memphis. Walker was Kefauver's point man for thousands of black voters, who decided for the first time during the Crump era to buck the machine.

The turnabout happened primarily because of Crump's stubborn objection to civil rights and his strident rejection of Harry Truman's presidential campaign—which included a strong push for integration. Walker represented the emergence of black leaders in Memphis who wanted to speed the tempo of the march toward racial equality. In the August Democratic state primary, Crump's candidates still carried Shelby County, but not by the numbers the machine normally tallied. Kefauver carried twenty-three city precincts—including three in predominantly black neighborhoods—en route to a decisive statewide victory.

And when Truman was elected president in a November squeaker, Crump, for the first time, tasted an embarrassing defeat at the polls. He accepted it somewhat gracefully and even tried to patch things up with African Americans. Shortly after the election, the city hired its first black policemen—although they were not allowed to arrest any white people. One of them was Ernest Withers, who went on to photograph some of the important moments of the civil rights movement. The fact that Crump was willing to accept black police officers in Memphis was a celebratory moment in the black community.

However, the Boss would never accept the idea of changing city government. And yet, more significant change to Memphis's way of life was coming, and Crump would be powerless to stop it. The Meeman-Burch-Orgill alliance had finally scored one against their invincible and cantankerous nemesis. But make no mistake, African American voters in Memphis again meant the difference between winning and losing. Only this time, seeds of political independence among the black electorate were starting to sprout.

CHAPTER 4

CHAOS AFTER CRUMP

THE MAN SITTING in the mayor's chair when Crump died was not Edmund Orgill, as the Meeman-Burch-Orgill alliance wanted. It was Frank Tobey. Orgill's time was coming. But this was the fall of 1954. And though Crump was becoming gravely ill by the day, his organization was still firmly in control of local government. The Boss reconciled with Watkins Overton in 1947—eight years after their highly publicized blowup that led to Overton resigning as mayor. On March 27, 1947, Overton became president of the Memphis City Schools Board Education with support from Crump.

As 1948—Crump's most difficult political year ever—drew to a close, the Boss asked Overton to again be mayor through an appointment by the city commission. He reluctantly said yes and was sworn in on January 15, 1949, replacing Mayor James Pleasants, who "resigned" to become city attorney. Before long, Overton and the commission were feuding again. And eventually Crump was up to his old habit of nitpicking Overton's every decision.

The commissioners criticized Overton for wanting to sell the city's asphalt plant property on Broad Street to Sears, Roebuck and Company. They also balked at allowing Overton to give Guy Bates, his young administrative assistant, a raise of $100 a month, boosting his monthly salary to $375. In Overton's mind, the dispute over the raise for Bates was pure spite. Bates was doing a good job and was a promising recruit to the Crump organization. Overton went public with a statement accusing the commissioners—and by extension Crump—of being stingy: "I am confident any fair-minded person would say a mayor of any city the size of Memphis should have the right to choose his own administrative assistant, and a salary of $375-a-month is certainly not excessive."[1]

Bates eventually got his raise. But Overton's foes on the commission continued to second-guess the mayor. Overton and the commission clashed over setting up pension and hospitalization programs for city employees. Commissioners were for them, Overton waffled on the issue. Overton also started talking openly about scrapping the city commission altogether and moving to a "strong mayor" form of government. Naturally, Crump disapproved, saying Overton had become obsessed with gaining absolute power. "No good man would want that authority and no bad man should have it," the Boss said.

In February 1953, the commission abruptly fired city personnel director Stanley Dillard—with approval from an ailing Crump. Overton was furious over Dillard's firing and soon after announced his resignation. "The present conditions are intolerable," the mayor said. "No man could continue to serve as mayor and keep his self-respect."

Enter Tobey, city commissioner of finance and former city controller. Crump, perhaps sensing that his health was irreversibly declining, was no longer interested in political hijinks. He wanted a serious-minded man in the mayor's office—someone experienced in the inner workings of city government who was also loyal to the Crump organization. Tobey fit the bill perfectly. He started with the city in 1924 as an engineer in the Department of Public Works. He worked his way up in government because he knew finances better that anyone else. He was the go-to man for anything related to budgets, bookkeeping, and finance.

He also was a religious man who loved to sing and loved cars. He was a native son in every sense, having been born in a house on the east side of Manassas Street just north of Poplar Avenue on September 25, 1890. His father owned the E. T. Tobey Coal Company at Main and Keel. His dad also ran a mattress company and owned a plantation in Walnut Bend, Arkansas. Both of his grandfathers fought in the Civil War and both died in the yellow fever epidemic.[2]

Tobey got along with everyone—blacks and whites—and Crump was sure that with him as mayor, the city would be in safe hands, even when the Boss was no longer around. The commission, in usual rubber-stamp fashion, appointed Tobey mayor on Thursday, February 20, 1953, and the appointment became official on Sunday, March 1. Later that day, he went to Idlewild Presbyterian Church, where he served as an elder, and sang "All the Way My Savior Leads Me" for the congregation.[3] Early the next morning, he got to work running the city. He worked day and night, including weekends, and he met with any group that issued an invitation. And yet the *Press-Scimitar* was not overly impressed with Crump's handpicked mayor. The paper credited Tobey for functioning well as city controller and getting off to a good start as mayor, but was quick to note that final decisions always "rested in the hands of one who was outside of government."[4] It was another obvious slap at Crump.

But Crump was becoming less accessible. And Tobey, by necessity, was becoming more assertive politically. After Crump died, Commissioner Joe Boyle, the Boss's closest lieutenant, tried to be the face of the organization. But he didn't have the temperament, and he certainly didn't have the support of black community leaders. Too many people remembered with disdain his days knocking heads—most of them black—while in charge of the police department. And they were not interested in that style of leadership running all of municipal government. Instead, the city rallied to Tobey. The Boss purposely had groomed no other obvious successor to his political empire. So Tobey assumed it by default—not with cunning or heavy-handedness, but with charm, responsiveness, and a calm demeanor. When black leaders complained about a body-snatching racket operating at John Gaston Hospital, Tobey broke it up.[5] When white citizens would approach him at the Little Tea Shop restaurant downtown, where he frequently met his wife for lunch, he would put down his fork, slide his dish of lemon pie aside, and listen to their concerns.

Beyond the niceties, Tobey wasted little time becoming an effective advocate for the growth of Memphis. Just two months after assuming the mayor's office, Tobey found himself at odds with President Dwight D. Eisenhower's administration over attempts by the president to significantly weaken the Tennessee Valley Authority (TVA). Eisenhower was seeking to kill a $30 million steam-generating power plant thirty miles outside Memphis that would enable the TVA to continue to meet the growing demand for electricity in the city.[6]

Tobey joined other Tennessee elected leaders in lobbying Congress to save the TVA power plant. Eisenhower supported instead the construction of a privately owned facility that became known as the Dixon-Yates electric-generating plant across the river in West Memphis, Arkansas. But Tobey refused to budge and proposed that the city build its own electric-generating plant. The Memphis Light, Gas and Water Division, led by Thomas H. Allen, and the utility's board voted in June 1955 to build the steam plant, and the city commission signed off on it as well.[7]

The move paid off, with Eisenhower—in a White House meeting with Tobey and Allen—agreeing to rescind his support for the Dixon-Yates plant on condition that the city not seek federal funds for construction of the municipal plant. The president also agreed not to cut funding to the TVA.[8] It was a huge political and economic victory for Tobey and the city.

The mayor scored another important economic coup in 1955, when entertainer Danny Thomas tapped Memphis as a possible site for a hospital to treat underprivileged children with cancer. Tobey committed to purchasing a tract of land that would be given free of charge to the hospital.[9] He even flew to Hollywood, California, to meet personally with Thomas. A reporter for the *Commercial Appeal* was also invited on the trip that included lunch with famed actors Walter Brennan and Jane Russell. Once he was back home, Tobey lined up support from prominent physicians and hospital administrators, and Thomas was well received when he visited the city in May 1955. The end result was construction of St. Jude Children's Research Hospital, which opened on February 4, 1962.[10]

The effort on behalf of St. Jude and electric power consumers in Memphis set Tobey apart as a mayor who got more done in a short period of time. Finally, the *Press-Scimitar* noted, "Tobey became the most accessible, most-seen-and-heard mayor Memphis has had in modern times. He went everywhere at all hours. Service clubs, civic clubs, neighborhood gatherings, business functions—all were visited by Tobey."[11] The frantic schedule finally took its toll on the mayor's already fragile health. On Thursday, September, 8, 1955, less than a year after his mentor's death, the affable singing mayor was taken to Baptist Hospital after suffering a heart attack at his home.

Tobey actually became ill while having dinner at his son's home earlier that evening, but he tried to brush it off. At the hospital, the sixty-four-year-old Tobey lapsed into a coma and died on Sunday morning, September 11, 1955. Most Memphians heard the news while leaving church services and hearing church bells tolling across the city. "History will say he probably worked himself to death," the *Commercial Appeal* wrote.[12] And Danny Thomas told the newspaper, "America has lost one of its finest sons."[13]

For the second time in less than a year, a shaken city was without its strongest and most respected leader. Walter Chandler stepped back in as interim mayor to calm a community that suddenly was uncertain—and uneasy—about its political future. Tobey had been expected to easily win a full four-year term as mayor in November 1955 with help from black voters—the same voters who had supported Crump candidates for decades.

But when Tobey died, the Crump machine's last hope for long-term survival died too. Edmund Orgill emerged as the favorite to capture the mayor's office. His anti-Crump coalition—led by Edward Meeman and Lucius Burch—was prepared and well financed. Watkins Overton surfaced once more seeking to win the office for a third time. He teamed with Stanley Dillard, his former personnel director, who sought one of four commission seats on the ballot. But voters had grown weary of Overton's combativeness. They acknowledged that Crump's interference was mostly to blame for the rancor while Overton was in the mayor's office. But it didn't matter. Memphians were finally ready to turn the page on the Crump era, and that included Overton.

On election day, Orgill got strong support in the predominantly black precincts and defeated Overton by 18,600 votes in the largest mayoral turnout ever in Memphis. The *Commercial Appeal* used the term "swamped" to describe Overton's embarrassing defeat.[14] The Orgill-Meeman-Burch alliance had finally achieved its ultimate goal—seizing control of city leadership and paving the way to a council-manager form of government. Orgill's longtime supporter, Frances Coe, also became one of two women to win seats on the Memphis Board of Education. The other was Jane Seessel. Coe had been working in the political trenches for several years for Democratic U.S. Senate candidates Estes Kefauver and Albert Gore. She got the endorsement of the Citizens League of Negro Voters and collected the third highest vote total in winning the Memphis City Schools Board of Education seat.

But votes in the 1955 city commission races produced the most significant and far-reaching results. Two old stalwarts of the Crump machine, Joseph Boyle and O. P. Williams, lost their bids for reelection, a definite sign that the Crump organization had faded. In their places, voters elected Stanley Dillard and Henry Loeb. The two would team with incumbents Claude Armour and John T. "Buddy" Dwyer to form a new commission for a new era in city government. Loeb was endorsed by the *Tri-State Defender*, which told its readers he would treat everyone fairly, regardless of race.

The election of Loeb, however, was surprising to those already in city leadership. He was not well regarded by the remnants of the Crump machine. Loeb, a World War II veteran, was an executive in his family's laundry business and commander of the American Legion Post No. 1 in Memphis. He married a former Cotton Carnival queen and in 1951 managed to snag an appointment to the influential Memphis Park Commission.

In that role, Loeb exposed commission chairman John B. Vesey for using park employees to do work at Vesey's home in Midtown. Those workers also used park material and equipment to perform various jobs, including planting trees, stripping paper off interior walls, floor repairs, general house cleaning, and "other odd jobs."[15] Loeb and fellow park commissioner Sam Nickey reported the findings to Mayor Tobey and the city commission.

The report proved to be a major embarrassment to an otherwise well-respected administration run by Tobey. But the mayor had no choice. He turned the findings over to his city attorney, Frank Gianotti Jr., who recommended administrative charges against Vesey. Tobey agreed and filed nine charges of official misconduct against Vesey and suspended him as park commission chairman.[16] But despite a trail of evidence, the city commission cleared Vesey of the misconduct charges and reinstated him, much to the dismay of many Memphians.[17]

Meanwhile, Tobey and the city commission opted not to reappoint Loeb to the park commission after his three-year term expired. The mayor's stated reason was that Loeb was contemplating running for a city commission seat. But the revelations against Vesey no doubt was a factor in the decision.[18] In addition, Boss Crump, before he died, let it be known to his lieutenants that he was not at all impressed with Loeb's leadership skills, his intellect, or his ability to work with people, particularly those in the black community. Little did the Crump faction realize that Loeb had already quietly begun assembling a political base of his own—one built around thousands of disaffected white Memphians who thought the city under Crump's rule had catered too much to blacks.

With the 1955 city election, the table was set for racial strife—which was already brewing across the South—to make its way into post-Crump politics in Memphis. Before Orgill could even be sworn in as mayor, young upstart black leaders were mobilizing around a serious push for integration. On November 19, 1955, ten days after Orgill's convincing mayoral win—thanks to black voters—the Memphis branch of the NAACP, led by its president Hosea T. Lockard, decided at its regular meeting to put two letters in the mail.

One letter was to the Memphis Park Commission formally requesting that all city parks, playgrounds, and cultural facilities be opened to Negroes. The other letter was to the Memphis Board of Education asking for a meeting "at the earliest possible date" to discuss the integration of city schools.[19] Lockard and his associates were determined to move swiftly. They were emboldened by a U.S. Supreme Court ruling handed down November 7, 1955—two days before the city election—declaring segregation unconstitutional in publicly owned parks, golf courses, playgrounds, and swimming pools. The ruling was an extension of the landmark *Brown v. Board of Education* decision a year and a half earlier. The local NAACP's calculated move requesting that the city start the process of ending segregation was the top story in the *Commercial Appeal* on November 30. "INTEGRATION SOUGHT," splashed the front-page headline. "Memphis Negroes Ask Park, Playground Use; School Talk Requested."[20]

The headline both disgusted and frightened the majority of white Memphians. They simply could not fathom the idea of engaging in the gentleman's sport of golf with black folks anywhere in sight—unless they were caddying or working as servers in the clubhouse. And they certainly could not envision white children going to school, swimming in public pools, and playing tag on a city playground with black kids.

Integration of this sort may have been something people tolerated up North, but not in the Deep South and certainly not in Memphis. Ironically, on the same day that the NAACP's letters were delivered, an all-white group of community and business leaders attended a dinner that evening at the Hotel Peabody to celebrate a chamber of commerce initiative called Forward Memphis! The overflow crowd in the hotel's ballroom learned that thirty-two of Memphis's top civic leaders had pledged support for the chamber endeavor "to make Memphis in the next 75 years a place with more industry, better homes, freer traffic and greater beauty." Mayor-elect Orgill was positively giddy. "It's a grand time to be mayor of Memphis," he told the crowd.[21]

The chamber's keynote speaker that night was Arthur Van Buskirk of Pittsburgh, an executive in the Mellon financial empire and chairman of the Allegheny Conference on Community Development. His message extolling the virtues of democracy, though unintended, provided an undercurrent to what was ahead for Memphis. "If democracy is strong in our cities, towns and hamlets, then democracy will be strong in the nation," Buskirk said. "It is not strong now—at least not strong enough for these crucial times. How can democracy be strong when we see the central business districts deteriorating and bordered by slums and blighted residential areas? These slums are cancerous to the body politic of our communities. They are breeding grounds for communism and forces of crime and corruption."[22]

No mention was made that night of the ominous integration push—at least not publicly. But the NAACP's move left city and school leaders flummoxed and tongue-tied. They had no idea how to react to this brewing civic crisis, and Boss Crump was no longer around to tell them what to do. When a *Commercial Appeal* reporter asked John T. Shea, the school board's vice president, for a comment, he responded with double-talk: "In accordance with the usual practice of the board, the letter requesting a conference will be presented and handled in the usual manner."[23]

Memphis Park Commission chairman John Vesey feigned ignorance about the Supreme Court's desegregation ruling and sought to pass the buck to the city commission. "The only thing I see to do is at our next meeting to refer the letter to the commission's attorney and ask him to advise us what do to," he stated. Vesey reminded the *Commercial Appeal* that the park commission "can't make the policy for the city. That has to come from the City Commission. We are not lawyers and it is not up to the Park Commission to interpret the law for the city."[24]

While both the *Commercial Appeal* and *Press-Scimitar* gave the NAACP's demands front-page coverage, neither paper's editorial board addressed the issue with an editorial. It was particularly surprising that Meeman, as editor of the far more progressive *Press-Scimitar*, chose not to take advantage of this crucial moment to address desegregation on his editorial page. And neither paper offered much follow-up reporting.

Instead, the *Commercial Appeal* devoted almost daily coverage to a segregated promotional program called Plant to Prosper, which highlighted area farm production, homemaking, and community activities. In its only major news story about the NAACP demands, the *Commercial Appeal* listed several city amenities that were already open to black citizens.

"Memphis has long permitted Negroes to use Overton Park Zoo one day a week—Thursday," the paper quoted Vesey as saying. "Plus, an amusement park at the Fairgrounds is open to Negroes one night each week. Negroes

are permitted entrance anytime to the Memphis Museum and the B
Art Gallery, and there is a Negro branch of the Cossitt Library on Vanc
enue." The paper added, "Negroes have the exclusive use of 18 playgrou
There are 39 for whites. The same supervised programs are in effect at b _ _
Negro and white playgrounds and equipment is identical.

"There are five white golf courses and one (nine-hole) Negro course. The
city has four swimming pools for whites and three for Negroes and now
is in the process of building a fourth pool for the Negroes. There are three
white community centers and one Negro center. There are 23 white tennis
courts and three Negro courts." The paper ended the story by noting that
about 40 percent of Memphis's population is Negro, according to the 1950
census.[25]

The demand to integrate public facilities came after years of neglect on
the part of the city in maintaining the few parks and playgrounds reserved
for African Americans. In late spring of 1952, the Bluff City and Shelby
County Council of Civic Clubs, a group representing thirty-one black civic
organizations, practically begged city officials to make improvements to the
"deplorable recreational facilities" set aside for Negro youths.[26] The council's
request noted that young black Memphians were becoming increasingly
disillusioned by the blatant racial discrimination that was a way of life for
them: "We cannot in all fairness to our children teach them the democratic
principles of our government and ask them to go along with us. We can't
even sell them on the Southern philosophy of separate but equal facilities
because they may be separate, but there is no equality."[27]

As a follow-up, the Commercial Appeal sent a reporter and photographer to
survey the fourteen playgrounds and parks provided for black Memphians.
They discovered that only three playgrounds were in excellent condition.
Others were nothing more than empty lots and many of them had no toilet
facilities and no drinking water.[28] In response, city leaders made a few minor improvements to black playgrounds but insisted they had no available
funds for lights at Negro ballparks. And desegregation of white parks and
playgrounds was out of the question.

Now, three and a half years later, the respectful request from black citizens for separate-but-equal facilities became an outright demand for full
integration. A week after the NAACP letters were delivered, about four
hundred white Memphians showed up at a park commission meeting to
vehemently protest against integrating city facilities. Only three of the

five commissioners were there—Chairman Vesey, Harry Pierotti, and E. C. "Chip" Barwick—but they represented a quorum. Commissioners Leo Bearman and John Gorman were conveniently absent. Some in the crowd of protesters claimed to be members of Pro-Southerners, a citizens group opposed to integration. They talked openly about trying to impeach the Supreme Court justices because of their desegregation rulings. The crowd filled every available space in the meeting room and spilled into hallways outside. It was an intimidating and imposing force.

Vesey read the NAACP letter in its entirety. Then he added, "I don't know how many Memphis Negroes belong to this organization. But I know it is influenced from the outside." Harry William Pyle, self-described chairman of the Pro-Southerners group, buttressed Vesey's claim. "The NAACP does not represent one percent of the colored people in Memphis," he shouted. "Pro-Southerners represent 10,000 people."

The three commissioners then voted unanimously to "mark for file" the NAACP letter. "That means no action is to be taken toward opening any of these facilities at this time," Vesey shouted loud enough for everyone to hear.[29] The crowd erupted into cheers and left the meeting satisfied that any talk of integration in Memphis had been put to rest. But they were sadly mistaken.

What they did not know was that Mayor Tobey, more than a year before his death in September 1955, had formally invited an all-black golfing association to hold its annual tournament in Memphis in July 1956, using one of the city's eighteen-hole courses where only whites were allowed to play. When the invitation became public knowledge, those same protestors—and hundreds others—were furious. Orgill was sworn into office in January 1956, and the handwritten invitation to the all-black Central States Golfing Association represented his first crisis as mayor.

The Sam Qualls Golf Club, a black golfing group in Memphis, was the tournament's local host and had been planning the event for two years. About 150 golfers were signed up to participate in the five-day event, requiring the use of an eighteen-hole course. Orgill was keenly aware that he could be branded an outright racist if he rescinded Tobey's invitation. But neither he nor Robert Wright, president of the Sam Qualls golfing group, wanted to stoke more anger among white Memphians. So at Wright's request, Orgill tried to rent a private course for the tournament.

"We're not trying to cause any trouble," Wright told the *Commercial Appeal*. The tournament had been held in Denver, Atlanta, Jacksonville, St.

Louis, Dallas, and Minneapolis without complaint. "If we bring these people in here, we don't want any ruckus," Wright said.[30] Orgill reached out to the privately owned Cherokee Golf Club located near Lamar and Prescott. But the club refused to accommodate black golfers, and Orgill had no choice but to secure one of the city's public courses.

This time, both the *Commercial Appeal* and *Press-Scimitar* editorialized in favor of allowing Tobey's invitation to stand. And both papers tried to help Orgill and other city leaders make the case to white Memphians that hosting a black golf tournament did not mean the city was moving toward racial integration. "This is a tournament for Negroes only and it is not a matter of desegregation," the *Commercial Appeal* noted in a four-paragraph editorial on February 10. "Memphis is big enough certainly and has the integrity to carry out its obligation and without untoward incidents. Memphis can entertain this tournament with tranquility and with honor as a community of our size and responsibility is expected to do."[31]

Four days later, the *Press-Scimitar's* editorial page added its voice to the contentious issue. "If the city 'flubs' its shot a handling the Negro tournament—golf course question, that flub will be heard around the world, and that's not the kind of noise we want going out of Memphis," the paper said. "The course of action is clear: The late Mayor Tobey obligated the city to furnish an 18-hole course for the play. He did it in a helpful spirit. This city is still obligated. It tried but couldn't rent a course. Therefore, the only sportsmanlike action is to allow use of one of the three public courses for the tournament. . . .

"Those opposed to the golf tournament have not hesitated to express themselves. They have gone to the commission meetings. But those who think that the promise made by the late Mayor Tobey should be carried out, whom we believe to be in the great majority, have not let their views be known to the same extent. They have not gone to the commission meetings, telephoned the commissioners, or written them letters. They should do so. They owe it to themselves and to their city to do so. Memphis needs fair and friendly relations between the races in order to be happy and prosperous."[32]

The calming editorial stances from both newspapers did little to appease the angry voices of dissent. And when the city commission met on February 14, the segregationists were ready. One of them was Dr. James Franklin, president of a group called We, the People. And he left no uncertainties about his stance on the issue. "We have reason to believe the tournament cannot be played on any white course without violence and bloodshed," he said. "(The tournament) would cause an influx of outside goon squads (from the NAACP). The city may receive a bloodbath." Orgill, however, was angered by Franklin's comments and challenged him to cite proof that people were planning violence. The *Press-Scimitar* reported the testy exchange between the two men: "Do you think you are being just to the police department? Would you be personally a party to violence and bloodshed?" Orgill asked Franklin. "I would not," he responded. The mayor then turned to others in the rowdy audience. "Would anybody in the room be a party to violence and bloodshed? If so stand up."[33]

No one did.

Others in the crowd then spoke in favor of holding the tournament in Memphis. They included civic leader and future congressman George Grider; Dr. Marshall Wingfield, pastor of First Congregational Church; Rev. Paul Carnes of First Unitarian Church; and Dr. Paul Tudor Jones of Idlewild Presbyterian Church. The back-and-forth arguments continued for more than four hours before the mayor and commissioners retreated to an executive session for another fifty-five minutes. When they emerged, commissioners voted unanimously to allow the black golf tournament in Memphis. A few days later, the park commission designated the Audubon Park Golf Course located at Park and Goodlett as the tournament site. Orgill favored that course because the surrounding area was not heavily populated.

"This is the right decision," the *Press-Scimitar* wrote in an editorial on February 15. Memphis keeps its word. Now all the country knows that. We should be proud to have a mayor and commissioners who had the courage, after hearing what citizens had to say on both sides, to do what was obviously right."[34]

The *Commercial Appeal* likewise hailed the vote as "the honest and honorable thing for the commission to do, and those who opposed the decision will, in time, come to recognize that. Memphis has handled its racial association with firmness and tranquility. We believe this action will strengthen that spirit of cooperation."[35]

Wright, whose all-black golf club would host the tournament, was delighted by the decision, telling the *Press-Scimitar* the local club "appreciates the responsibility placed in its hands by the city commission and the park commission. We want to assure them that we will respond by conducting a fine tournament."[36] And that they did. The tournament was a first-class event held July 16–20, 1956, with no reported incidents. It also received sparse newspaper coverage. When it was over, the *Commercial Appeal* reported deep inside its sports pages that Memphian Elton Grandberry was the winner in the men's division and another Memphian, Bubba Jeter, finished second. Gail Patton of St. Louis was victorious in the women's division.

Orgill, other city leaders, the clergy, and the editors of both newspapers were relieved that the tournament went off without any confrontations. In their minds, a racial tempest was now behind them. Except it wasn't. The original NAACP request for desegregation was still on the table and still being ignored. And a growing number of African Americans in Memphis came away from the contentious golf tournament issue disgusted at the very idea that they could not use public facilities for which their tax money was being used to maintain. While Orgill, in the end, stood firmly in favor of the tournament, he was still waffling on full desegregation. As a result, the black voices of discontent and impatience were not abating. They were only getting louder.

CHAPTER 5

WHITE BACKLASH

I N LATE 1955 and early 1956, as Memphians grappled with their own relatively minor racial issues, the cry throughout the South for civil rights was poised to become a full-fledged movement. But white resistance to it was getting stronger and increasingly more violent. On August 28, 1955, black Chicago teenager Emmitt Till was brutally murdered in Money, Mississippi, by a couple of white hotheads.

Till was not trying to integrate the local school or swim in a whites-only pool. His offense was whistling at a white woman. And for that, he was snatched from a relative's home, beaten severely, and shot in the head. The killers then tied a bulky cotton gin fan to the boy's body using barbed wire and threw him into the Tallahatchie River. An all-white jury later acquitted the killers, J. W. Milam and his half-brother, Roy Bryant, whose wife had been the object of Till's whistling.

A majority of whites in Memphis, 125 miles north of Money, seemed oblivious to the growing national outrage over Till's murder. And as 1955 drew to a close, they were instead panicking over the notion that city parks, playgrounds, swimming pools, and—God forbid—public schools would soon be forced to integrate. As white Memphians were stewing over allowing a black golfing association to use a whites-only golf course for its tournament, people elsewhere in the South—thanks to Supreme Court's desegregation rulings—were being forced to finally address the race issue. And the inclination of most white Southerners, including those in Memphis, was to fight.

In late December of 1955, U.S. Senator James Eastland of Mississippi, the most powerful political leader in the state, along with Senator Strom Thurmond of South Carolina, organized a secret two-day meeting at the Peabody Hotel in downtown Memphis to lay the groundwork for a new organization that would vigorously oppose integration throughout the South.[1]

The group named itself the Federation for Constitutional Government and consisted of "the most vehement collection of right-wing activists in the nation."[2] A tip relayed to Commercial Appeal reporter James Gunter led to a news story in the December 29 edition exposing the private meeting. The following day, the New York Times picked up the story and quoted Eastland as saying the federation was designed to "fight the Supreme Court, fight the CIO, fight the NAACP and fight all conscienceless pressure groups who are attempting our destruction."[3]

Meanwhile, two months later in February 1956, Autherine Lucy, the first black student to enroll at the University of Alabama, was suspended from classes, and eventually expelled after repeated threats of violence by white mobs. And in South Carolina, a state park was ordered closed rather accommodate blacks. The *Commercial Appeal* took note of escalating racial violence and denounced it, not necessarily because of the black people who were being hurt or killed but because it was giving the South a bad name. "Mob action is clumsy," the paper said in one editorial. "There are orderly, legal methods of attacking the Supreme Court's attempts to write a law on school segregation."[4]

Memphis was now being run by a progressive mayor, Edmund Orgill, who rose to power with the help of a progressive lawyer named Lucius Burch and a progressive newspaper editor named Edward Meeman. But although Orgill had nothing but praise for the black voters who helped put him in office, or the black workers at his family's business, Orgill Brothers, the mayor was still powerless—and in most cases hesitant—to make any meaningful moves on behalf of desegregation in Memphis. A clear majority of the white population would not allow it, Supreme Court or no Supreme Court. And the mayor was unwilling to stick his neck out too far to help blacks achieve even small measures of equality.

When Orgill sought to appoint Joseph E. Walker, the highly respected head of Universal Life Insurance Company, as the first black board member of John Gaston Hospital, every member of the city commission balked. The mayor's reasoning was sound. African Americans made up nearly 40 percent of the city's population in the mid-1950s and represented 85 percent of the hospital's patients. But none of that mattered. The backlash from many white Memphians was loud and intimidating. And Orgill had little choice but to drop the Walker nomination.[5]

For a majority of whites, separate but supposedly equal was working just fine. They also believed that most black Memphians were content with segregation. Indeed, older leaders in the black community felt they could not afford to press too hard for change for fear of violent retaliation from white extremists. After all, it had happened before in Memphis. So black leaders in 1956 felt they had little choice but to go along with the formation of the Greater Memphis Race Relations Committee, a group set up to promote interracial discussions and harmony but was really designed merely to keep the peace and to put off full integration as long as possible.[6]

Both daily newspapers supported the committee. And each paper's editor—Frank Ahlgren of the *Commercial Appeal* and Edward Meeman of the *Press-Scimitar*—were founding members. The group held its first meeting a week after the golf course controversy was resolved and as racial animosity continued to brew throughout the South. A *Commercial Appeal* editorial on February 24, 1956, said the committee "will be a vehicle for expressing the will of that great majority of citizens who desire nothing more than a continuance of Memphis's orderly progress, and which they know can come only in an atmosphere free from agitation and threat of violence."[7]

The same day the editorial appeared, the *Commercial Appeal* published a story from its Washington bureau that U.S. Representative E. C. Gathings, a Democrat from Arkansas, stood up on the floor of the House and called for a congressional investigation of the NAACP. Gathings said the investigation was warranted after the names of scores of NAACP members and officers had been cited in the records of the House Un-American Activities Committee. Gathings, in essence, was alleging that the civil rights organization was full of communists.

"I feel such a thorough investigation is necessary to protect the Southern Negro and others who have been duped, victimized and exploited by and through the promotional schemes of the NAACP," Gathings said. "Having lived among these people, I am convinced they would not knowingly contribute to or take part in the activities of any organization upon which there is a question mark." Gathings's comments sparked a spirited debate over integration in the South, during which a Georgia representative blurted out, "If the Supreme Court continues to usurp the powers of Congress, our way of life is doomed."[8] Just days before the heated House floor debate on integration, the Mississippi legislature passed a bill essentially forbidding the FBI from conducting civil rights investigations in the state, including the Emmitt Till murder six months earlier.[9]

In Memphis, however, community leaders—black and white—were determined to prevent racial hostility from taking root. They also wanted to keep the courts from forcing integration on a city clearly not ready for it. As a result, some of the city's most influential business and religious leaders signed on to the Race Relations Committee. They included Rabbi James Wax, Msgr. M. F. Kearney, Dr. Donald Henning, Everett Cook, Kenneth Orgill (a cousin of Mayor Edmund Orgill), and Harry Pierotti. Dr. Hollis Price, the black president of LeMoyne College in Memphis, also was among those who agreed to participate. "I suspect most Negroes here are quite content with a gradual approach to integration," he said. Even more significant, Lt. George W. Lee, arguably the most respected black political leader in Memphis at the time, also tacitly agreed with the group's aims. "We'll play along with the (Race Relations) committee as long as we feel it will do something," he said.[10]

In reality, Lee was skeptical. He believed that the committee was nothing more than a feel-good effort to calm fearful whites and appease restless blacks. Besides, Lee preferred to play politics at the national level and had no illusions that the white establishment in Memphis was remotely interested in full racial equality. A protégé of black millionaire Robert R. Church Jr., Lee had succeeded Church as the recognized leader of the Republican Party in Shelby County. His influence stretched across Tennessee and even to Washington.

Just as Church before him, Lee controlled the appointments to federal jobs in Shelby County when a Republican was in the White House. White Republicans outside Memphis respected his political know-how and considered him an asset to their cause. But he was marginalized by most whites in Memphis, despite the fact that both Memphis newspapers chronicled his impressive life story and frequently sought him out for comment on the pressing civic issues of the day.

There was absolutely no reason—other than pure racism—why Lee was never tapped for appointment to a city board or commission. He was smarter than most, if not all, of the white men in city government. He was a decorated war hero, an eloquent orator, and wordsmith who wrote the history of Beale Street. He was cited for bravery during World War I while serving as a liaison officer to General Henri Giraud, brigade commander of French and American troops. Years later, the *Commercial Appeal* reported the story of Lee's valor in detail:

"It was the night of Sept. 25, 1918 in the Argonne when Lee won his promotion from second to first lieutenant liaison officer for the 368th Infantry of the 92nd Division. The French and Americans had advanced to the little village of Benarville on the outskirts of the Argonne after fighting through the forest.

"It was Lee's job to go back to regimental headquarters and report the advance and get further orders. Lee filtered through a barrage of enemy artillery and machine gun fire to reach his objective. The forest was being shelled by the Germans and Allied artillery both. (Lee) also had a running fight with a German sniper in a tree. A bursting shell inflicted a slight wound to his leg, but he kept going. Lee continued to exchange shots with the sniper and he didn't know whether or not he hit him, but the sniping stopped."[11]

The story of Lee's World War I heroism was repeated often around Memphis, and he became beloved throughout the black community. In an equal society, he could have easily become mayor or a member of Congress. But the majority population of Memphis never once considered him for public office and—perhaps knowing the outcome—he never offered himself as a candidate.

For years, Lee was the director of the local branch of the Atlanta Life Insurance Company. When the company wanted to transfer him to the home office in Atlanta in 1948, a campaign was launched to keep Lee in Memphis. The effort was led by Matthew Thornton, the unofficial "mayor of Beale Street" and president of the Cotton Makers' Jubilee, the black version of the segregated Cotton Carnival. Thornton's petition drive collected about three thousand letters demanding that Lee stay put. "We just can't let Lieutenant Lee leave Memphis," Thornton told the *Commercial Appeal*. "We need him too much . . . and we will do everything in our power to keep him here."[12] The petition drive worked, and Lee remained with the Memphis office.

One reason blacks wanted Lee to stay was because he spoke out forcefully on their behalf, and he was not afraid to criticize whites for their racist behavior. In 1957, when U.S. Marshal John T. Williams balked at hiring

Frank LaMondue as the first black deputy marshal in the Memphis office, Lee dispatched a stinging letter to Republican representative Kenneth Keating of New York, who was a ranking member on the House Judiciary Committee: "Better than 50 percent of the people who pass through the federal courtroom are Negroes and if Mr. Williams does not feel that he can serve as marshall (sic) with the Negro deputy, then it seems reasonable to me that he should resign."[13] LaMondue got the job.

In 1946, Lee almost singlehandedly paved the way for East Tennessee congressman Carroll Reece of Knoxville to become Republican national chairman by convincing prominent black Republicans in the North to support the appointment of a white southerner. Reece solicited Lee's help in a letter that acknowledged his considerable influence in the party. "As you know, my voting record on federal legislation has been good . . . having supported both the anti–poll tax and anti-lynching bills over all the years," Reece wrote.[14] Lee eagerly agreed to assist. He wrote to thirty-two Negro GOP leaders in New York, Indiana, Michigan, Pennsylvania, and Missouri asking that they support Reece. "Strange as it may seem," Lee wrote in one letter, "some of the most outstanding liberals in America are from the South."[15] The letter-writing campaign worked. The black Republicans in the North did not oppose Reece's appointment and he served as GOP chairman for two years.

Such political influence was nothing new for Lee, the son of an Indianola, Mississippi, preacher. In 1929, Lee and his mentor, Robert Church Jr., wrote to President Herbert Hoover criticizing him for ignoring the plight of Negroes. They were especially critical of Hoover's proposed $500,000 memorial to dead soldiers of color. "The dead are safe," Lee and Church wrote. "But the living are with us to contend for recognition as citizens."[16]

Lee also held considerable sway with Boss Crump. In a letter to Crump in July 1941, Lee noted that the Boss planned to start patriotic singing in Court Square: "I think this is a most significant move in the face of the lack of National unity; and I believe other cities will catch the spirit. For if our country is to survive, there must be forged a stronger brand of Nationalism. Might I also suggest that a similar program of singing be inaugurated in Handy Park (near Beale Street where black Memphians often congregated). While the Negro's loyalty through the years has never been questioned, yet I feel we are in need of some stimulation."[17]

Lee showed patriotism with more than mere words. Two weeks before writing the letter to Crump, Lee withdrew $5,000 from his personal savings and purchased national Defense bonds. "Our country needs funds,"

Lee told a reporter for the *Press-Scimitar*. "I think every citizen should be defense-conscious and give every aid possible to make our nation secure against the great wave of autocracy that sweeps over 4,000 miles of ocean and is now crashing sullenly against our shores."[18]

Years later, Lee described Crump as "perhaps the kindest of political leaders in an age when Negroes were not considered in the political life of the city." According to Lee, Crump "lived only in the fear of God and brooked no interference from any man. A hard-driving individual who held Memphis and Shelby County by its political coattails . . . and he who dared foul his philosophy or block his onward march would face fury like a dozen cyclones."[19]

Lee's crowning moment in the national political spotlight came in 1952, when he was selected to give a speech at the Republication National Convention in Chicago seconding the nomination of Robert Taft for president. The convention, however, selected Dwight Eisenhower as the party's nominee. After his election, Eisenhower appointed Lee to an advisory committee for the U.S. Small Business Administration. And Lee oversaw the president's 1956 reelection campaign in Memphis. G. Wayne Dowdy, in his book *Crusades for Freedom*, described Lee's work for Eisenhower this way:

"For decades Lee had employed grassroots electoral techniques, and he used all of his considerable political talents during the 1956 presidential campaign. Workers fanned out across the city and county, ringing doorbells, and distributing eighty-nine thousand pieces of campaign literature. Large rallies were held in the African American wards, while Lee negotiated with ministers to use their influence to get out the vote on election day. The negotiations worked. The Friday before the election, over one hundred black religious leaders issued a statement requesting their parishioners to vote for the president."[20]

Lee also authored newspaper editorials and gave speeches imploring Shelby County voters to cast their ballot for Eisenhower. The effort paid tremendous dividends. Eisenhower became the first Republican in history to carry Shelby County, with a nearly four-thousand-vote margin over Democrat Adlai Stevenson. Most of the president's support came from African American wards and white suburban voters.[21]

But despite Lee's national reputation as an effective political operative, he was viewed by white power brokers in Memphis as merely one of the rare Negroes who dressed impeccably, spoke well, had been to college, and had a decent job. To most of them, he was still just a black man deserving of no meaningful voice in city government affairs. His clout in national Republican politics would eventually come under serious threat as well by an emerging group of white lawyers and businessmen who wanted to seize control of the local party.

Lee and many others in the black community, including the highly respected Blair T. Hunt, believed radicalism was not the way to approach the segregation question in Memphis. They hearkened back to their cordial relationship with Boss Crump, who would at least listen to them and often tried to make life better for black folks. As long as Mayor Orgill and those of his ilk remained in office, most black Memphians clung to the belief that their plight would gradually improve.

That was so even after Orgill was forced at a heated city commission meeting on April 2, 1957, to emphatically state his position on racial integration. Once again, desegregation of city parks was on the agenda that day. And Warren Webb, secretary of a prosegregation group called the Tennessee Federation of Constitutional Government, put the mayor on the spot with one simple question: "What I'd like to know is the mayor's stand on integration."

Orgill's response focused only on school desegregation, an issue he knew was politically toxic. "I do not believe in integration of our schools," he said. "I think it would be bad for two principal reasons. First, the predominant public opinion is against it. And second, it would hurt the quality of our teaching." The mayor then quickly pivoted to patronizing comments about the perceived racial harmony in Memphis. "We've had remarkably little racial trouble in Memphis. This is due in large part to the wisdom of our Negro leaders of today. We employ Negroes as firemen and policemen. We have both charity and pay hospitals for Negroes. We have a training school for Negro nurses. Eighty percent of John Gaston Hospital is occupied by Negroes. We have planned facilities for Negro interns.

"Most of our public housing is for Negroes. Political leaders of the past urged Negroes to vote and they register and vote now without hindrance. They serve as election officials. . . . These things seem to indicate wisdom on the part of the political leaders of the past. The Negro has felt that his needs were being looked after by elected officials. We haven't had any trouble and I sincerely hope we will continue to be wise enough to conduct ourselves so we will not have trouble.

"I think that if a man has colored skin, he is still a son of God. It is my hope I will always conduct myself so I will not hurt his feelings or make him feel he is not one of God's children. In this period of tension we need to do what we have been doing. Things are going along very good as it is. The less talking we do, the better."[22]

Orgill's lengthy remarks also noted that Dr. Martin Luther King Jr., fresh from his leadership of the successful bus boycott in Montgomery, Alabama, was planning a speech in Memphis in two weeks. And the mayor tried to assure Memphians that King's visit would be peaceful. "I talked to some of the Negro leaders of Memphis about this and ventured the thought that if (King) should decide to do so, he could help us instead of hurt us. I think having a contact with the leaders of the Negroes is worth something to the city government. My guess is they will respond to fair treatment and I pledge my efforts in that direction."[23]

Once the commission meeting was over, Orgill took a deep breath and left the room feeling that his political tap dance around the integration question would settle things down in Memphis—at least for a while. He was also relieved that no reporters followed him out of the room to ask follow-up questions. Privately, though, Orgill fretted over King's pending Memphis visit, even though he got additional assurances that the speech would not incite a racial uprising in Memphis.

Three black fraternity chapters in Memphis—Alpha Phi Alpha, Kappa Alpha Psi, and Phi Beta Sigma—were sponsoring the King visit at Metropolitan Baptist Church, a stone's throw from LeMoyne College in a well-to-do black section of South Memphis near Mississippi Boulevard and Walker Avenue. The organizers of King's visit were from the best-educated segments of black Memphis—a younger generation that wanted to remain respectful of the black-white relationships that had been carefully nourished over the years by Boss Crump, Blair T. Hunt, Lieutenant Lee, and others. Still, their agenda was clear. Racial change in America was inevitable and they didn't want Memphis to be left out.

Between sixteen hundred and seventeen hundred people showed up at Metropolitan church on the evening of April 19, 1957, which was Good Friday, to hear the dynamic young Baptist preacher and emerging civil rights leader. Both the *Commercial Appeal* and *Press-Scimitar* recognized the news value in King's speech and sent two of their top reporters to cover it. But not surprisingly, the *Press-Scimitar* gave the event more coverage in its Saturday editions.

Reflecting on the bus boycott, King told the audience the move created lots of hardship for blacks in Montgomery, but the cause was much larger than one city. "It is more honorable to walk in dignity than ride in humiliation," he said. "And we are determined to win freedom in this generation. If democracy is to live, segregation must die. Segregation is a tragic evil, a festering sore that debilitates the white man as well as the Negro. Segregation is a tragic cancer in the body politic which must be removed before democracy can be realized."[24]

King also called for continued local support of the NAACP and its gradual effort to desegregate parks, libraries and schools. And he urged the audience to use the power of the vote—something black Memphians had been doing for decades, even if once directed by Crump. Only now, it was time to start making the black vote in Memphis pay off for black candidates in Memphis. "We must gain power by gaining the ballot," King said. "One of the more decisive steps that a Negro can take is the short step to the ballot box." He closed his speech with this admonition: "Let us make sure that as we go, our methods will be rooted deep in the soils of the Christian faith. Be sure your hands are clean in this struggle."[25]

Other than two newspaper stories, King's visit created little stir among white Memphians—much to the delight of Mayor Orgill and the police department. The coming months brought little if any change to Memphis's segregated way of life, although Orgill's popularity throughout Tennessee was on a definite upward spiral. In early 1958, a group of East Tennessee businessmen floated the idea of drafting Orgill to run for the Democratic nomination for governor. When the idea reached Lucius Burch, Orgill's biggest supporter in Memphis, he was ready to seize the moment.

On April 2, 1958, Burch convened a group in Nashville to officially demand—with Orgill's blessings, of course—that the mayor get into the governor's race. Joining Burch at the Nashville meeting were fellow Memphians George Grider, Dr. Henry Gotten, and Frances Coe.[26]

Orgill remained coy to the press. But three weeks later, he announced his entry into the gubernatorial race against Buford Ellington and segregationist judge Andrew "Tip" Taylor of Jackson. The Orgill campaign captured the attention of voters in Middle and East Tennessee. But among white voters in Shelby County, Orgill's perceived waffling on the issue of race cost him the election, even though he kept insisting that he had not advocated for school integration and would never do so if elected governor.

Still, Taylor's campaign distributed to white voters in Shelby County copies of the black-owned *Tri-State Defender* newspaper's endorsement of

White Backlash

Orgill. The *Commercial Appeal* endorsed Taylor while conveniently ignoring his staunch views against integration. Ed Meeman's *Press-Scimitar*, as expected, endorsed Orgill. But all three Memphis newspapers missed the mark. On election night, Orgill lost the Democratic nomination to Ellington by about seven thousand votes. In Shelby County, Orgill carried the black vote handily. But he lost badly to Taylor among segregation-minded white voters, and as a result, Orgill lost the county by about three thousand votes, thus ending any hopes for statewide office.[27]

After a short vacation on the Atlantic coast, Orgill returned to his job as mayor. And Burch sought to reignite the dormant race relations committee, which had failed to make any progress in 1956, mainly because white members refused to even meet in the same room with African American members.[28] Black demands for desegregating public institutions and major businesses were gaining momentum and would eventually lead to lawsuits, student sit-ins, and community rallies.

Burch put out a call in late 1958 to form a truly biracial group known as the Memphis Committee on Community Relations (MCCR), and more than fifty people—including NAACP leaders, the newspaper editors, and Memphis Chamber of Commerce members—responded with a pledge to participate.[29] Most whites in the group still wanted to move slowly on integration. And the daily newspapers downplayed black protests in order to help keep the peace. But as the sit-in movement to integrate city libraries and other facilities grew more intense and disruptive, the MCCR stepped up the call for desegregation, including at major department stores such as Goldsmith's and Lowenstein's downtown on Main Street.[30]

Meanwhile, by early 1959, interest was starting to build toward a municipal election that would be a defining moment in the black-white relationship in Memphis—a relationship that was growing more strained by the day. Commissioner Henry Loeb tapped into the white hostility simmering across the city over continuing demands for racial equality—and Orgill's reluctance to take a firm stand one way or the other. By spring, Loeb announced that he would oppose Orgill for mayor in the August 1959 city election. With the Crump machine, which once tried to derail his political ambitions, all but obliterated, Loeb was convinced the time was right to mount a campaign based mostly on white resistance to civil rights.

Loeb's candidacy got an unexpected but gigantic boost when Orgill became ill while campaigning on July 3. During a three-hour handshaking tour of the city, Orgill lost feeling in his right hand, and the next day checked himself in to Methodist Hospital. Tests revealed a blocked carotid artery that could have led to a massive stroke. The mayor underwent surgery but was forced to drop out of the mayor's race six weeks before election day. With no other major contender in the race, Loeb instantly became the prohibitive favorite. He had the support of both the *Commercial Appeal* and *Press-Scimitar*, along with a majority of the city's business leaders. Orgill's withdrawal caught members of his campaign committee completely off guard, but many of them still wanted a say in who the next mayor would be. So within two weeks of the mayor's withdrawal, his committee had revamped itself into a new citizens' group known as the Dedicated Citizens Committee.

Rather than commit to another mayoral candidate, the committee distributed a list of questions to all of them. Loeb, probably by design, was the first to publicly respond, and both newspapers published his treatise word for word. Loeb addressed in detail such issues as changing the form of government (which he favored), annexation, consolidation of city and county governments (which he also favored), and city planning. On the subject of racial segregation, however, Loeb had little to say. "My position with regard to the Negro citizens of our community is a matter of day-to-day record, not theory," he stated. "It is well known, both in private and public life, that I have treated the Negro fairly and squarely."[31]

That was it. No elaboration at all on desegregating schools, public parks, swimming pools, libraries, and playgrounds. No discussion whatsoever on integrating lunch counters or appointing African Americans to public boards and commissions. Loeb's steamrolling campaign was deftly silent on the important issue of race. And his supporters liked it that way. But the subject would prove unavoidable—all because of Loeb himself. His quest for mayor meant that his elected position as commissioner of public works became a free-for-all. And with that open seat, Memphis's young black political upstarts finally saw a possible opening to win an elected office.

Memphis elections did not provide for a runoff, so the candidate with the most votes—even if not a majority—would win. Russell Sugarmon, a Harvard-educated lawyer, was the only black candidate to file for Loeb's commission seat against five white candidates, four of whom were considered viable contenders. Sugarmon led the all-black Volunteer Ticket of candidates, which also included Dr. Benjamin L. Hooks for juvenile court judge, Rev. Roy Love and Henry Bunton for the Memphis City Schools Board of Education, and Eliehue Stanback for city tax assessor.

White Backlash

The group opened its headquarters on Beale Street across from Robert R. Church Park and campaigned hard but acted pragmatically. The chances that all five would win were remote. But with a strong black voter turnout, Sugarmon had the best chance because his four major opponents—William Farris, Will Fowler, John Ford Canale, and Sam Chambers—would split the white vote. Once white Memphians realized that Sugarmon had a legitimate shot, they shifted to crisis mode.

Among black Memphians, however, there was genuine excitement for an election in which for the first time a black candidate—or two—had a chance to win. The Volunteer Ticket capitalized on the growing fervor with large get-out-the-vote rallies. The first one was scheduled to be held at Martin Stadium at Wellington and Crump Boulevard, home to the Memphis Red Sox of Negro League baseball. Thousands of tickets were distributed for the event, but B. B. Martin, a black businessman who owned the team and the stadium with his brothers, refused to allow the rally to be held there. When asked why by a reporter from the *Tri-State Defender*, Martin shouted, "Because it's mine."[32]

The rally was held instead at Mason Temple on July 31, 1959. Several hundred black residents showed up to hear fiery campaign speeches from some of the city's finest black orators, including Dr. W. Herbert Brewster and George W. Lee. "We're going to fight till hell freezes over and, if necessary, skate across the ice in order to keep freedom moving in the right direction," Lee told the pumped audience. "Many people still think of Memphis as Mr. Crump's town and us as Mr. Crump's Negroes. That ain't so now."[33]

The main speaker, however, was Martin Luther King Jr., who was personally invited by Sugarmon and Hooks. Sugarmon and King had briefly attended Morehouse College together—King was a sophomore when Sugarmon was a freshmen. They became friends before Sugarmon was kicked out of the school. The reason for his expulsion? Sugarmon and other students were caught drinking beer in a bell tower that had been rendered off limits to students. Sugarmon and the others were there chugging beer while watching crosses being burned in the distance by the Ku Klux Klan.[34]

Instead of returning to Memphis, Sugarmon took an instructor's advice and applied to Rutgers University—a place where he would be challenged more academically. The admissions officer was dubious that a black student from the South could compete at Rutgers but agreed to give Sugarmon a semester to make the grade. He graduated with a degree in political science then obtained a law degree from Harvard.

When King heard that his former Morehouse mate was trying to win political office in Memphis, he readily agreed to help. He urged the Mason Temple crowd that evening to go to the polls in record numbers to put Sugarmon, Hooks, and the other black candidates in office. King and other civil rights leaders, including Rev. Fred Shuttlesworth, Rev. Ralph Abernathy, and Rev. T. J. Jemison, included Memphis as part of their goal to register some three million black voters in eleven southern states by 1960 and recruit black candidates to run for offices in those states.[35]

News coverage of the massive Mason Temple rally created even more uneasiness in the white community. And the next day, Loeb announced that, if necessary, he would endorse one of the white candidates in the public works commissioner's race to keep an African American from winning. To avoid having to get involved in the race, Loeb urged at least two of the white candidates to voluntarily withdraw. If not, he warned, the odds were good that Sugarmon would win: "Suppose there are 100,000 votes cast and 25,000 of these are colored and the rest are split four ways. You have something that is not good."[36]

The *Commercial Appeal* and *Press-Scimitar* joined with Loeb in the call for the white candidates to "thin their ranks." The *Commercial Appeal* even went so far as to suggest that the election of any one of the black candidates would produce "real fear in the white community." It was simply unthinkable, the paper said, that a Negro juvenile court judge would be exercising supervision over broken white families. Instead, the newspaper suggested setting up a separate division in juvenile court "for Negro problems with members of that race administering the offices."[37]

Despite repeated urging, no white candidate was willing to drop out. Candidate Sam Chambers issued a statement saying he refused to be "pressured out by professional politicians and two Scripps-Howard newspapers." He added that all of the attention being paid to the commissioner's race might allow a Negro to "slip in the back door in the Juvenile Court and school board races."[38]

Loeb, who was virtually assured of becoming the next mayor, kept up the pressure. On August 13, one week before the election, he convened a meeting at the Claridge Hotel in downtown Memphis with the four major white candidates for public works commissioner. The meeting was open to reporters because Loeb wanted to assure white Memphians that he was

White Backlash

working feverishly on their behalf to keep Negroes out of elected office. But the meeting produced no withdrawals.

Two days later, however, Fowler, who had insisted that he was the leading candidate based on a *Commercial Appeal* poll, dropped out, saying he was doing it for the good of Memphis. Fowler's withdrawal did the trick. It eliminated the need for Loeb, the mayor-in-waiting, to personally endorse one white candidate over the others. And the race was all but decided two days before the election when Mayor Orgill and key supporters for Loeb and Commissioner Claude Armour endorsed Farris, who earlier was endorsed by both the *Commercial Appeal* and *Press-Scimitar.*[39]

The *Tri-State Defender*, however, endorsed the Volunteer Ticket with a front-page editorial. The African American newspaper also endorsed Partee Fleming for mayor, proclaiming in a front-page headline that "Loeb is not for us." The paper urged blacks to "flock to the polls" to vote against Loeb hoping "some miracle may work itself to keep Loeb out of office." The paper noted, however, that some in the black community were unhappy that Volunteer Ticket candidates Rev. Roy Love and Henry Bunton were running against two white women on the Memphis City Schools Board of Education who had been sympathetic to black Memphians, rather than opposing two white men, Julian Bondurant and John T. Shea.[40]

On election night, August 20, Farris got 58,951 votes to win the seat over Sugarmon, who finished second with 35,237 votes. Other black candidates on the Volunteer Ticket also finished second in their races but lost by substantial margins in what was the heaviest voter turnout in the city's history. Hooks, for example, lost the juvenile court judge race to Elizabeth McCain by twenty-one thousand votes. The *Commercial Appeal* trumpeted the outcome with a front-page headline that read, "Negroes fail in bid for city posts."[41] An editorial the following day sought to justify the paper's stance in the election by insisting that it would have been unfair for a relatively small number of black voters to decide the outcome.

"We are opposed to bloc voting," the paper said. "Of course, minorities want to make their views known and in this election Negroes got together, flexed their muscles and showed a capacity for using the election processes. It was a situation which could have had embarrassing consequences, but the outcome was satisfactory if the white community now realizes that Negroes are due more participation in municipal government."[42]

The editorial was mere wishful thinking because Loeb, who was elected mayor in a landslide, had no intention of giving black Memphians any kind of significant voice in city government. The political influence of the so-called white progressives, led by Lucius Burch, Edmund Orgill, and Edward Meeman, turned out to be only fleeting. Loeb and the city's white majority were perfectly satisfied with a segregated society and a white-dominated government in Memphis. In their minds, blacks and whites were getting along because everyone—except for a few radicals—knew their place. Nothing was going to change because Loeb and his backers had the voting numbers on their side to stave off any future attempts by these young, upstart blacks to gain a foothold in local government.

The white backlash against civil rights and racial equality was working. But it wouldn't last.

CHAPTER 6

CAUGHT BY SURPRISE

HENRY LOEB WAS SWORN IN as mayor on the first day of a new year in a new decade—January 1, 1960. But for African Americans, very little had changed. Loeb was keenly aware of who had put him into office and they were not from the black community. So he felt no need to offer an olive branch to black leaders, and they felt no hesitancy in criticizing the new mayor for perpetuating segregation.

When Loeb took office, a few blacks had been part of the police department for a dozen years, although their authority was limited. The new mayor flatly refused to appoint any African Americans to positions in his administration or to board memberships that the mayor's office controlled. And unlike most of the preceding mayors, including Walter Chandler, Watkins Overton, Frank Tobey, Edmund Orgill, and even Boss Crump himself, Loeb had no one in the black community he could rely on as a confidante. And that was just fine with him. In later years, however, he did consult from time to time with black businessman Fred Davis, and occasionally took his advice on city issues.[1] But that was as far as it went.

The pent-up demand in the city's black community for racial equality was poised to gain new foot soldiers as sit-ins were taking place elsewhere around the South. For example, on February 1, 1960, four black college students staged a sit-in at a Woolworth's lunch counter in Greensboro, North Carolina, where they were refused service. Thirteen days later, black students entered the Kress, Woolworth's, and McLellan's stores in Nashville and sat down at those lunch counters. They were denied service, and about two hours later, the counters were closed.

And on March 18, 1960, seven black students from Owen Junior College in South Memphis entered a McLellan's on Main Street and sat down at the "whites only" lunch counter next to white patrons.[2] The police response was swift and the store manager promptly closed the business. The students left without being arrested.[3] Claude Armour, the city commissioner in charge of public safety, issued an immediate statement saying police "will not tolerate this type of unlawful demonstration. Our men have been instructed to be firm but fair and to enforce the law. We of this department had hoped there would be no incident of this type to occur in Memphis."[4] Armour warned that if the sit-ins continued, the demonstrators would be charged with loitering, disorderly conduct, and breach of the peace. "We have had excellent race relations in our city and sincerely hope this will continue," he said.[5]

The following day, however, nearly forty male and female students, mainly from Owen and LeMoyne College, staged a sit-in at the Cossitt branch library downtown and the main library at Peabody and McLean in Midtown. And within an hour, they—along with editors and photographers for the *Tri-State State Defender* and *Memphis World* newspapers—were arrested and charged just as Armour had promised.[6] The incident spurred an almost overnight change in the thinking of many African Americans in Memphis about the stubborn resistance to racial integration. Until then, older and more established members of the black community had been leading the desegregation charge in a deliberate, nonconfrontational fashion. Now young black college students were getting involved. And the entire city had to take notice.

The NAACP and the black clergy offered immediate support to the students and raised money to post their bail. At his Sunday morning worship services at East Trigg Avenue Baptist Church, Pastor W. Herbert Brewster said the students "were merely applying Gandhi and Nehru's tactics of passive resistance to compel the white race to live up to its own political and religious philosophy."[7] Brewster and other black ministers urged members of their congregation to show up in large numbers for the city court hearing the following day. More than two thousand spectators did, but they were turned away by police.[8]

Inside the courtroom, NAACP lawyers, including H. T. Lockard and Russell Sugarmon Jr., argued that the students had a legitimate civil right

Caught by Surprise

to enter the libraries. But after the five-hour hearing, Judge Beverly Bouche made his feelings clear. "I'm not concerned at all with civil rights," he said. "I'm not here to listen to arguments over integration or segregation."[9]

He fined thirty-six students twenty-six dollars each for disorderly conduct and called their sit-in "an attempt at mob rule (and) an open invitation to violence. There is no doubt in my mind that this was a concerted effort to use this court as a platform for your propaganda. I have said many times from this bench and I will repeat, we will not tolerate anything in this city that smacks of mob rule or gangsterism, and race, creed and color has nothing to do with it." Bouche also fined Lutrelle F. Palmer, editor of the *Tri-State Defender*, fifty-one dollars merely for talking to the student demonstrators during the sit-in.[10]

Mayor Loeb and the city commission offered wholehearted support for the police action in hauling the demonstrators to jail. And both the *Commercial Appeal* and *Press-Scimitar* published editorials supporting Judge Bouche's decision to fine the students. The *Commercial Appeal* wrote that the demonstrations "accomplish nothing and negate the fruits of many years of sincere community striving for racial goodwill."[11] The *Press-Scimitar*, while calling the sit-ins ill advised, said it was time to end racial segregation at publicly owned facilities: "It does not make sense that Negroes, who can shop for evening dresses and fur coats at fashionable stores in the city on an equal basis with white customers, cannot shop freely for books in libraries supported by taxes they help to pay."[12]

Six months after the student sit-ins began, the slow-moving MCCR helped secure an agreement to desegregate public libraries. Integration at the zoo followed, and finally the major downtown retailers.[13] Loeb, however, remained unmoved. His relationship with the black community became even more strained after the mayor gave a condescending speech to the Memphis Rotary Club on August 1, 1961, in which he chastised blacks in Memphis for being irresponsible, for "asking and never giving," and for failing to meet "the white community half way on what is best for all of us."[14]

The *Commercial Appeal* published a full transcript of Loeb's speech in which he suggested that the civil rights movement was just another attempt by northern whites to exploit helpless blacks in the South: "Following the Civil War men known as 'carpetbaggers' came down from the North. Posing as friends of the rights of the Negro, they placed the Negro in places of political responsibility for which he was not prepared. It did not take the Negro long to discover that he was being used. He discovered that his real friends were not the politicians black or white trying to use him, but those vast numbers of Southern white people who began the struggle to give him better schools and better economic opportunities.

"Surely our Negro citizens will not forget that lesson of history so soon. Again the real friends of the Negro are those vast numbers of whites who strive not to elevate a few, but to elevate all of the race to new heights of educational and economic opportunity.

"I choose to be with those moderate, decent, level-headed people who desire to elevate all of the races. When we choose this road, we know that we shall have to endure the slander of the lunatic fringe of both races. To this way I am committed because I believe that it is right, that it is the American way and that it will win. While mayor of this city, I believe that the greatest service I can render to all races, colors and creeds is to strive to have in places of highest trust those who by their qualifications and efficiency are best prepared to lead and thereby to serve. Those who know me best know that I will not budge one inch in doing my duty. In the end it may not be said of me that I was popular, but I hope it may be said of me as it was said of Henry Hudson, the explorer of this new world: 'He kept the courage of a certain aim, amid the peril of uncertain ways, and sailed ahead, and left the rest to God.'"[15]

Loeb's heavily publicized speech only further inflamed black leaders, both the old guard and the younger freedom advocates. Three days later, George W. Lee, the most respected and most outspoken black political leader in Memphis, responded to Loeb's comments—not so much with anger, but with facts about the vast contributions that black people had made to the city.

Lee's response was given during a gathering of the Memphis Underwriters Club and was published verbatim in the *Press-Scimitar.* Lee reminded white Memphians that black people had safeguarded their homes and businesses after whites fled the city during the yellow fever epidemic, and that black millionaire Robert Church Sr. had provided much-needed financial help that allowed the city to recover after the epidemic. Lee also reminded whites of the bravery of Tom Lee, who had rescued more than thirty whites from a sinking tugboat in the Mississippi River in 1925, and of the efforts of Joseph E. Walker, founder of Universal Life Insurance Company and cofounder of Tri-State Bank. The two businesses had provided $25 million in loans to build homes in Memphis.

"I believe any fair-minded white person will say that Negro leaders stand not only acquitted of the indictment of failure to assume their responsibility, but as having established in addition the positive fact of their usefulness to the community," he said. "It is our earnest hope that our mayor, who says he is the mayor of all the people, will exert a more wholesome and hearty influence in these days when some very good and sincere white people are genuinely distressed."[16]

Despite Loeb's recalcitrance where racial equality was concerned, incremental progress against segregation continued to take place in Memphis. In October 1961, thirteen first graders became the first African Americans to integrate Memphis City Schools. They were enrolled at the previously all-white Bruce, Gordon, Rozelle, and Springdale elementary schools. Scores of white parents immediately withdrew their children from the schools, but for the most part, this baby step toward school integration was carried out peacefully in Memphis.

Unlike in other parts of the South, including just across the state line in Mississippi, white politicians and business leaders in Memphis who had spoken out so forcefully in the past against race mixing in the schools realized it was foolhardy to defy the Supreme Court. The strategy by NAACP leaders to begin the integration process in elementary schools, using the best and brightest first graders they could find, was brilliant. The chances that children so young, well dressed, and studious would be harassed and intimidated were low, and the calculation proved correct. It would be another ten years, however, before court-ordered school desegregation would fundamentally change Memphis schools forever.

A far more shocking and unexpected change in city government took place in the fall of 1963. The president of Loeb Laundry-Cleaners, a highly profitable business owned by the mayor's family, died suddenly. Loeb then had an equally sudden political decision to make—whether to end his bid for reelection and take over as president and general manager of the family business. On the morning of October 3, he made the decision public before scores of supporters who gathered at his campaign headquarters at 26 South Cleveland. He would leave the mayor's office immediately. "Sometimes in life you come to a conflict of responsibilities and so it is here," he stated. "One responsibility is the path I had chosen—which I love—serving Memphis to the best of my ability. I have done my best for eight years. The other responsibility is to my family which I cannot turn aside. I have no alternative but to withdraw my name from the mayor's race."

Loeb, however, cautioned his critics to not get too ecstatic. "This doesn't mean I'm through with politics. I hope someday to run again."[17] Still, the decision was welcome news in the black community, where leaders were marshaling support for city court judge William B. Ingram, who was considered a long shot for mayor and remained so even with Loeb out of the race. With Loeb's withdrawal, Commissioner William Farris emerged as the front-runner. He was enthusiastically endorsed by both the *Commercial Appeal* and *Press-Scimitar,* and there was strong sentiment to make him interim mayor.

Loeb, however, opposed the idea, saying it would give Farris an unfair advantage with the city election just a month away. The commission agreed to allow Commissioner Claude Armour to serve as interim mayor then after the election appoint the mayoral winner to the post immediately. Most of the city's power brokers were still thinking that would be Farris. But on election night, Ingram pulled an upset, thanks to an impressive voter turnout in black precincts, particularly in southwest Memphis and Frayser.

Loeb's withdrawal from the race actually depressed the white vote, and Ingram received a final tally of 57,513 to Farris's 50,637. Ingram attracted black voters for one primary reason. Blacks who came into his courtroom were treated fairly. Unlike other Memphis judges, including Beverly Bouche, Ingram would not automatically side with police who made arresting blacks for the pettiest of crimes a local pastime. Ingram once told a reporter that when he first went on the bench someone told him, "It's always best to believe the testimony of police officers. You can't believe what people charged with offenses testify. They'll say anything to get off."[18] However, Ingram routinely did the opposite and constantly drew the ire of Commissioner Armour and his henchmen in the police department. "If police are supposed to win every case," Ingram said, "there's no need for judges."[19]

Black Memphians loved that kind of talk and supported Ingram at the ballot box because of it. But once again, the effort by black voters to get one of their own elected fell short. In the November 1963 city election, Benjamin Hooks was again on the ballot, this time as a candidate for Memphis City Court judge. He finished a close second to Ray Churchill, who got 43,396 votes to 41,515 for Hooks. It was an admirable showing for Hooks, who received virtually no votes in predominantly white precincts. Many in the black community became resigned to the notion that getting an African American elected to a city office under the current system was impossible. Their focus instead would remain on full integration of schools, parks, museums and restaurants. In the mayor's office, at least, blacks were content for the moment knowing that they now had an ally and not an enemy sitting there.

A more super-sized victory for black citizens came about eight months later, when President Lyndon B. Johnson—who had become commander in chief after the November 22, 1963, assassination of John F. Kennedy—signed the landmark Civil Rights Act into law on July 2, 1964. The act officially outlawed discrimination in voting, public accommodations, schools, employment, and all public places. Most whites, it seems, were caught completely by surprise, while black leaders had been planning for the moment. The next day, a group of black Memphians, led by local NAACP president Jesse Turner, visited several segregated restaurants and ordered meals. The black customers were served at every place except one, the Normal Tea Room at 593 South Highland.[20]

Across the state line in Mississippi, mobilized NAACP leaders from other states poured into Jackson, the state capital, and successfully checked into the previously segregated King Edward, Sun-N-Sand, and Heidelberg hotels. Blacks were served at the Sun-N-Sand's restaurant, but the hotel quickly closed its swimming pool and stationed two armed guards at the pool to keep people out.

Charles Evers, the brother of slain civil rights leader Medger Evers, was in charge of escorting the out-of-state NAACP heads from the Jackson airport to the hotels. During one airport run, he was stopped by Jackson police and arrested allegedly for speeding. Evers posted a twenty-seven-dollar bond and continued his shuttles. The one major Jackson hotel that opted to close rather than integrate was the Robert E. Lee Hotel.

Resistance was equally strong elsewhere in the South, including Atlanta, where outspoken segregationist Lester Maddox confronted two black customers at the door of his restaurant. "Stop right where you are," Maddox shouted. "You are not going to eat in my place tonight, tomorrow night or any other time." Maddox had his hand on a holstered pistol the entire time. Finally, a police detective told the blacks to leave and they did.

Meanwhile, the owner of the Heart of Atlanta Motel Corporation immediately filed a lawsuit asking for an injunction to stop enforcement of the public accommodation section of the Civil Rights Act. The lawsuit maintained that desegregation would ruin motel president Moreton Rolleston's business, his reputation, and his goodwill.

In Memphis, however, Kemmons Wilson, owner of the fast-growing Holiday Inn hotel chain, took the bold step of immediately ordering all of his hotels nationwide to end segregation with "careful tact and restraint. Seldom does a democracy enjoy unanimity on any question, but we all know that the successful operation of a democratic nation requires that its people abide by its law, popular or unpopular."[21]

President Johnson's signature on the Civil Rights Act of 1964, more than anything, changed the landscape of national party politics and gave Republicans their first real inroad to southern white voters. James L. Dickerson, in his book, *Dixie's Dirty Secret*, wrote that the shift actually began during the 1960 presidential campaign after Massachusetts Democrat John Kennedy telephoned Coretta Scott King, the wife of Martin Luther King Jr., after his arrest in Atlanta for marching without a permit. During the call, Kennedy reaffirmed his intention to end racial segregation if elected president.

"That telephone call marked the precise historical point at which Southern Democrats packed their racist, Old Confederacy baggage and put it on the conveyor belt to the Republican Party," Dickerson wrote. "In the years to come, the Democratic Party would become the pro-black, liberal party and the Republican Party would pick up the racist, radical-right ideology of the Democratic Party."

Indeed, civil rights became the number-one topic among delegates and the press at the Republican National Convention in San Francisco in mid-July 1964. Memphis's struggle with racial politics figured prominently in the convention's cumbersome debate on the subject. And at the center of it all was prominent black Memphian George W. Lee.

Lee had been a stalwart in the Republican Party for decades, and a convention delegate six consecutive times. He was counting on being a significant player at the 1964 gathering, even if it became the last convention hurrah for the sixty-seven-year-old political titan. However, almost a dozen years earlier, emerging white Republicans in Shelby County started maneuvering to take control of the local party away from Lee. The move was spearheaded by young attorney Lewis Donelson, who had been a Democrat until 1951, when he realized his political views were "more in tune with conservatism and nonregulatory policies of the Republicans than the Democrats who preached big government, business regulation and lots of handouts."[22]

Donelson, and others who formed the New Guard Republican Association in Shelby, were convinced that Lee and his Lincoln League Repub-

Caught by Surprise

lican group were only interested in patronage and controlling jobs at the post office and had no interest in seeing the party gain local strength and power.[23] The battle for control between the New Guard Republicans and Lee's group—also known as the Black and Tans—went on for years, with the New Guards gaining more recruits each year.

In his 2012 memoir *Lewie*, Donelson wrote that as the 1964 GOP convention approached, he and lawyer Harry W. Wellford, a fellow recruit to the New Guard Republicans, visited Lee "to work out an understanding. We took the position that we represented the majority of Republicans in the county and wanted the majority of representation in the party structure. We offered Lieutenant Lee a significant minority with adequate representation, including election as a delegate to national conventions, but he rejected that proposal. We said to him—probably I said to him, 'If you are not willing to make a reasonable compromise, move over because we are going to take over the party and freeze you out.'"[24]

Lee would not budge. And later at a local delegate selection meeting, county Republicans refused to appoint Lee and Ann Moody as delegates and instead chose Donelson and Robert James. The move meant that an all-white delegation would represent Tennessee at a GOP convention for the first time in fifty years.

Both Lee and Moody were furious, as were Benjamin Hooks and David Marks, who were vying to be alternate delegates. Millsaps Fitzhugh, a former chairman of the Shelby Republican Party, spoke out against the rejection of Lee and Moody, saying the process was "illegally conducted" and that Lee was a victim of racial discrimination.[25]

Lee traveled to the convention anyway, determined to expose the wrongdoing. He was an outspoken opponent of Arizona senator Barry Goldwater's bid for the 1964 presidential nomination and instead supported William Scranton of Pennsylvania. Both James and Donelson were committed to Goldwater, and Scranton's people were all too eager to expose the racial turmoil among the Tennessee delegation as another example of Goldwater's anti–civil rights stance.

When he arrived in San Francisco, Lee was kept secluded in Henry Cabot Lodge's hotel suite while others appeared before the Credentials Committee in the Italian Room of the St. Francis Hotel to contest Lee's ouster as a delegate. The attorney who represented Lee at the three-and-a-half hour hearing was white Republican R. C. Smith Jr. of Knoxville, which was no surprise given that Lee's strongest allies in the party had always been from East Tennessee. When the impeccably dressed Lee—sporting a brown silk suit, two-tone shoes, and yellow tie—appeared before the Credentials Committee, the *New York Times* described it as a "long and disjointed account of events leading up to the state Republican convention's rejection of his bid for a seat" at the convention.[26]

Harry W. Wellford, the grandson of prominent Memphian Walker Wellford, represented James and Donelson at the hearing and strongly denied that race played a role in the rejection of Lee. "We have had a number of local disputes in Shelby County," Wellford said, "but we do not fight on the basis of race."[27] The committee then voted sixty-six to nineteen in favor of seating James and Donelson. Committee members told the press that convention rules prevented them from considering whether the rejection of Lee was done improperly.

Wellford, who went on to become a Richard Nixon appointee to the federal court bench in Memphis in 1970 and years later a judge on the U.S. Sixth Circuit Court of Appeals, now reflects differently about the local party's treatment of Lee. He now believes that race did indeed play a prominent role in Lee's ouster from local and state party leadership, and he's sorry that it occurred because Lee had been a dedicated and influential Republican.[28] Lee, however, left the 1964 convention dejected, and he remained opposed to Goldwater, who won the nomination over Scranton. "The convention and the committees are so thoroughly in the hands of the Goldwater people that it is like trying to pluck a star from the firmament and put it in a sack for the truth to get a hearing," he told the *Commercial Appeal*.

More than anything, Lee's very public ouster became the final catalyst for turning blacks in Memphis away from the Republican Party. Lee himself fueled the defection wherever he went by encouraging black voters to choose Lyndon Johnson over Goldwater and, in a local congressional race, Democrat George Grider over Republican Bob James. Lee described both Goldwater and James as right-wing extremists.

It didn't take much coaxing. Blacks in Memphis and elsewhere in the South were deathly afraid that a Goldwater presidency would undo all of their civil rights gains. Local Democrats issued a written invitation for Lee to make a clean break with Republicans and become part the "the great Democratic Party of John Kennedy and Lyndon Johnson." He graciously declined. "I'm a Republican born and bred, and I'll be a Republican 'til I'm dead," he said.[29]

Black political groups that had been splintered in past campaigns took the cue from Lee and flocked en masse to the Democrats. They also quietly coalesced behind a plan to once again put one of their own into elected office. The groups conducted massive voter registration drives and held a series of voter education seminars in black neighborhoods. They also tapped into Sunday morning worship services at black churches where the campaign for Democrats was openly endorsed from the pulpit.

Among the groups' leaders was Russell Sugarmon Jr., head of the Shelby County Democratic Club. Their local candidate of choice was civil rights attorney Archie W. Willis for a Memphis seat in the Tennessee House of Representatives. With all of the attention in the white community devoted to angst over desegregation and the push to get Goldwater elected president, whites failed to focus on the mobilization occurring in the black community.

On general election day in November, 212,804 votes were cast in Shelby County, which at the time had 231,351 total registered voters. Close to 73,000 general election votes—a third of the total—were cast by blacks, which represented a stunning 91 percent black voter turnout, according to the *Commercial Appeal*. The white turnout was even higher at 92 percent, but while the white votes were split between both political parties, 99 percent of the black vote went to the Democratic Party ticket. As a result, Johnson took Shelby County en route to a landslide victory over Goldwater.

More significant for black Memphians, Willis defeated Republican Garvin Crawford to capture a seat in the state house, becoming the first black candidate to win elected office in modern-day Memphis. And H. T. Lockard narrowly defeated A. Arthur Halle to win a seat on the Shelby County Quarterly Court, thus becoming the first black candidate elected to public office in Shelby County government since Reconstruction. Willis collected 97,373 votes to 94,668 for Crawford, which meant that more than 24,000 thousand white Memphians actually voted for a black man. Lockard defeated his opponent by just 189 votes out of 48,200 total votes cast in that race.

Most white conservatives were dumbfounded by the results, while elation and a strong sense of civic accomplishment were evident throughout the black community. One white Republican, speaking anonymously to *Commercial Appeal* reporter Angus McEachran, said, "Frankly we're in a state of shock. . . . What we now have to consider is that the Negroes now control the way of political life in Memphis and Shelby County. They elect you and if you don't go down the line with them, they will vote you out of office with one big sweep."[30]

With that, the newspaper immediately assigned one of its best writers, William Thomas, to dig deeper into an election outcome that the white press—and hence the white community—never saw coming. Thomas concluded that the civil rights issue drove black voters to the polls in the same way that blind loyalty to Boss Crump drove them there in decades past. "The Negroes won more than an election," Thomas wrote. "They established themselves firmly as a political power which could mean a whole re-shuffling of political attitudes. The mammoth Negro vote, which included thousands of persons who went to the polls for the first time, is perhaps the most significant development in latter-day Shelby history."

Thomas also wrote that while bloc voting was not new in Memphis, the difference in 1964 was that blacks "ran their own show. They chose their sides and they conducted a campaign with startling effectiveness."[31]

Willis agreed that the fight for civil rights was a huge motivator for black voters in 1964, but it wasn't their only cause. Negro voters, he said, also feared that if Goldwater had been elected, they would lose their pensions and Social Security, "and for many of them, this is all they have." Willis added that blacks voted as a bloc for the Democratic ticket because they had no choice: "(They) voted for a philosophy that to (them) meant survival. (They) voted for Social Security, welfare, Medicare and TVA, which . . . meant lower electrical bills. We picked up this pulse beat of the Negro at thousands of rallies and we channeled this enthusiasm into action at the polls. The Negro was afraid of Goldwater and afraid of the bomb."[32]

James E. Irwin, the white chairman of the Shelby County Democratic Party, assessed the election outcome in blunt terms. "The Republican Party left the Negro and there was no place for him to go but to the Democrats," he said. Conversely, James Harpster, a Shelby Republican Party leader, said Negroes were victims of a fraud: "The Democrats and East Coast liberals did a good job of painting conservatism as extremism. When this highly emotional state dies down and the Negro realizes what a fraud has been practiced upon them, they will again vote Republican."[33]

As for Lee, Thomas wrote that his decision to "retire to the sidelines" after being rejected as a Republican convention delegate meant that no other black person in Memphis was available to take his place, and the Republicans were left without a Negro rallying point. Still, Lee insisted that blacks would not leave the party completely. "Negroes have voted Republican before and they'll do it again," he said, adding that the party needed to "reshape itself into a more moderate mold. Negroes voted against Goldwaterism, not the principles of the Republican Party."[34]

The election results so angered and embarrassed Bob James, who lost his race for the Ninth District congressional seat to Democrat George Grider, that he issued an off-the-cuff statement to the *Commercial Appeal* insisting he had "won the support of an overwhelmingly high percentage of the respectable people of the community." His clear implication was that black voters and whites who voted for Grider were not respectable. But James wasn't through venting.

He told *Commercial Appeal* reporter Angus McEachran that Grider had gotten support from "only three white groups—a substantial element of the Jewish group, the old people who couldn't see their way clear to vote any other way except Democratic and the labor leaders."[35] A day later, James apologized, saying he meant to say "responsible people." But the damage had been done. Harry Wellford, the calmer head among the new Republican Turks, tried to further clarify and temper James's insulting comments. For the sake of the party's changing image, Wellford knew he had to do damage control and he ended up blaming James's remarks "on the frustration of losing."[36]

In all, the events of 1964 represented a watershed moment in both local and national politics. Results in the presidential election launched the mammoth shift of white southerners from the Democratic Party to the Republican side, and the GOP's southern strategy was born. At the local level, black Memphians in 1964 flexed their political muscle like never before and allowed themselves to think realistically about gaining additional elected offices.

Bob James, Lewis Donelson, and other new guard Republicans also got what they wanted—white control of the local Republican Party. To their credit, they turned the party into a powerful political force that attracted more white voters, particularly in growing East Memphis, with each election cycle. Their work helped get Republicans elected locally and statewide for the first time in nearly a century.

Also to their credit, most of the candidates they backed were moderates, including Winfield Dunn for governor and Howard Baker and Bill Brock for the U.S. Senate. After unsuccessful tries for state senate and house seats, Bob James settled into a comfortable spot on the Memphis City Council, as did Donelson, who had no regrets about wresting the local party from

Lieutenant Lee. Donelson made the point that he and the New Guard Republicans were supportive of desegregation as early as 1956, while white Democratic politicians supported segregation.[37]

Meanwhile, the new generation of black leadership, led by A. W. Willis Jr., Russell Sugarmon Jr., Benjamin Hooks, Jesse Turner, H. T. Lockard, and Vasco and Maxine Smith, celebrated their first election victories in 1964—alone with their political independence out of the shadows of Blair T. Hunt and George W. Lee. And for the first time, black Memphians fully realized what was possible with political unity. The sobering question became would the unity continue or would it fade?

CHAPTER 7

THE VILLAIN RETURNS

FROM A RACIAL PERSPECTIVE, the mid-1960s were relatively peaceful times in Memphis. As turmoil swirled around the region in such places as Birmingham and Selma, Alabama, as well as Jackson and Philadelphia, Mississippi, the Bluff City was experiencing growth in both the black and white populations—even though much of that growth came through annexation. Young blacks, escaping the plantations and oppression in Mississippi, the western counties in Tennessee, and rural East Arkansas, flocked to Memphis. Other blacks continued farther north to St. Louis, Chicago, Milwaukee, and Detroit. But Memphis claimed more than its share of new black residents looking for jobs that did not come with a mule, a plow, and a cotton sack.

To rural blacks, Memphis offered manufacturing and warehouse jobs and represented fancier living, even if it was in a public housing project. It also represented freedom from hostile defiance of the Civil Rights Act of 1964 and growing racial violence that had already seen church burnings, death threats, and lynchings.

The growing black population in Memphis gave black community leaders the confidence that they could make additional political demands on the white power structure—including reforms to city government that would ensure black representation. Their quest meshed with the longstanding efforts of white liberals such as Lucius Burch Jr., Edmund Orgill, and Edward Meeman, who had been pushing to get rid of the city commission form of government since the 1940s.

With Boss Crump long gone and his surviving cronies losing political clout with each election, 1966 became the year that government reform was finally achieved. But getting there was a struggle that created more division than unity between blacks and whites. Meeman's *Press-Scimitar* newspaper had long supported government reform with stories, columns, and editorials. But when the *Commercial Appeal*, the larger and more influential of the two daily papers, finally jumped on board, the movement gained the traction it needed.

Commercial Appeal editor Frank Ahlgren could always be counted on to favor the Crump way of running government, which included keeping the city commission structure in place. He also catered to conservative business leaders in town and was unwilling to do anything to support the black community or advance desegregation for fear of reprisal from the business establishment. Plus, his newspaper had long been openly hostile to African Americans while supporting every effort to keep whites in absolute power.

And yet Burch was finally able to convince the cautious editor to see the benefits of discarding the outdated and myopic city commission. Ahlgren assigned city hall reporter Jack H. Morris to write a series of stories that analyzed urban government and the need for reform. After the articles— and accompanying editorials—appeared in the fall of 1965, Burch helped bring together more than two hundred local leaders, black and white, to select a twenty-five-person committee that would draft a new city charter. The group became known as the Program of Progress (POP) Citizens Committee and selected Downing Pryor as its chairman.

After some thirty-five meetings, the POP committee issued the final draft of a new charter calling for a mayor-council form of government. Under the plan, seven council members would be elected from seven individual districts starting with the 1967 city election. Six council seats would be elected at-large. Gone would be a commission system in which all members were elected at-large and oversaw both the administrative and legislative functions of government.

Mayor William B. Ingram was strongly opposed to the charter change but gave in to demands that the issue be put before voters in a ballot referendum during the general election for federal and state offices on November 8, 1966. The proposed change produced some unlikely alliances. Former mayor Henry Loeb, who was quietly eyeing a second run for the office, supported the new charter along with local NAACP leaders. Also on board were sitting city commissioners Hunter Lane Jr. and Claude Armour and former commissioner William Farris.

Black leaders favored the change because it all but guaranteed that up to three of the new elected city council members would be black. The *Press-Scimitar* was all-in on the charter change, and the *Commercial Appeal* finally gave its support once it became clear that at least some council members would be elected at-large. The paper's endorsement editorial said the POP charter "will give growing Memphis a chance to operate its public business with far more efficiency and with a system of checks and balances which will minimize political logrolling."[1]

Mayor Ingram, however, remained dubious. He sided with opposition groups that were convinced the change would lead to wasteful spending, racial strife, and more crime. The groups keyed in on the $6,000 annual salary for each part-time council member as evidence of unnecessary spending. Just before the referendum vote, the opposition began distributing leaflets around the city, one showing the image of a young white girl labeled "Miss Memphis." She was depicted walking past a building with the acronym "POP" scrawled on it. Lurking behind the building were three menacing images identified as narcotics traffic, organized vice, and race riots. A caption at the bottom of the leaflet read, "Keep Memphis safe and sound. Vote NO against POP."[2]

Ingram, meanwhile, actively campaigned against the charter change, particularly among black voters who had put him into office in 1963. Shortly before the vote, he went on both WDIA and WLOK, the city's two black-oriented radio stations, with a paid sixty-five-minute program during which he called POP supporters "Goldwaterites." The mayor reminded black listeners that Memphis had a mayor-council form of government before the Civil War and it had allowed slaves to be sold on Main Street. He also said that Los Angeles was divided into council districts, and one of them was Watts, where riots occurred in 1965.[3]

Ingram, however, badly miscalculated the biracial clamor to change city government. Memphians approved the POP referendum by a vote of 56,808 favoring it and 39,211 opposed. Turnout was heavy in black precincts, but even more so among white voters. As a result, Shelby County's new look Republican organization—made up exclusively of white professionals—scored its first major successes. Republican Dan Kuykendall unseated one-term congressman George Grider for the Ninth District seat. In winning,

Kuykendall became the first Republican congressman from Memphis in the twentieth century. In addition, the white turnout helped Republican Howard Baker win a Tennessee seat in the U.S. Senate.

The upstart Republicans considered themselves moderates, but they attacked Grider for supporting the liberal agenda of President Johnson, including civil rights, Medicare, and antipoverty programs. That was ammunition to turn just enough white voters against Grider. Kuykendall got 46,578 votes to 42,716 for Grider. Once the results were announced, shouts of joy spread through the Republican Party headquarters in Midtown. "I don't know how I feel," Happy Jones, the local party's secretary, told a *Commercial Appeal* reporter. "We never won an election before."

A stunned Grider was less than conciliatory. He said his defeat represented a desire "for a return to the good old days when Southern congressmen voted against everything but cotton legislation and public works bills. This isn't meant to sound like sour grapes. I got beat. I got beat good and I got beat fair and square."[4] The defeat effectively ended Grider's political career.

Also in that election, Memphis voters approved a runoff for all future city races in which a candidate does not receive 50 percent of the vote. The change also called for moving city elections to October to make way for runoff voting in November. Whites strongly supported runoffs, recalling the 1959 election in which black candidate Russell Sugarmon Jr. came close to grabbing a city commission seat against four white opponents. The switch to runoffs would have a profound impact on future elections, but the press and voters were focused more on the charter change. The *Press-Scimitar*, reflecting on the crusade launched by its now-former editor, Edward Meeman, hailed the decision as a huge step forward for the city. "Memphis will no longer have a five-headed government trying to handle legislation and administration at the same time," the paper's post-election editorial said. From now on, there will be the "council to fix policies and the mayor to carry them out."[5] Meeman died one week after the election.

Before the vote totals became official, the jockeying had already begun to claim each of the 13 new legislative seats in city government. Mayor Ingram made it clear that he intended to seek reelection no matter how the charter vote went. Despite splitting with the black community on the charter change, he was still counting on Negro votes to return him to office. But two forces were building that would significantly cripple Ingram's chances—and he was completely blindsided by both of them.

Former mayor Loeb, an outspoken segregationist, had made a strategic decision to publicly support the POP proposal. His face graced POP campaign ads in the newspapers and he endorsed the plan everywhere he went throughout the city.[6] As a young ambitious politician, Loeb had been spurned by Boss Crump in the 1950s. But now he had the upper hand on the remnants of Crump's fading organization. Naturally, if the old Crump boys were against government reform, Loeb was for it.

Loeb was also getting antsy sitting on the political sidelines. Running the family's laundry and dry cleaning business was financially rewarding, but it was nowhere near as fulfilling as running city government. So Loeb sold his interest in the company. On July 17, 1967, he gathered a flock of supporters at his old Cleveland Avenue campaign headquarters and summoned the press to announce he would again seek the mayor's office. Loeb told the assemblage that his campaign would be built around law and order in Memphis.[7]

He also promised equal enforcement of the law for all races, a statement meant to show that he was not the racist villain that was being portrayed in the black community. Black Memphians, however, weren't buying it. Loeb had already cemented his reputation as an unwavering opponent of civil rights. There was not a single black vote that he could confidently count on, and he knew it. What's more, he didn't much care.

Meanwhile, the emerging, middle-class black leadership—emboldened by the successes at the polls in 1964 and 1966—decided that now was the time to run its own candidate for mayor. These black leaders looked across the country and saw that Carl Stokes was leading in his race to become the first black mayor of Cleveland, Ohio, and Walter Washington was favored to become the first black mayor-commissioner of Washington, D.C. So A. W. Willis Jr. offered himself as the first serious black mayoral candidate ever in Memphis.

Willis believed he could capitalize on his stunning victory for a state legislative seat in 1964. At age forty-two, he had all the qualities necessary to be an attractive candidate—a good education, a charming, picturesque family, a record of public service and political know-how. He and his strategists believed that black voters would abandon Ingram's campaign if there were a capable black man running. Both developments—Loeb's reemergence and Willis's daring move—spelled trouble for Ingram. Yet he marched on, hopeful that black leadership springing for the NAACP and its allies among a growing cadre of young black lawyers, would not turn African Americans of more meager means from the Ingram camp.

One tactic that Ingram's supporters devised was a gossip campaign to spread the word in the black community that Willis was being paid by Loeb to run. It was a far-fetched notion given the fact that Willis and Loeb had been involved in a very public dispute six years earlier when Loeb was mayor. In July 1961, Willis was angling to become the first black board member of the Memphis Transit Authority. Commissioners John T. Dwyer, James W. Moore, William W. Farris, and Claude Armour initially voted to appoint Willis to the seat. But Loeb considered Willis to be part of a group of "Negro extremists."[8] The mayor convinced all four commissioners, during a six-hour private meeting late on a Friday night, to rescind the vote and instead appoint A. Maceo Walker, who in Loeb's mind was a more acceptable Negro.[9]

Willis was livid. This was no longer the Crump era when black folks were hesitant—or fearful—to speak out. The young black lawyer issued a statement to the newspapers saying he pitied the four commissioners: "They have been victimized and intoxicated with fear in a so-called 'moonlight commission meeting' where they were swallowed up and driven to change their convictions. Out of the darkness came four once courageous men now reduced to boys, soaked in the soup of race hatred, prepared by the hands of Mayor Loeb."[10] Willis also predicted that the compromise would galvanize the black community. "(It) has given us a shot of courage that will lead us down the road to democracy and freedom," he said. "We would rather be dead than to kneel and humble ourselves to a racist dictator."[11]

It was implausible to think that—six years later—Willis and Loeb would be conspiring with each other to get Ingram out of the mayor's office. But that was the story trotted out to black voters—with Ingram's blessing—after Willis announced as a mayoral candidate on August 29, 1967. Cornelia Crenshaw, a black community activist, along with a group calling itself the Memphis Unity League, distributed racist fliers depicting Willis as a *Hambone*-type puppet sitting on Loeb's knee saying "Yassir boss" to whatever Loeb wanted. The caption on the flier, which supported Ingram, made it clear: "It's impossible for a Negro to win the mayor's office at this time. Why waste your vote on Willis."[12]

First-term city commissioner Hunter Lane Jr. also entered the mayor's race on the strength of his support for switching to a mayor-council form of government. He too tried to make racial voting an issue, only his attack was against Ingram. A day before the election, Lane took out a full-page ad in both the *Commercial Appeal* and *Press-Scimitar* aimed at white voters. "Hunter Lane is the only man who can beat Mayor Ingram," the ad proclaimed. "Loeb can't get any black votes, and no candidate can win with one-third of the vote solidly against him." The ad listed several members of Lane's campaign committee, including Harry W. Wellford, Lucius Burch Jr., and Edmund Orgill.[13]

Also in the mayor's race was first-term sheriff Bill Morris. But the national attention was focused on Willis because no other black candidate had seriously tried to become mayor of a major southern city since Reconstruction. And although Willis started his campaign late, he assembled an impressive biracial campaign committee. It included campaign co-chair Dr. Darrell Daugherty, a white assistant professor of religion at Southwestern at Memphis, and finance committee co-chair Mrs. Julian Hohenberg, the wife of a wealthy Memphis cotton broker. A. Maceo Walker was also a key member of Willis's campaign committee.

One week before the election, *Jet*, a popular black magazine, produced a multipage spread on Willis's campaign. "A. W. Willis can win the race if 75,000 Negroes vote for him," the headline read. The article's first paragraph stated, "Memphis is on the spot. A young aggressive Negro lawyer is running for mayor and the whole nation is watching."[14] The *New York Times* also carried a story a week before the voting pointing out that Willis still had not succeeded in convincing black Memphians that he could win.

"This campaign is raising for the first time the real problems of racial inferiority," Willis told the *Times*. "The Negro has been taught to be inferior. He thinks the white man's ice is colder, his sugar is sweeter, his medicine is better. When I step out and say I want to be mayor of the town, that's way ahead of most Negroes' thinking. They've first got to believe in themselves, they've got to believe that a Negro is capable of running the city."[15] The *Times* article also laid bare another of Willis's campaign hurdles—his perceived disconnect with the average black voter: "He is well bred, successful and wealthy. Most of the Negroes here definitely are not, and one of them told a lawyer friend of the candidate's that he could not support 'that man' because 'he's forgotten about us.'"[16]

By election day, the battle lines were clearly drawn. The *Tri-State Defender* endorsed Mayor Ingram for reelection over Willis. The *Press-Scimitar* endorsed Commissioner Lane, declaring he and the city's new governing body "naturally belonged together."[17] And the *Commercial Appeal* endorsed Morris, Shelby County's thirty-five-year-old sheriff, noting he has "the vigor of youth to get things done and the maturity to do them right."[18] Editorially, both daily newspapers dismissed the candidacies of Ingram and Loeb, and they couldn't have been more wrong. After the votes were counted, Loeb received 47,778 to Ingram's 36,074, putting them both in a November 2 runoff. Morris finished third with 30,979 votes, Willis was fourth with 17,744 votes, and Lane finished a disappointing fifth with 8,795 votes.

It was a crushing loss for Willis, who was beaten by Ingram two to one in most black precincts. Ingram was aided by a large group of black ministers who convinced their parishioners that because Negroes made up only 34 percent of registered voters, Willis could not win. A few black preachers also helped spread the rumor that Willis was paid $35,000 by Loeb to get in the race and split the black vote between himself and Ingram.

In response, Willis called the preachers "Uncle Toms." He refused to endorse Ingram in the runoff and harbored resentment against his critics in the black community for years. Willis knew he was fighting a losing battle all along, but he was fighting it for the right reasons. "He knew he couldn't win, but he was running to pave the way for other black politicians," said his wife, Miriam DeCosta-Willis, who was a co-chair in the campaign and became heavily involved in politics with local NAACP leader Maxine Smith.[19]

In a post-election analysis by the *Commercial Appeal*, the paper pinpointed another culprit, saying jealousy by some blacks toward Willis led to his defeat: "Many Negroes may feel that Mr. Willis and other successful Negroes have little understanding of the problems of someone who makes five dollars a day and cab fare."[20] The assessment was spot on. There was a growing disconnect between the average black Memphian and the young black legal Turks who had seized leadership roles in the black community.

The runoff contest between Ingram and Loeb produced even more racial polarization. Both newspapers endorsed Loeb, with the *Press-Scimitar* declaring he would provide "strong effective leadership" to help Memphis compete with Atlanta, Dallas, and New Orleans: "We have watched him grow. He has boundless enthusiasm and personal charm."[21] The *Commercial Appeal* wrote that Loeb "would serve Memphis with greater efficiency and distinction than the incumbent."[22] Ingram still pulled virtually all of the black vote. Loeb, however, received 90 percent of the white vote and defeated Ingram 78,470 to 66,628.[23]

Both the October election and the November runoff produced the largest voter turnouts—well over 60 percent each time—for a municipal-only election in the city's history, which meant the outcome was no fluke. Loeb's appeal to conservative whites—who constituted a sizable majority of Memphis voters—was a clear sign that blacks could not win citywide elections without voting as a bloc. Splitting their votes between Willis and Ingram in 1967 meant that their influence in the mayor's office was gone. And their villain had indeed returned.

CHAPTER 8

MEMPHIS'S DARKEST DAYS

THE 1967 MEMPHIS ELECTION marked yet another turning point for the black community, which had long desired to be part of decision making in city government. The switch from a self-centered commission form of government to a more inclusive one, with a mayor and thirteen council members, resulted in the election of three black councilmen—Fred Davis, James L. Netters, and J. O. Patterson Jr. The remaining ten white council members were mostly conservatives with ties to the new-look Republican Party in Shelby County that had seized control from black GOP leader Lt. George W. Lee, a successful businessman and World War I hero.

Two of the new councilmen—Lewis Donelson and Robert James—were directly responsible for pushing Lee from Republican power, but neither man was closely aligned with returning mayor Henry Loeb and his power base among local segregationists. Another new councilman was Wyeth Chandler, whose father Walter Chandler enjoyed an amicable relationship with black Memphians, particularly black preachers.

Collectively, the council was determined to make city government work for all citizens in ways that the old self-serving commission never could. But just a month into the new governmental structure, the worst racial turmoil since the days of Ida B. Wells began to unfold in Memphis. It started at the most unlikeliest of places with the most unlikeliest of people—in the city's Sanitation Department among black garbage workers.

This was a group with arguably the most menial jobs in town, lugging tubs full of filthy garbage and trash from the back yards of Memphis residences to a waiting truck. Their average pay amounted to no more seventy dollars a week and their benefits were virtually nonexistent. Most of the sanitation work force had come to Memphis from the plantations in surrounding counties. They were considered the lowest of the low among municipal employees and they were taken for granted by both black and white Memphians.

On February 1, 1968, black sanitation workers Echol Cole, thirty-six, and Robert Walker, thirty, were part of a detail collecting garbage near Colonial and Quince in East Memphis. A heavy rain started, and the two men sought refuge in the rear of the garbage truck. Inexplicably, a compressor inside the truck activated and Cole and Walker were crushed to death before co-workers could shut off the device. The *Commercial Appeal* reported the accident on the first page the following day, but other than that, little else was said. And when the city refused to provide insurance benefits for the dead men's widows, the last straw had finally been pulled.

Former garbage worker Thomas O. Jones had been trying for years to unionize his fellow employees. He and more than thirty others were fired in 1963 for attempting a job action.[1] This time, however, most of the thirteen hundred garbage men were united. On a Sunday evening, ten days after the tragic deaths of Cole and Walker, Jones called a strike meeting.

About four hundred workers showed up, and together they created a list of demands. It included city recognition of Local 1733 of the American Federation of State, County and Municipal Employees (AFSCME) through a dues check-off system, more hourly pay, and better working conditions. Jones left the meeting and took the demands to Sanitation Department leaders, who flatly rejected them without discussion. Jones returned to the meeting empty handed, and the angry workers agreed to strike.[2]

The following morning, fewer than two hundred garbage workers reported for duty, a move that caught the mayor, the newspapers, and city residents—black and white—totally off guard. For the first time in modern Memphis history, a demand for racial equality didn't spring from the black upper crust, the black clergy, or the NAACP. The uprising this time came from the invisible public servants who had always done what they were told by their white bosses—for meager pay.

However, it didn't take long for the city's civil rights leaders to realize they needed to hop aboard this freedom train because the garbage men were serious and they had a cause that could be cloaked around the civil rights movement, which many people believed had peaked. Memphis garbage men may have spent their work days in filth, but they were sick and tired of being treated like dirt.

White Memphians, however, were incensed. And they counted on Mayor Loeb to quickly put these striking Negroes in their place. Loeb immediately declared the strike illegal and ordered the men back to work or else their jobs would be given to others willing to work. He had no intention of giving in one inch to any union, particularly one made up of black garbage men. When national representatives from the AFSCME arrived in Memphis and wanted to negotiate with the mayor, he agreed to meet but basically told them to get lost.

On Tuesday, February 13, Loeb met with P. J. Ciampa, field staff director, and William Lucy, director of legislative and community activities for the AFSCME. Their discussion was heated from the beginning and continued that way throughout the day. The men reminded the mayor that political leaders had just settled a garbage strike in New York City, to which Loeb replied, "I don't care what (New York City Mayor John) Lindsey did, I don't care what (New York Governor Nelson) Rockefeller did. You're talking to a country boy. This is not New York, this is Memphis. I live here and my kids live here and I am not going to play around with the health of this city."[3]

That morning, hundreds of striking workers marched nearly five miles from a union hall to city hall in protest. They wanted to talk to the mayor themselves and were directed to nearby Ellis Auditorium. Loeb left his meeting with Ciampa and Lucy to address the strikers directly for the first time. He was convinced he could use his domineering, paternalistic personality to persuade the men to come to their senses and end the walkout.

"You are in effect breaking the law," Loeb told them. "Your work is essential to the health of this city and not doing your work constitutes a health menace to the city." The men responded with boos and catcalls. Reporters who were there said some of them laughed at Loeb and that angered him even more. "I have sat here and taken quite a bit of abuse and I don't appreciate it," he said. "And I have not given any abuse back. Your jobs are important." Ciampa and Lucy, who followed Loeb to the auditorium, then tried to address the crowd, but the mayor pushed them aside and continued talking. As he did, his voice grew to a shout. His jaw was jutted and the veins stood out in his neck. "I promise you the garbage will be picked up," he declared. "Bet on it."[4]

It was a losing bet because strike breakers, replacement workers, and managers couldn't keep up. On the first day of the strike, thirty-six garbage trucks were on city streets collecting trash. The next day, ten were out, and the third day, just four. When moderate and liberal white Memphians, including E. W. "Ned" Cook, Edmund Orgill, and Lucius Burch Jr., tried to seek an end to the crisis, Loeb rebuffed them as well.

The majority of white Memphians had the mayor's back. So did the *Commercial Appeal* and its conservative editor, Frank Ahlgren. The newspaper's editorial page turned a blind eye to any suggestion that the sanitation workers were waging a civil rights struggle. To Ahlgren and his editorial board, this was a labor issue, pure and simple: "There is no doubt about the current Memphis garbage strike being illegal. Mayor Henry Loeb has taken the proper stance in refusing to bargain with disgruntled sanitation workers under union pressure. The issue is public health and welfare. The main object of the union appears to be to unionize workers and get the city to act as collector of dues."[5]

The strikers, however, and their growing cadre of black supporters, were undeterred. They held regular meetings in black churches, collected thousands of dollars in donations for the striking workers, and launched boycotts of downtown businesses, including the *Commercial Appeal* and *Press-Scimitar*. Even blacks who had opposed each other during the mayoral election the previous year came together in support of the strikers. The fledgling city council did nothing to resolve the strike. When the three black councilmen, Fred Davis, J. O. Patterson Jr., and James L. Netters, tried to convince their colleagues to urge the mayor to give in to the demands and settle the strike, only one—Jerred Blanchard—sided with them. He was ridiculed by his white colleagues and labeled as the "fourth nigger on the council."[6]

The community meetings continued almost nightly, mostly at black churches around the city. During one gathering, Dr. Vasco Smith, a leader in the NAACP and head of the Shelby County Democratic Club, urged the strikers to stand firm. "Don't let them hoodwink you," Smith said. "You are living in a racist town. They don't give a damn about you."[7] When the city council met to discuss the crisis on February 22, scores of protesters and union leaders showed up and staged a sit-in in the council chambers, bringing in bologna sandwiches for lunch. The meeting was abruptly halted until the following day.

The next morning, the *Commercial Appeal* published an editorial cartoon showing an overweight black man sitting on top of a garbage can as trash is littered around him. Thin, crooked lines depicting the stench of the garbage shot up from the trash to form the word "ANARCHY." The caption above the cartoon read, "Beyond the Bounds of Tolerance." An accompanying editorial declared, "Memphis garbage strikers have turned an illegal walkout into anarchy, and Mayor Henry Loeb is exactly right when he says, 'we can't submit to this sort of thing.'"[8]

Later that day, the council resumed the meeting in front of hundreds of protesters and voted nine to four to give Mayor Loeb sole authority to handle the strike. None of the protesters were allowed to speak. The group left city hall filled with anger and started a spontaneous march along the sidewalks of Main Street heading to Mason Temple.

A police car followed the protesters, and when it got too close—one witness said the car ran over a woman's foot—protesters rocked the squad car from side to side. Officers then converged and arrested some of the protesters. Others, including bystanders, were beaten and sprayed with Mace. A photographer for the black-owned *Tri-State Defender* snapped a picture of an angry officer coming toward him with the night stick. Officers threatened the *Defender*'s photographer while allowing white photographers to do their jobs without interference.[9] An editorial in the *Press-Scimitar* the next day, however, ridiculed the protesters and praised the police action. "Memphis can take deep pride in the prompt and efficient way its law enforcement officers handled the situation," the paper noted.[10] The arrests continued, but in most cases, city court judge Bernie Weinman released the detainees on their own recognizance, a move that angered Fire and Police Director Frank C. Holloman: "They're letting them go on their own recognizance faster than we can keep pace on the streets. Every arrest so far has been in the line of duty—in the public interest."[11]

The escalating racial tension in Memphis was not occurring in isolation. On February 29, 1968, the *Report of the National Advisory Commission on Civil Disorders*, also known as the Kerner Report, was released. The groundbreaking, 426-page document was commissioned by President Johnson following inner-city unrest in the mid-1960s in such places as Newark, New Jersey, Detroit, and the Watts section of Los Angeles. The report concluded, "Our nation is moving toward two societies, one black, one white—separate and unequal."[12]

And as the sanitation strike dragged on and uncollected garbage piled up, the crisis started to gain attention outside of Memphis as national black leaders digested the Kerner Report and took an interest in the sanitation workers' plight. The *New York Times* and *Wall Street Journal* sent reporters to Memphis to cover the standoff. On March 14, Roy Wilkins, executive secretary of the NAACP, and Bayard Rustin, an official with the A. Philip Randolph Institute who organized the 1963 March on Washington, addressed a rally of more than nine hundred at Mason Temple.

"The city of Memphis ought to be ashamed of itself," Wilkins said. "If I were the mayor of this city, I would be ashamed. You have given enough in forbearance. I don't mean go out and tear up the town. . . . Don't foul your nest, but don't give an inch. I didn't come here to make threats. But anybody who runs around picking on peaceful people is building for trouble."

Rustin compared the sanitation strike to the 1955 bus boycott in Montgomery, Alabama, and said the crisis in Memphis is "one of the great struggles for the emancipation of the black man today. This becomes the symbol of the movement to get rid of poverty. The record here shows that in Memphis this fight is going to be won because the black people in this community and the trade unions stand together. It is written that where there is justice, order will maintain it; where there is injustice, disorder is inevitable."[13]

On March 18, Martin Luther King Jr. flew to Memphis and spoke to an even larger audience, telling the crowd that "all labor has dignity." Addressing directly the striking sanitation workers, he added, "You are demanding that this city will respect the dignity of labor. You are reminding not only Memphis, but you are reminding the nation that it is a crime for people to live in this rich nation and receive starvation wages."[14] King then promised to return and lead a march through downtown. The march was set for Friday, March 22, but a crippling snowstorm forced a cancellation. It was reset for March 28.

Loeb strongly opposed the march, predicting that violence would occur. And he was right. Young militants who were upset that they had not been included in the planning showed up the morning of the march. Some were participants, others walked along beside the march. As the group made its way down Beale Street near Main, suddenly there was the sound of shattered glass. Chaos erupted and the police used tear gas and Mace to disperse the crowd. The *New York Times* reported that King "was whisked away from the march at the first sign of trouble." In the confusion, sixteen-year-old Larry Payne was shot to death. The official police account said Payne was shot after he was caught looting a store and attacked a policeman with a butcher knife."[15]

The incident was gut-wrenching on several fronts. In addition to Payne's death, the city was thrust into the national spotlight as the site of racial violence, and the striking workers and their supporters took the brunt of

Memphis's Darkest Days

criticism for creating the upheaval. The incident also embarrassed King, who was planning a poor people's march on Washington the following month. The *Commercial Appeal* put it bluntly: "Martin Luther King Jr. came to Memphis to star in what was billed as a 'dress rehearsal' for his April 22 'Poor People Crusade' on Washington. By his own nonviolent standards, the rehearsal was a flop."[16]

But King would not concede. He promised to return and lead a nonviolent march in Memphis. Loeb and other city leaders vowed to stop it. They went to federal court on April 3 and got a temporary restraining order preventing King for leading a second march. King returned to Memphis that morning as arrangements were being made to retain lawyers from the Burch, Porter and Johnson and the Ratner, Sugarmon and Lucas firms to get the restraining order lifted.

The request to represent King in federal court came to young attorneys Mike Cody and Charlie Newman. But before accepting, they both consulted with Lucius Burch, their firm's senior partner, who was hesitant to handle the case without first meeting face to face with King. Burch wanted to satisfy himself that the march was really important to King and the civil rights movement because involvement by Burch's firm was sure to cost him clients in Memphis.

Late in the afternoon on April 3, Burch, Cody, and Newman, along with lawyers David Caywood, Louis Lucas, and Walter Bailey, went to the Lorraine Motel and met with King, Andrew Young, Ralph Abernathy, Jesse Jackson, and James Lawson. They sat "knee-to-knee" in the small room, 306, as King spoke passionately that the march was essential—for both the striking sanitation workers and the movement. After the meeting, Burch was convinced and agreed that his firm would handle the court hearing pro bono.[17]

That night, King gave his now-famous "Mountaintop" speech at Mason Temple to a packed audience that had braved a severe thunderstorm to hear the nation's premiere civil rights leader. "We've got some difficult days ahead," King said. "But it really doesn't matter with me now, because I've been to the mountaintop. And I don't mind. Like anybody, I would like to live a long life. Longevity has its place. But I'm not concerned about that now. I just want to do God's will. And He's allowed me to go up to the mountain. And I've looked over. And I've seen the Promised Land. I may not get there with you. But I want you to know tonight that we, as a people, will get to the Promised Land."[18]

The next morning, King's Memphis lawyers appeared along with three city attorneys before federal judge Bailey Brown, a former partner in the Burch firm. The hearing lasted most of the day before Brown called the lawyers into his chambers and told them the march could proceed the following day.

Cody then drove Andrew Young, who had been a witness at the hearing, back to the Lorraine Motel and dropped him off before heading home. A few minutes later, at 6:01 p.m., King was shot to death by sniper James Earl Ray while King stood on the balcony outside his motel room. And almost instantly, violence erupted in Memphis and throughout the nation, including the big cities of Chicago, Detroit, Pittsburgh, and Baltimore. The rioting left several people dead, hundreds injured, hundreds more arrested, and millions of dollars in property damage. Dust-to-dawn curfews failed to curtail the unrest. An Associated Press report published April 6 on the front page of the *Commercial Appeal* started this way: "Negroes roamed the streets of many American cities . . . in outbursts of grief, violence and vandalism." The article said violence was reported in at least forty-one U.S. cities.[19]

The intense national and international news coverage of the assassination and the unrest that it spawned was devastating to the image of Memphis. In response, the largely toothless Memphis Committee on Community Relations announced it would hold a "Memphis Cares" rally on Sunday, April 7 at Crump Stadium. The MCCR also took out a full-page newspaper ad calling for one hundred days of love and prayer in the city from April 10 to July 18.[20] At the Crump Stadium rally, some six thousand people, black and white, showed up to hear speakers, including automobile dealer John T. Fisher, James Lawson, and Benjamin Hooks, plead for unity and also an end to the sanitation strike. "I call on the mayor to immediately settle this strike," Hooks demanded. "This could have been settled three days after it started."[21] Predictably, Mayor Loeb did not attend, but he did proclaim three days of public mourning in Memphis.

In the days following the assassination, Loeb came under heavy pressure by the city council, Memphis clergy, the White House, the local newspapers, and others around the country to settle the strike. King's death forced much of white America to finally acknowledge the horrible impact of racism. Fisher appeared before the all-white Memphis Rotary Club on Tuesday, April 9 and called for the involvement of African Americans in the day-to-day public affairs of the city. "Don't underestimate the resolve that these people have," he said. "They only want the things that I have, opportunity and privilege, but they don't want the dole. They want to share in the planning."[22] That same day, the *Commercial Appeal*'s editorial page, employing a bit of revisionist history, read, "As we have said for years, our Negro community deserves more attention that it has received under any administration."[23]

Finally, on April 16, Loeb and the sanitation workers reached an agreement, called a "Memorandum of Understanding," to end the strike. It included the following terms:

- Recognition by the city of the AFSCME union as "designated representative" for laborers, truck drivers and crew chiefs of the Sanitation Department "for negotiations on wages, hours and conditions of employment."
- A payroll deduction of union dues through the credit union.
- A grievance procedure to be set up at each level of employment, with union officials getting reasonable time off to handle grievances.
- A 10-cents across-the-board pay raise starting May 1, and another 5-cent increase on September 1.
- Promotions on the basis of merit and seniority.
- No recrimination against the strikers and no discrimination based on race, sex, age, marital status, religion, national origin or political affiliation.

After two months and five days, the strike that had created long-lasting and deep racial divisions in Memphis and led to the assassination of an iconic national leader was over. The lowly sanitation workers prevailed. But the cost was tremendous and Memphis was changed forever. The strike and its aftermath marked the beginning of massive white flight from the city and ended Henry Loeb's political career. After leaving the mayor's office for good in 1971, he taught a political science class at Christian Brothers College and continued to hold his Dutch treat luncheons where politics and public policy were discussed weekly. Loeb also considered making a run for governor in 1974 but chose not to enter the race.

Thus the man considered by Boss Crump to be ill tempered and ill prepared for public office eventually left public life and left behind a racially fractured city. He moved to a farm in Forrest City, Arkansas, and died on September 8, 1992, at Baptist Memorial Hospital in Memphis.

The tragic events also forced editors at both the *Commercial Appeal* and *Press-Scimitar* to reexamine their hiring and news-coverage practices. It finally dawned on them that there was no one in their newsrooms who knew anything about the black community. So both papers made concerted efforts to hire African American reporters, and the *Commercial Appeal*, which had published the racially demeaning *Hambone's Meditations* cartoon series since 1917, finally dropped the strip on April 30—more than three weeks after the King assassination.

A story in the paper's May 1 editions insisted that the daily cartoon, which showed an elderly black man in overalls spouting homespun philosophy in virtually unintelligible broken English, was never intended to be malicious or racist. Instead, the paper said, it was merely wit and wisdom intended to "mellow the day." Still, the paper acknowledged it was bowing to societal change in deciding to end the strip.[24]

But the racial animosity that had always defined Memphis persisted. A special report on the sanitation strike prepared by the Southern Regional Council, an Atlanta-based civil rights organization, and dated March 22, 1968, summed up the sanitation crisis perfectly: "If one were required to say in one word what the strike and the marches and the mass meetings in Memphis were all about, that word would have to be dignity."[25]

Black Memphians had spent decades begging for dignity and a rightful place in the city's political process. And the fight was only beginning.

CHAPTER 9

YELLOW BUSES AND WHITE FLIGHT

INTEGRATION CAME SLOWLY and reluctantly to Memphis, just as it did in other southern cities. Blacks and whites lived in separate worlds. They had separate schools, separate swimming pools, separate fairs, parades, and carnivals, and separate parks and playgrounds. At movie theaters, including the Orpheum, black patrons sat upstairs or in the back rows away from whites. Blacks were allowed at the Memphis Zoo only on Thursdays.

On Tuesday, August 26, 1958, a group of African Americans tried to enter the zoo, but police quietly escorted them to their cars, which bore Louisiana license plates, and told them to leave. "Thursday is colored day," city police commissioner Claude Armour told a reporter after learning of the incident at the zoo.[1]

And on January 28, 1962, Mayor Henry Loeb threatened to veto any action by the city commission to voluntarily desegregate a restaurant at Memphis Municipal Airport. Nine days earlier, the airport's Dobbs House restaurant had refused to serve a black man, who happened to be Carl T. Rowan, a deputy assistant secretary of state in the John F. Kennedy administration and at one point the highest-ranking black person in the U.S. government. The Dobbs House incident led to a lawsuit filed by local NAACP leader Jesse Turner that resulted in a Supreme Court decision outlawing discrimination at the restaurant.

It mattered little that the high court in 1954 had declared separate but equal schools to be unconstitutional and several months later extended that ruling to other public accommodations. In Memphis, Rowan was just another Negro who would not be allowed to mix with whites at a public restaurant—even one inside a public airport—and Loeb was content to keep it that way. "I am not interested in the Justice Department or the Kennedy Administration," the mayor told a local television station. "I am interested in Memphis."[2]

But without question, the fiercest battle over desegregation in Memphis involved the city schools. The Supreme Court's *Brown v. Board of Education* decision was virtually ignored in the Bluff City, as it was in much of the South. In Mississippi, for example, full integration of public schools state-wide was not implemented until the fall of 1970. White private schools sprang up as a result, and in less than five years, many public school districts around the state were resegregated.

Members of the all-white Memphis Board of Education justified their nullification of the Supreme Court's *Brown* ruling by convincing themselves that blacks did not want to go to school with whites any more than whites wanted to go with blacks. "We believe our Negroes will continue using their own school facilities since most of them are located in the center of Negro population areas," school board president Milton Bowers said in response to the *Brown* decision. He basically promised the white community that the schools would never be integrated.[3]

It proved to be a hollow promise because on the morning of September 3, 1958, Marjorie McFerren, a black woman who worked as a secretary at Tri-State Bank, tried to enroll her eight-year-old son Gerald in all-white Vollentine Elementary School. She was turned away by assistant super-intendent Harry Sharp, who told her she did not have the proper transfer papers from the district's central office. Two days and several runarounds later, McFerren submitted a formal application seeking transfer papers for Gerald to leave all-black Hyde Park Elementary and attend Vollentine—not so much as a test case for integration, but because Vollentine was closer to their home.[4] The application was promptly denied by Superintendent E. C. Stimbert. The denial and the pretext behind it, however, set the stage for a protracted legal showdown over the integration of Memphis City Schools.

On March 31, 1960, eight black lawyers representing eighteen black school children and their parents filed suit in federal district court in Memphis accusing the board of education of operating a biracial school system in violation of the Supreme Court's ruling. The suit asked that the entire school district be fully integrated. It was filed by lawyers Thurgood Marshall, Constance Baker Motley, A. W. Willis Jr., H. T. Lockard, Russell B.

Sugarmon Jr., Benjamin Hooks, Ben F. Jones, and Ira Murphy. The case was styled *Deborah A. Northcross et al. v. The Board of Education of the Memphis City Schools et. al.* The named defendants were Superintendent E. C. Stimbert and school board members Walter P. Armstrong, John T. Shea, Frances Coe, Jane Seessel, and Julian Bondurant.

The complaint created uneasiness in the city's white neighborhoods, while most of black Memphis took a calmer wait-and-see attitude. To most blacks, Milton Bowers had been partially correct. They did prefer their own schools, but if integration meant an end to substandard textbooks, equipment, and facilities, better job opportunities, and more say-so about the district's operations, then bring it on.

School board members and their attorneys convinced themselves that the lawsuit was merely a minor annoyance. In its written response to the suit, the board claimed it was following Tennessee's Pupil Placement Act allowing school boards to assign students to schools any way it saw fit, so long as the assignments weren't based on skin color. Plus, parents could appeal to change any assignment. It was a specious argument because school administrators had no intention of putting black children in white schools and certainly wouldn't dream of putting white kids in black schools.

The lawsuit was assigned to federal judge Marion Speed Boyd, a lifelong Tennessean who grew up in Covington. Boyd had served in both houses of the Tennessee legislature and became a city court judge in Memphis during the heyday of the Boss Crump political machine. On issues of racial equality, Boyd was far from open-minded. But whether he was a bona fide racist is difficult to determine. Born in 1900, he was a product of his segregated upbringing. His longevity in elected and appointed office forced him to confront many thorny racial issues. But Boyd always preferred to believe that any perceived mistreatment of blacks could be easily explained, and that the white power structure was doing its best to remedy inequities with all deliberate speed. In other instances, Boyd believed that segregation was allowable because of tradition. In 1956, he dismissed a racial discrimination lawsuit filed by black activist O. Z. Evers, who was ordered to either move from his front seat on a city bus or get off the bus. Evers chose to get off. The incident happened just months after the end of the Montgomery, Alabama, bus boycott, yet Judge Boyd ruled that Evers had no case.[5]

In 1961, Boyd had to be forced by the Sixth Circuit Court of Appeals to issue an injunction preventing the eviction of hundreds of Negro sharecroppers from rented land in Haywood County. White landowners kicked the sharecroppers off their property because they had registered to vote in the 1960 presidential election. Boyd had refused to issue the injunction, saying he could not get involved in private rental contracts. The appeals court, siding with the Justice Department's Civil Rights Division, ruled, however, that "there was sufficient evidence of threat, intimidation and coercion to require the trial judge to grant a restraining order against the landowner defendants."[6] Boyd did as the higher court ordered.

The cautious judge took the same approach with the desegregation lawsuit against Memphis City Schools. He ruled in favor of the school board. Boyd acknowledged that the board now had a legal obligation to end racial segregation, but he gave the board an out by stating that it was doing the job satisfactorily by following the state's pupil placement law. Of course that wasn't the case, but Boyd's upbringing, his political bent, and his long association with segregated white society meant he could rule no other way. He was not about to become the first white judge in Tennessee to instantly grant equal rights and equal access to black folks.

Once the judge's decision was made public, most of white Memphis sighed with relief. But the school board realized that it could no longer stonewall every legitimate request by blacks to enroll at a white school. So in October 1961, thirteen first graders, carefully selected by the NAACP, walked into history by becoming the first Negroes to integrate Memphis City Schools. They were enrolled at four elementary schools—Bruce, Gordon, Rozelle, and Springdale. School leaders were relieved. The children had enrolled without a serious racial incident and Judge Boyd had put a stop to dreaded wholesale integration. But the NAACP lawyers weren't through. They appealed Boyd's ruling to the Sixth Circuit Court of Appeals. And on March 23, 1962, almost two years after the case was filed, the appeals court overturned Boyd's ruling. The court declared that Memphis was in fact running a segregated school system and ordered Boyd to oversee plans to more fully integrate schools.

"The inescapable conclusion is that at the time of the judgment in this case, the schools of Memphis were open on a basis of white schools for white children and Negro schools for Negroes," the court said. It also called the state's pupil placement law a farce: "Negro children cannot be required to apply for that to which they are entitled as a matter of right. The burden rests with the school authorities to initiate desegregation. The admission of thirteen Negro pupils (to four white schools) after a scholastic test which the white children did not have to take . . . is not desegregation nor is it the institution of a plan for non-racial organization of the Memphis school system. We are impressed that the defendants honestly and sincerely desire to comply with the law, but they have pursued the mistaken belief that full compliance as required by the Supreme Court can be had under the pupil assignment law."[7]

Again, Judge Boyd proceeded, ever so slowly, to do as he was told by the higher court. But he stepped down from the bench in 1966 before any headway was made toward full desegregation. The case languished until it was assigned to Boyd's replacement, Judge Robert Malcolm McRae Jr. A native Memphian and product of the city schools, McRae served in the U.S. Navy during World War II and spent time in both the Atlantic and Pacific theaters. Like Boyd, he grew up in a segregated environment. But unlike his predecessor, McRae developed a strong distaste for overt racism. He got elected to the Shelby County Circuit Court bench in 1964. Two years later, his strong family ties to Democratic Senator Albert Gore led to his nomination to the federal court bench. He was appointed by President Lyndon Johnson and was sworn in on November 10, 1966.

Initially, Judge McRae also moved the school desegregation case along slowly. But the pressure from black community leaders continued to escalate. It reached a crescendo the fall of 1969, when the Memphis chapter of the NAACP, spearheaded by Maxine Smith, Ezekiel Bell, and others, stepped up demands for black representation on the city school board and the hiring of more black teachers. When the board refused to discuss the issues, black students staged a spontaneous boycott of classes that soon evolved into weekly "Black Monday" protests in which up to sixty-seven thousand students and several hundred teachers stayed away from schools.[8]

The protests had a major financial impact on city schools, because state funding was based on average daily attendance. "Black Monday" protests ended only after the Memphis City Council agreed to name two black advisory members to the board, and the board itself agreed to hire more black teachers.[9] In 1971, the school board expanded from five members to nine, and three African Americans—Maxine Smith, George H. Brown Jr., and Carl Johnson—won seats.

But full integration of the school district remained on hold and the Sixth Circuit Court of Appeals was losing patience. Under pressure from the higher court and his own sense of fairness, McRae finally made it known in a December, 10, 1971, ruling that city schools would be desegregated and the method to get that done would be busing. The judge noted that of the 162 city schools, 67 of them had a student population that is 90 percent or more black, and 61 schools had a population that is 90 percent or more white.

"By state and local law, and entrenched custom and practice, Negroes were denied many privileges and opportunities which were available to all white persons," McRae wrote. "Furthermore, the Negro schools were not equal from an educational standpoint. In addition to this unequal educational opportunity, the Negroes were by custom and practice denied most of the employment opportunities which permitted whites to purchase more expensive housing. The city and its economic structures were dominated by white persons."[10]

McRae's written ruling also noted, as an aside, that in 1947, the Memphis Board of Censors banned a movie from being shown in the city "for the reason stated by the chairman of the Board of Censors as follows: 'I am sorry to have to inform you that (the census board) is unable to approve your "Curley" picture with the little negroes as the south does not permit negroes in white schol (sic) nor recognize social equality between the races even in children.'"

The fact that McRae included the census board's misspelling of the word "school" in his ruling was his way of exposing the ignorance of those who believed Negroes were intellectually unequal to whites. "The law is clear and emphatic," McRae said, "that a school board may not continue to maintain a segregated system because there is disagreement with the necessary methods of desegregating the system."[11] And busing was now necessary in Memphis.

McRae's explosive ruling escalated the white community's angst to all-out panic. It was panic far greater than that displayed during the black park controversy of 1914 or the dispute over the black golf tournament at Audubon Park in 1956. For most white Memphians, having Negroes attending their schools would be distasteful enough. But sending their children to black schools was an abomination.

School leaders tried to tell McRae during a December 1971 hearing that whites won't stand for wholesale school desegregation. They will sell their homes and move to the suburbs, they declared. School board witnesses admitted that white flight was the primary reason the district kept avoiding integration—to "stabilize communities."

One witness, Dr. Robert Guthrie, an urban sociology professor at Memphis State University, made the argument, rather patronizingly, that segregation is a natural and historical phenomenon. At one point, he explained to Judge McRae that segregation was a voluntary grouping from the inside, based to a large extent on "ethnocentrism, a sense of allegiance or grouping together around things that are familiar to certain groups."[12]

McRae was far from impressed and did not like being lectured to on the human tendencies of segregation. He told the entire courtroom that white flight cannot be a factor in any desegregation plan that the school board develops. Sixth Circuit Court judge Paul Weick of Akron, Ohio, had essentially said the same thing six months earlier. "It has not been suggested that the board can stop (white flight) or that it should chase after them," he said.[13]

As the school board, under McRae's order, tried to develop two busing plans, white Memphians mobilized like never before in Memphis. The most vocal of the white protest groups was Citizens Against Busing (CAB), whose leaders were as emphatic as McRae's written ruling. They intended to make sure there would be no busing in Memphis. But on April, 20, 1972, McRae approved Plan A, which called for busing nearly fourteen thousand city school students to achieve desegregation.

The judge rejected a second plan offered by the district to bus about thirty-nine thousand students and rejected the NAACP's plan to bus sixty-one thousand students. Frances Coe was the only white school board member to vote against appealing McRae's decision. She sided with black board members Maxine Smith, George H. Brown Jr., and Carl Johnson, who argued the board needed to get on with the business of fully desegregating schools. Coe's decision was based on two factors. "It is obvious, due to the geographic and population facts, that some transportation is necessary if we are to make progress in achieving a desegregated school system," she said. "Second, the practicalities of the situation have been recognized and we have not been ordered to do more than we are currently capable of doing."[14]

Whites—those with school-aged children and those without—were incensed. A month before McRae imposed Plan A, Citizens Against Busing buried a beat-up old yellow school bus some sixteen feet deep on property just off James Road. And on May 17, the group staged a massive rally at Poplar Plaza. About one thousand protesters then marched down Poplar to the board of education building on Avery. They carried with them their children's new school assignment cards for the coming school year torn into pieces.

Some of the marchers also carried placards with a picture of George Wallace, who as governor of Alabama had stood in the doorway to block black students from enrolling at the University of Alabama. Along the march route, supporters handled out free ice cream and soft drinks. A car dealer along Poplar opened his snack machine and gave away treats to the marchers. Ken Keele, president of CAB, said the march was intended to "send a message to the judge, the school board and liberals everywhere that this community is not going to have busing."[15]

Other white Memphians tried to temper the anger among the adults and ease the fear among white students. On November 27, 1972, school board member Hunter Lane Jr. met with white students at Frayser High School who were about to start attending classes with students from all-black Manassas High. Lane encouraged the students to show leadership and accept the Manassas children. "I'm one who believes there are some basic differences between the races," Lane told the students. "But there are many other common similarities. If you look for common ground instead of differences, you may be amazed at what you find."[16]

White adults, however, continued to vilify McRae for imposing the busing order. He received constant death threats and was escorted to work by U.S. marshals, who took a different route to his judicial chambers at the federal building every day. The judge also was shunned by parishioners at his own church.[17] And yet, the chaos in Memphis was relatively tame compared to far more volatile responses elsewhere to school desegregation orders. In Little Rock, Arkansas, for example, the reaction when nine black students integrated Central High School in 1957 was worse than anything experienced in Memphis. Angry white mobs took their cues from Orval Faubus, a segregationist governor who declared a state of emergency and sent in the state National Guard to keep the black students from enrolling at Central. Only after federal troops, dispatched by President Dwight Eisenhower, arrived were the students allowed in—and even then, they were mercilessly taunted by the hostile white demonstrators.

New Orleans also was the scene of violence in November 1960, when four black first graders desegregated two previously all-white elementary schools in the city's Ninth Ward. A group of angry white women gathered at the school every day for months and spat at, shoved, and shouted ob-

Yellow Buses and White Flight

scenities at the small black children.[18] Cities including Atlanta, Charlotte, San Francisco, Detroit, and Chicago also had their share of contention over integrating public schools.

But perhaps nowhere was the backlash against school desegregation more contentious than in Boston in the fall of 1974. Like Memphis, Boston was placed under a federal court order to achieve school desegregation through widespread busing. In response, "wild, raging mobs of white men and women confronted armies of police, while youths in their teens and younger hurled rocks, bottles and racial epithets at buses carrying terrified black youngsters to school."[19]

Blacks and whites alike were beaten and stabbed. A white man was dragged from his car and beaten to death, and a black lawyer was beaten on the steps of city hall and struck with the staff of an American flag that was used as a spear.[20] That attack was captured by a photographer and became an enduring image of northern white reaction to racial integration. Nothing that extreme happened in Memphis. However, whites left the city schools by the thousands. When the first wave of busing was implemented in January 1973, most of the seven thousand students who boarded the spiffy yellow vehicles on the first day were black. Private schools sprang up everywhere, and the prophecy of white flight came true as white Memphis residents flocked to the Shelby County suburbs and to welcoming DeSoto County, Mississippi.

According to the 1960 census, Memphis had a total population of 497,524, of which 312,799 were white and 184,320 were black. By 1970, with the annexation of Whitehaven, the total population had grown to 623,497, of which 379,199 were white and 242,505 were black. And by 1980, the total population had grown to 641,400, but the white total had shrunk to 333,769 and the black total stood at 307,671.[21]

The demographic pattern was now set. When the 1990 census was taken, blacks officially became the majority population of Memphis with sixty-six thousand more residents than whites. School desegregation, along with busing that was used to achieve it, cannot be blamed for all of the white flight from Memphis. Worries about crime, blight, and higher taxes also fueled the out-migration—along with the simple desire for more space and newer surroundings. A sizable number of black Memphians also left for the suburbs.

But the assassination of Martin Luther King Jr. in 1968 and forced busing four years later were the one-two punch that sent most white Memphians packing. Meanwhile, the steady growth of the black population, through births and in-migration from rural areas in Mississippi, Arkansas, and West Tennessee, meant that Memphis politically was poised to change for good. As a result, several disparate political factions within the black community started to plan in earnest for the day when they could put more of their own into elected office.

As for Judge Robert M. McRae Jr., he remained on the federal bench until the last day of December 1994. Before his death in 2004, he told a reporter for the *Commercial Appeal* that his only regret about the desegregation order is that he didn't do it sooner. He recounted for the reporter the statement by city school board president Milton Bowers in 1954 that blacks had their own schools and that's the way it should stay. Bowers's comment, McRae said, suggested that blacks "were no longer independent. They were in bondage. They wouldn't go to 'our' schools. They would go to 'theirs.' I developed a terrible disapproval of discrimination like that because it was illegal and immoral."[22]

McRae also wrote his own book about the *Northcross* desegregation case. In it, he relates a story from his childhood in which his father severely admonished him for being too chummy "with niggers" after the young McRae put his arms around a black man who was working at his father's garage. "I was coming from the belief that blacks were inferior to whites socially and probably otherwise," McRae wrote, describing it as the "white racism syndrome." But he adds, "The definition of white racism syndrome does not indicate that it is an incurable disease."[23]

Finally, McRae told the *Commercial Appeal*, "There are some people who say I ruined the school system," but he hoped his book will portray him as "somebody who did something that had to be done because the law required it. There are some people who don't want to understand that. I don't think I'll be a hero. But I think history will treat me as somebody who followed the law."[24]

Yellow Buses and White Flight

E. H. "Boss" Crump (right) with Shelby County Commission Chairman
E. W. Hale on election night in November 1944.

E. H. Crump gives his famous wave while going for a ride with children
and adults at the Fairgrounds Amusement Park (later renamed Liberty-
land) in October 1939.

E. H. Crump celebrated a 1943 birthday with a Mississippi River boat ride for 3,000 orphans, wounded soldiers, shut-ins, needy Memphis residents, and other politicians.

(*Clockwise from top left*) Walter Chandler, Watkins Overton, Cliff Davis, and E. H. Crump all wore the Memphis mayor's hat during a 39-hour span on the first two days of 1940.

Lucius Burch, Edward Meeman, and Edmund Orgill, who led the movement to topple the Crump machine, in 1949 (Courtesy Special Collections, University of Memphis Libraries)

Mayor Watkins Overton in front of the mayor's office after he resigned on Feb. 28, 1953. He served as mayor from 1928-1940 and 1949-1953. (Courtesy Special Collections, University of Memphis Libraries)

Lieutenant George W. Lee at a dinner in his honor at the Holiday Inn
Rivermont in September 1973

Chief Deputy U.S. Marshal George Tallent (*left*) watches over attorneys (*standing from left*) A. W. Willis, Ben L. Hooks, B. F. Jones, Russell B. Sugarmon Jr. and H. T. Lockard (*seated*) on March 31, 1960 as they check summons forms after filing a desegregation suit in Federal Court against the Memphis Board of Education and city school superintendent.

City Councilman and future mayor Wyeth Chandler talking with local AFSCME president T. O. Jones (*center*) at a city Public Works Committee meeting attended by some 700 striking sanitation workers on February 22, 1968. Union representative Joe Warren is listening in.

One day after the assassination of Dr. Martin Luther King Jr., Mayor Henry Loeb—a shotgun beneath his desk—greeted about 300 black and white ministers in his office on Friday, April 5, 1968. He is shaking hands with Rev. Joseph P. Toney while Father Nicholas L. Vieron (*behind the clasped hands*) looked on.

NAACP leader Maxine Smith participating in a "Black Monday" protest against racial inequality in Memphis City Schools on November 15, 1969.

Roy Wilkins (*left*), executive director of the national NAACP, chats with Jesse Turner (right) at The Sheraton-Peabody on May 22, 1969 during a testimonial banquet honoring Turner.

On October 27, 1975, Minerva Johnican was sworn in by Judge H. T. Lockard to fill the Shelby County Quarterly Court District 6 seat, becoming the first African-American woman to hold county office.

Mike Cody (*left*) congratulates Congressman Harold Ford on election night in 1976.

Mayoral opponents Otis Higgs (*left*) and Wyeth Chandler in October 1979.

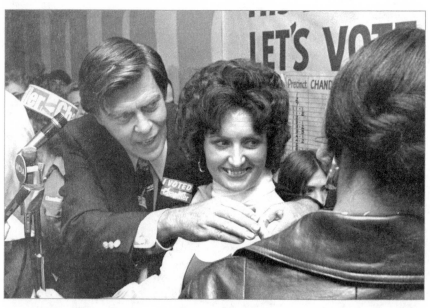

Mayor Wyeth Chandler, with wife Linda, after winning reelection to a second term on November 6, 1975.

Dr. Willie W. Herenton standing on the steps of his childhood home on the south side of E. H. Crump Boulevard near South Third Street on December 7, 1978.

Mayor Dick Hackett with his wife, Kathy, and children on September 24, 1987, during his successful campaign for reelection to a second full term.

U.S. Rep. Harold Ford (*left*) with W. Otis Higgs on April 20, 1991

U.S. Rep. Harold Ford, with his jacket off, confronts Election Commission Chairman O. C. Pleasant Jr. about uncounted absentee ballots in the Memphis mayor's race on election night, October 3, 1991. Others immediately behind Pleasant and Ford are (*from left*) Reginald French, Tarik Sugarmon, and Frank Banks

W. Otis Higgs is seated in the pulpit at Bloomfield Baptist Church in South Memphis during Harold Ford's long-awaited Black Leadership Summit on June 15, 1991.

Dr. Willie W. Herenton's supporters at The Peabody Hotel cheer after hearing that their candidate had taken the lead in the vote count on election night, October 3, 1991.

Mayor Dick Hackett leaves the podium with his wife, Kathy, in the early morning hours of October 4, 1991, after learning that Dr. Willie Herenton had apparently defeated him in the mayoral election.

Dr. Willie W. Herenton being sworn in as mayor on Wednesday, Jan 1, 1992, by Judge Luke C. Moore. Herenton's mother, Ruby Harris, (*left*) held the Bible as her son took the oath of office.

The author in the newsroom of *The Pittsburgh Press* in 1991.

CHAPTER 10

THE FORD MACHINE

"**T**HANK YOU, JESUS! Thank you, Jesus!"

Those words of praise came from an unidentified woman crowded inside the Harold Ford for Congress campaign headquarters at Angelus Street and Poplar Avenue on the evening of November 5, 1974. It was election night in Memphis, and the twenty-nine-year-old Ford had just scored the biggest political victory in modern history for a black man in the Bluff City. He would represent almost the entire city of Memphis in the U.S. House of Representatives—a position previously held by a succession of white men, several of them handpicked by E. H. "Boss" Crump because of their service and loyalty to the Crump machine. Crump himself even held the office for two terms before discovering he'd much rather be the big dog in Memphis instead of a small fish in Washington.

Now, twenty years and three weeks after Crump's death, fellow Democrat Harold Ford surprised all of Memphis—blacks and whites alike—and Washington politicos as well by defeating four-term Republican representative Dan Kuykendall for the Eighth District congressional seat. In winning the seat by the slimmest of margins, Ford also stretched his political coattail just enough to carry two brothers, Emmitt and John, to victory in their respective state legislative races. Harold Ford was now officially on his way to assembling a newer and more expansive political machine than the one Crump maintained for nearly fifty years.

Kuykendall miscalculated virtually every aspect of his fifth campaign for Congress. He grossly underestimated the black community's fervor—

which mostly went unreported by the white media—to push Harold Ford to victory. And he grossly overestimated his ability to attract the same black support he had gotten in past elections or to continue wooing crossover white Democrats who up to now could not see themselves voting for a black man.

Most of all, he underestimated Ford's smarts and tenacity as a campaigner. Once the final results were in and he grudgingly accepted defeat, Kuykendall even misjudged what the Memphis congressional district would look like in the future. He boldly predicted that the Eighth District would become a "yo-yo seat," alternating between Democrats and Republicans. "I don't see any stability in this district," he told the press.[1] History would prove that he couldn't have been more wrong. No Republican has held the congressional seat since Kuykendall.

The reality that a young black man from a large, poor southwest Memphis family could pull off such a stunning and historic victory spoke volumes—about Ford's burgeoning campaign skills, but even more about the evolution of black political dreams in Memphis. African Americans, from those too young to vote to those too old and frail to do it without assistance, were united in pulling for Ford. And like Crump before him, Ford put together an impressive campaign organization capable of getting his supporters to the polls on election day.

But how did he do it? Ford did not have the legal background of others—Benjamin Hooks, A. W. Willis Jr., Russell Sugarmon Jr., and H. T. Lockard—who started making political waves in Memphis when Ford was still a kid in grade school. But Ford had something the others didn't—perfect timing and a built-in connection to the entire black community through his family's funeral home business.

After graduating from Geeter High School, Ford attended Tennessee State University in Nashville, where he earned a bachelor of science degree in business administration. At twenty-two, he was immediately off to Philadelphia in the summer of 1967 for a job at IBM, thinking he was gone from Memphis for good. But before he even started with IBM, Ford answered a call from his mother, Vera Ford, to return to Memphis and help his father, N. J. Ford, run the growing funeral home.[2]

His parents were sure that Harold's charismatic personality and leadership skills were just what the business needed. They had seen him in action a year earlier as manager of N. J. Ford's campaign to defeat Sugarmon for state representative. Harold absolutely sparkled as a campaign organizer for his father. Other family members also pitched in, and the elder Ford captured an impressive 28 percent of the vote in the Democratic primary in losing to Sugarmon, who was far more politically established. The experience gave Harold a mild thirst for politics, so it was easy for him to say yes when his mother asked him to come home.

Ford obtained an associate degree in mortuary science and was off and running as a funeral director. But another venture into politics was waiting. In the fall of 1968, both Sugarmon and Willis lost their legislative seats— Sugarmon to Alvin King and Willis to James I. Taylor. *Jet* magazine took notice of the upsets, saying they were the result of black Memphis voters "still seething over the prolonged garbage strike that ended in the murder of Dr. Martin Luther King Jr."[3]

The fact that voters would blame Sugarmon and Willis for the sanitation strike was far-fetched. The more plausible reason for their defeat was that ordinary black voters in their respective legislative districts could not relate to a couple of highly successful lawyers who didn't mingle much in their circles. Plus, a whispering campaign about their marital lives did not help them at the polls either. Still, the lost was particularly devastating for Willis, who in 1964 became the first black Memphian elected to the state House since 1884. Willis also had lost a bid for Memphis mayor in 1967 and would never hold elected office again.

In 1970, Ford saw an opening. Taylor, a black school teacher and real estate agent, was vulnerable in the South Memphis legislative district. Ford successfully painted Taylor as a do-nothing representative, pointing out that of more than two thousand bills introduced in the legislature, Taylor's name was on only three—and none of them passed. Ford was sure he could win, and he did so with ease. In the August Democratic primary, Ford took advantage of the family funeral home's connections, his own growing popularity, and an endorsement from the *Memphis Press-Scimitar* and trounced Taylor by nearly sixteen hundred votes. Embarrassed and angry, Taylor claimed that he had been cheated out of the seat. He then ran as an Independent candidate against Ford in the November general election. But Ford got 73 percent of the vote, and that was the end of Taylor's brief political career.

The following year, Ford's older brother John followed him into politics by defeating incumbent Rev. James L. Netters for a seat on the

Memphis City Council. Netters had the support of several fellow preachers, the *Press-Scimitar* and the two other black councilmen, Fred Davis and J. O. Patterson Jr. The *Press-Scimitar* argued that Netters presented a better image for the majority black council district. But the charismatic Fords and their growing ability to get out the vote overcame all of that, and John Ford beat Netters by twenty-one hundred votes. The *Commercial Appeal* noted that Netters was "ousted by a younger, more aggressive Negro . . . who comes from a highly politically motivated family."[4]

Among many black voters, John Ford's victory over Netters overshadowed a rather tame mayoral race. Incumbent mayor Henry Loeb opted again to not seek reelection, mostly because of intense criticism of his handling of the sanitation strike that led to the assassination of Martin Luther King Jr. With the black community's arch villain out of the picture and no black candidate in the race, the mayoral campaign was almost a ho-hum affair in the black community. Loeb and practically all of his supporters rallied behind the mayoral campaign of City Councilman Wyeth Chandler, a hard-driving and hard-drinking politician from the old school of city leadership. The daily newspapers predicted that Bill Morris, making his second try for mayor, would get the majority of black votes.

But instead, most African Americans went for Kenneth Turner, a juvenile court judge. Chandler and Turner ended up in a runoff, even though Chandler received twenty thousand more votes than Turner. Morris finished a disappointing third. The November runoff was as racially polarized as any previous election in Memphis history and produced one of the closest finishes since the Crump days. Chandler got less than 3 percent of the black vote, while Turner was beaten five to one in most white precincts.

When the votes were counted, Chandler was ahead, but only by 1,833 votes out of 166,649 cast.[5] Turner refused to concede, preferring to wait until a special audit was done. But the audit a week later only gave Turner 2 additional votes, while 13 votes were deducted from Chandler's total. The final tally was 84,228 for Chandler and 82,410 for Turner, who immediately conceded.

Once the new city council was sworn in, it didn't take long for John Ford to make waves, with most of the sparring coming between Ford and fellow black councilman Fred Davis. At a meeting on February 6, 1973, Ford got into a heated shouting match with two white councilmen, Jack McNeil and Chairman Thomas Todd. Ford became upset when Todd repeatedly ignored his demands to speak against a request for the city to help fund new private schools organized by Citizens Against Busing.

The Ford Machine

During the dispute, McNeil intervened and appeared to be chastising Ford. "Why don't you just shut the hell up," Ford responded. Todd then ordered the council's bailiff to remove Ford from the chambers if he "cursed" again. "The bailiff ain't gonna remove me," Ford angrily told Todd. "You have the bailiff put his hand on me and we'll remove each other."[6] Todd backed down and Ford was allowed to speak against any taxpayer money going to the private schools, which were set up solely in opposition to the desegregation of Memphis City Schools. Ford called claims by CAB leaders that the new schools were integrated a fallacy.

Ken Keele, president of CAB, asked the council for an unspecified amount of taxpayer money to help pay teacher salaries and buy supplies. Several councilmen—including Ed McBreyer, Billy Hyman, and Robert Love—supported the proposal. "We have appropriated funds to help illegitimate children and criminals," councilman McNeil said. "But I'm sure the Federal District judge (Robert M. McRae Jr.) won't allow us to do this." Along with Ford and Fred Davis, Councilwoman Gwen Awsumb also opposed the funding, saying she believed it was illegal.[7] The ideal was eventually tabled.

But when the council reconvened the following week, even more chaos erupted when Harold Ford, accompanied by Rev. Samuel Billy Kyles and about one hundred other followers, showed up demanding to speak in support of Ford's brother John. Harold Ford repeatedly asked Chairman Todd to suspend council rules to allow the group eight minutes to speak. But Todd repeatedly refused as chants from the clenched-fisted Ford supporters grew louder in the rear of the council chamber. "Mob rule does not get us anywhere and I feel you are trying to intimate this council or me," Todd said. John then shot back, "Don't call these people a mob." Both Fred Davis and J. O. Patterson Jr. sided with Todd and also swapped verbal jabs with Harold Ford. "I ask council to reconsider. I represent 40,000 people," Harold said. "I represent 90,000 people," Davis responded. When Todd asked Harold to sit down, he said, "I'll sit down. But I don't think I can control the audience. You and two black members have voted not to let black folks speak." Davis then shouted, "That's just so much bull."[8]

The confrontation ended with neither Harold nor anyone else in the group getting to speak on John's behalf. But Harold had accomplished his objective. Throughout the entire encounter, he was persistent, but not belligerent. He was there to help his brother stand up against using public money for white private schools, and he clearly got under the skin of Todd, Davis, and Patterson. The incident garnered heavy media coverage, and state representative Harold Ford was now viewed by black Memphians as their unquestioned political leader.

The following year, with two terms in the Tennessee General Assembly under his belt, Harold grew restless and started looking for bigger challenges. It came in late spring of 1974 when close friends and political allies, including fellow state representative Alvin King, suggested that he challenge Dan Kuykendall for the Memphis congressional seat. The Ford family was all-in as well. Brother Emmitt would seek Harold's state house seat and brother John would run against his nemesis J. O. Patterson Jr. for the state senate. All of the districts overlapped allowing the Ford brothers to run as a team.

Before Harold would fully commit, he knew he needed support from white Memphians, particularly liberal Democrats who just might think the time was right to support a black candidate for higher office. Ford and his father N. J. went to see Lucius Burch at his downtown law office. Burch was the top white liberal Democrat in Memphis who fought the Crump machine for years. He had helped Edmund Orgill get elected mayor and Estes Kefauver elected to the U.S. Senate—despite opposition from Crump in the waning years of the old political machine. If Harold had any chance of becoming a congressman, he needed Burch's support and his political connections.

Burch listened to young Ford for several minutes and then called into the room one of the rising stars in the Burch law firm, Mike Cody. Cody had been part of the legal team that represented King in federal court the day of his assassination. Cody also was chairman of the Shelby County Democratic Party, and his political views were as liberal as they come. Both Burch and Cody were immediately impressed by the young black candidate's political savvy and organizational skills. Burch agreed to give Cody all the time necessary to help the campaign. Ford in turn named Cody a campaign co-chairman.[9]

As the campaign progressed throughout the summer of 1974, Burch and Cody were in awe of Ford's organization. "E. H. Crump was good," Burch told Cody. "But I think this young man will be better in terms of organizing people in wards, precincts and neighborhoods."[10] Ford took the best of Crump's political strategy and added even stronger constituent services along with one-on-one campaigning.

He and wife Dorothy stomped for votes at bus stops in the morning and went door to door in the evening. Most of all, like Crump, Ford knew that his political success depended on almost unanimous backing from black voters—and he worked tirelessly to get it. The work paid off in the August primary when Ford trounced five opponents to win the Democratic nomination. He received 35,120 votes. His closest challenger, Charles Burch (no relation to Lucius), got only 8,156 votes. Sister Mary Ann Guthrie, a Catholic nun running for the nomination, got 7,534 votes.[11] After the primary, Guthrie joined the Ford campaign.

In his primary victory speech, Ford talked directly to his white supporters, downplaying the impact that race would have on his campaign to unseat Kuykendall. He was keenly aware that he had just gotten fifteen thousand more primary votes that Kuykendall, who easily won the Republican nomination over Joe Cooper and Duncan Ragsdale. Ford needed to project the voice of a leader who could represent all of Memphis.

"Inflation knows no color. Gasoline pumps know no color," Ford said. "The voters have spoken loudly today. They are tired of a situation where the price of everything is rising and yet salaries remain the same." He then declared to everyone in Memphis that he did not win the Democratic nomination because he's black. It was because he represents a need for new, dynamic leadership.[12]

Still, the general election campaign would be daunting for the twenty-nine-year-old political phenom. Kuykendall was fifty years old, had been in Congress nearly eight years, and had plenty of Republican money behind him. Plus, white voters still outnumbered black voters in the district 55 to 45 percent. Kuykendall also had handily defeated black city councilman J. O. Patterson Jr. in the 1972 general election, and Patterson, in theory, had just as much name recognition—of not more—than Ford.

But Ford had several things working in his favor that Patterson did not. White flight to the suburbs because of the 1972 busing decision had increased the black voting population from 29 to 45 percent in just two years. And the people leaving the district were Kuykendall voters. In addition, President Richard Nixon was forced to resign from office because of the Watergate scandal one week after the August 1974 primary, and Republican candidates—including Kuykendall—had to endure the scent of scandal throughout the fall campaign.

Ford's biggest advantage, however, was his extensive reach into the black community through the funeral home and black churches. The Ford organization perfected Sunday morning campaigning. Ford or a member of the family would hit several churches in one day and that proved invaluable in reaching large blocks of voters simultaneously. Congregations were more than receptive. No doubt someone in every black church in the city had a relative or friend who had been buried by N. J. Ford and Sons Funeral Home. Kuykendall had no answer for it.

To no surprise, however, both the *Commercial Appeal* and *Press-Scimitar* endorsed Kuykendall. Then less than a week before the election, the Republican got what he thought was a giant boost among black voters. A. W. Willis Jr., the city's first black state legislator in modern times, publicly endorsed Kuykendall. "I've watched both men carefully and I've checked their voting records," Willis told a meeting of Democratic and Independent voters in East Memphis. "I think Kuykendall will do a better job than Ford in this critical time of inflation and economic problems." Willis insisted that Ford was not quite up to the task of dealing effectively with national issues.

Ford was unfazed by the endorsement, saying it was because Willis had gotten an eighty-five-thousand-dollar federal grant through Kuykendall for the Beale Street urban renewal project. Ford said Willis "has no credibility in either the black or white communities and I say 'right on' for his endorsement of Kuykendall."[13]

Endorsing Kuykendall might have been a sound business decision by Willis, but politically it was a colossal mistake. His widow, Miriam DeCosta-Willis, believes he should not have endorsed the incumbent because it did nothing to help Kuykendall, or her husband for that matter, among black voters.[14] Black radio executive Art Gilliam, who had a regular column in the *Commercial Appeal* in 1974, wrote after the election that Willis's attempt to vilify Ford "was a dirty, self-serving political move. A few years ago Willis would have been regarded as an Uncle Tom. Today he's too insignificant in local politics to be regarded."[15]

Indeed, Ford's biggest concern was not Willis. It was the fear that black voter turnout would not be large enough to overcome Kuykendall's massive white support. Mike Cody and other liberal whites had worked to get Ford a respectable 15 percent of the white vote. The rest was up to black Memphis.

In strategy sessions, Ford and his advisers concluded that the key to increasing the vote was to attract black women to the polls. In a brilliant, last-minute campaign move, the organization recruited soul singer Isaac Hayes to cut a radio commercial for Ford. The ad was played only on election morning on black radio stations, including WDIA. In the spot, Hayes uses his deepest, sexiest voice to ask black women to get up, get dressed, and get to the polls to vote for Harold. It worked beautifully. Black women flocked to the polls.[16]

Hayes also accompanied Ford to several precincts on election day, including Ford's voting place at the Riverview Community Center in South Memphis. Ford's mother, Vera, also recorded an effective radio ad asking voters, particularly black women, to elect each of her three sons—Harold for Congress, John for the state senate, and Emmitt for the state house.

After the polls closed, Ford was confident. But the tenseness was excruciating at the campaign headquarters. It changed to outrage when every television station in town started reporting that Kuykendall had apparently won. Ford's own accounting firm, which was keeping a running track of estimated precinct numbers, told Ford he was slightly ahead. So Ford, Alvin King, Willie Miles, and Rev. R. C. George Jr. went to the election commission headquarters and confronted commissioners over the TV news reports. Ford and the commissioners then discovered that six precinct boxes, each containing votes and a tally sheet, were sitting in the basement uncounted. Poll workers who had turned them in, had failed to take the tally sheets out of the boxes.

Ford, however, went on live television and alleged that the tally sheets had been tossed into a garbage can in the basement. Both Democratic and Republican election commissioners disputed the claim, calling the missing tally sheets an innocent mistake. "I could have killed him when he said that on television," Commissioner Jack Morris III, a Democrat, later told the *Commercial Appeal*. "I can't understand a man who was treated so nice acting like that."[17]

Ford's anger and distrust were understandable. All six of the uncounted boxes were from black precincts, and there had been rumors of something similar happening during the 1972 congressional election. Earlier in the evening, Kuykendall had been declared the winner by about five thousand votes. But shortly after 11:00 p.m., the election commission reported the final unofficial tally: Ford—67,715, Kuykendall—67,141.

The young, upstart politician from a poor black family of seventeen had defeated a white incumbent congressman by a scant 574 votes. (The numbers were later adjusted to show that Ford won by 744 votes.) Jubilation erupted throughout the city. Thomas BeVier, a *Commercial Appeal* reporter who spent part of election night at the Ford campaign headquarters, described the scene as "like the 1960s without the anger."[18]

Car horns blared across Memphis and people took to the streets to celebrate. At the headquarters, BeVier reported, a matronly black woman bowed her head and shouted, "Thank you Jesus. Thank you Jesus." Sister Mary Ann Guthrie then led the campaign staff in prayer: "Heavenly Father, we thank you from the bottom of our hearts. This reflects more than the election of Harold Ford to Congress. . . . We are one people under you. We ask you to bless Harold Ford, his wife Dorothy . . . (and) we thank you for the looks on the faces of the young people here. Amen."[19] Kuykendall was stunned almost beyond words and asked for a recount. He later thought better of it and reluctantly accepted defeat while lamenting the fact that he had gotten only about half of the black vote he received two years earlier. "I don't know how. I worked twice as hard for it and lost it," he told a reporter.[20] The *Commercial Appeal's* post-election editorial grasped for an explanation of Ford's victory: "Many a Democrat smothered personal doubts and came out publicly for Harold Ford, thus assuring him of more than the usual white liberal vote for a black candidate." The paper said the outcome reflected the greatest party unity since the New Deal era.[21]

In his first meeting with reporters as U.S. representative-elect, Ford tried to conceal the smugness but couldn't. He had done the unthinkable and he wanted all of Memphis to know it. Referring to his doubters, black and white, Ford simply said they "can say all they want, but I won and I am congressman."[22]

Kuykendall, however, did not leave gracefully. In what Ford called a "last-minute political potshot," the ousted representative had all of the furniture removed from his Memphis congressional office in the federal building on New Year's Eve—two days before Ford had scheduled an open house in the office. Kuykendall purchased the furnishings—including an eighty-one-inch leather sofa, five chairs, a wooden desk, and two IBM Selectric typewriters—for $1,440 and was shipping them to a private office in Washington.[23] The move forced Ford to cancel the open house but also allowed him to score even more political points with his black constituency by painting Kuykendall as vengeful and disrespectful of the first African American congressman in Memphis.

In retrospect, the November 5, 1974, election showed once again that the local white-owned press had failed to detect or understand the growing power of the black electorate in Memphis. All the signs were there that black voters were ready to flex that power on a much grander scale with the election of the first black congressman ever from Tennessee. That election marked the real beginning of the Ford political dynasty. Its leader, Harold Ford, had shown Memphis how it's done. He had taken Boss Crump's ingredients for building an enduring political machine and made it work for black Memphians. But the elusive prize remained the mayor's office, and now the black community—much of it, at least—was clamoring for more.

CHAPTER 11

CHANDLER VERSUS HIGGS

WYETH CHANDLER SQUEAKED into the mayor's office in 1971 thanks to strong backing from his predecessor, Henry Loeb, and most of Loeb's old campaign apparatus. Loeb personally told Chandler of his decision not to run again before he announced it publicly. During that meeting in the mayor's office, Loeb committed his support to the ambitious city council chairman with the hope that some of Loeb's old cronies would be kept on in a Chandler administration. Few of them were.[1]

In the 1971 election, nearly 90 percent of white voters cast their ballot for the son of one of Memphis's most popular mayors from the past, Walter Chandler. But the Loeb endorsement was the kiss of death in the black community. In three successful campaigns for mayor, Wyeth Chandler never got more than 3 percent of the black vote—despite making promises to help mend the city's deep racial divide. Shortly after taking office in January 1972, he appointed Rev. James L. Netters as an administrative assistant after Netters lost his city council seat to John Ford. Netters, however, was the only black member of Chandler's all-male cabinet.

Black lawyer D'Army Bailey, who succeeded Art Gilliam as a regular columnist in the *Commercial Appeal*, severely chastised Chandler for his indifference to Memphis's black population. "Throughout his first term of office, Chandler has failed to give blacks a fair shake with top city jobs," Bailey wrote. "He has appointed one black among 10 city division heads. From among 50 department heads, there are only 10 blacks and 6 of these are in sanitation. There are no black department heads in fire, police or public works."[2]

Even Chandler's staunchest allies acknowledge that he never wanted to schmooze the black community. He really was never good at glad-handing for votes anyway. But his supporters always insisted that Chandler, the politician, tried to make life better for at least some black Memphians. He considered the sanitation department as the most important function in city government—even ahead of police. And he worked to improve pay inequities among black sanitation workers after the 1968 strike. His administration also ended a segregated practice in the police department in which white and black officers were not allowed to ride together in patrol cars.[3]

As the 1975 city elections approached, Chandler and Loeb had long parted ways. They didn't speak to each other for nearly four years, mostly because Chandler had gotten rid of Loeb's top men and never really sought the former mayor's advice. Plus, Loeb was a button-down conservative while Chandler preferred the life of a late-night carouser. The bar hopping frequently got Chandler into scrapes—some of which were reported in the newspapers and some of which were kept secret. There was the fist fight involving Chandler while he was socializing with women at the Lafayette Music Room on Madison Avenue in Overton Square in December 1972. Chandler, who was married four times, denied that a fight occurred, but several witnesses said it did.

A month later, in the wee morning hours, there was an even more bizarre incident in which a woman, who later became Chandler's wife, sent out a police broadcast saying, "The mayor needs help." Chandler had been drinking heavily and passed out behind the wheel of his city-issued car. Chandler's companion intended to use the car telephone to call for help but mistakenly picked up the police microphone, and in doing so summoned almost every available police car in Memphis to assist the inebriated mayor.[4] Chandler also once picked a fight at the old Western Lounge near Madison and Cleveland and wound up on the losing end of the brawl.

Two city police officers, Johnny Williams and Bobby Sides, were assigned as bodyguards for Chandler. But they were also his drinking buddies and helped the mayor get into trouble more than keep him out of it. The word around the police department was that Williams and Sides kept a manila folder containing the names of women who frequently socialized with the mayor. Occasionally, however, Chandler enjoyed a night out by himself.

Chandler versus Higgs

There was one instance when, after leaving an event at the Holiday Inn Rivermont, he got out of his car and locked the doors before realizing he had left the keys in the ignition. Without hesitating, Chandler took out his gun and shot out the car window to get back in the vehicle. The shattered window was quietly repaired the next day.

During business hours at city hall, however, the mayor was all about the business of running the city. He knew all the ins and outs of city government and he had assembled a capable and loyal executive staff. Still, as the 1975 election approached, Chandler's old partying habits, along with the closeness of the 1971 election, created some doubt that he would remain the people's choice. Judge Kenneth Turner decided to make another run for mayor. With his strong showing among black voters, all he needed to do was to reach out to more whites—particularly among the city's growing moderate and liberal factions in Midtown, the Memphis State University area, and portions of East Memphis.

The strategy initially paid off. Turner early in the campaign raised almost twice as much money as Chandler. But former mayor Loeb's large bloc of conservative white voters remained loyal to Chandler, oblivious to the fact that the two men weren't on speaking terms. And as the filing deadline neared, Turner was blindsided when black criminal court judge W. Otis Higgs abruptly resigned from the bench and announced his candidacy for the mayor's office. There had been no black candidate in the 1971 mayor's race, and once Higgs determined that Harold Ford's political organization was not interested in fielding a candidate, he made his move. Sporting his signature afro hairdo and stylish two-piece suit, Higgs invited television cameras along when he filed his qualifying papers at the Shelby County Election Commission office downtown. In interviews, he said he was offering himself as part of the emerging black political leadership in Memphis.

Higgs had been appointed to the criminal court bench in 1970 and was the only African American in Tennessee serving in that role at the time. But he desperately wanted more and eagerly obliged when close friends urged him to run for mayor. The problem was that his late entry into the race fueled suspicion and rumors that he was only in it to split the black vote with Turner and give Chandler an easy ride to reelection. Higgs called the accusations blatant lies.

Despite having little money and no visible help from other well-known black city leaders, particularly Harold Ford, Higgs's campaign quickly gained momentum in the black community, where the quest to put one of their own in the mayor's office was just as strong as ever. Higgs got crucial backing from the political arm of the American Federation of State, County and Municipal Employees, the union representing city sanitation workers. Union members manned phone banks, put out yard signs, and raised money while Higgs took his message to receptive black churches throughout Memphis.

A series of preelection opinion polls by the *Commercial Appeal* showed Chandler with a comfortable lead while Higgs and Turner were running even. Turner disputed the polls and predicted he would hang on to his black support while also attracting moderate white voters. Both daily newspapers endorsed Chandler. The *Press-Scimitar*, while offering effusive praise of Higgs's accomplishments, cautioned that the criminal court judge "lacks the administrative experience the job of city mayor demands." Under Chandler, the paper said, "there has been comparative peace between the races—not perfect by any means, but still much better than the way things were.[5]

On election night, Chandler—as expected—finished first but did not get enough votes to avoid a runoff. Higgs finished second, more than twenty thousand votes behind Chandler but an impressive thirty-one thousand votes ahead of Turner. The results were far better than even Higgs expected and they buoyed his campaign. If he could just snag three-fourths of Turner's votes, he would win the runoff.

Both Higgs and Chandler campaigned vigorously for the second election, even making several joint appearances before mostly white audiences. Chandler's overtures to black voters were neither given nor wanted. During one forum before college students at Southwestern at Memphis, Higgs got the better of the mayor over the long-simmering issue of an expressway through nearby Overton Park. Chandler told the crowd that he supported the original plan of running the expressway through the park. Higgs, however, said he strongly opposed the idea, and the students erupted in cheers. It was one of Chandler's few campaign missteps, because many of the mayor's most loyal white supporters objected to the idea of expressway traffic going through the inner-city park and zoo.

The expressway comments, however, created no lasting campaign damage for Chandler. On October 15, Turner and most members of his campaign committee announced their support for Chandler,[6] and Higgs got virtually no help from Harold Ford's organization in getting out the black vote. Both daily newspapers repeated their endorsements of the incumbent, and on November 6, 1975, Chandler easily won reelection—by a 31,000-vote margin over Higgs. Total turnout was more than 58 percent, and Chandler got about 112,000 votes to 81,000 for Higgs. The mayoral voting was completely along racial lines, and again both the *Commercial Appeal* and *Press-Scimitar* encouraged Chandler to do more to bridge the racial gap in Memphis.

The mayor was an avid newspaper reader, but was never chummy with the top editors. He preferred hanging out with the papers' veteran beat reporters who covered city hall and politics and, to put it mildly, were some of the best alcohol connoisseurs in town. But the mayor realized he needed to do something tangible to improve race relations in Memphis. He just didn't know what or how. As he was building his political career, he never established any kind of rapport with black Memphians the way his father had done more than thirty years earlier.

As mayor and a loyalist to Boss Crump, Walter Chandler communicated frequently through the exchange of letters and personal visits with several black preachers. Some of the correspondences were patronizing, of course, but the black ministers and their congregations appreciated the gesture. Wyeth Chandler could never approach his father's level of camaraderie with black Memphians. But aides told him he could at least begin to build trust in the black community by making changes in the police department.

Memphis police had a horrible reputation in the black community, as did police in many major cities with sizable black populations across the country. There were only a handful of black police officers and none of them were in the top ranks. Plus, the black community was still seething over the beating death of seventeen-year-old Elton Hayes by Memphis police and Shelby County sheriff's deputies in 1971. Hayes's death spotlighted the fact that the city police had a history of brutality against black citizens. Chandler, a councilman at the time, could claim some credit for working to calm tensions in the city after Hayes's death.

One of his administrative assistants was E. Winslow "Buddy" Chapman, a United States Naval Academy graduate who had gotten the commission thanks to Chandler's father. Chapman worked in Wyeth Chandler's first mayoral campaign in 1971 and he earned the administrative assistant job as a reward. But from the beginning, Chapman wanted to be police director and he told Chandler so. The mayor, however, refused to even consider it. He had been content to keep things as they were with Jay Hubbard, a transplant from California, as police director, and two holdovers from the old city commission form of government—Bill Price, the police chief, and William O. Crumby, the deputy chief.

Once Hubbard came on board, Price retired, and Crumby ascended to police chief. But like Price, Crumby had no use for the director's role no matter who was in it. He had come up through the police ranks and detested the idea of a civilian director—even one with a military background—running the whole department and giving him orders. Crumby and Chandler were old classmates at Snowden School, which meant the new police chief—in his mind, at least—had free rein within the department.

Hubbard and Crumby could not coexist. Both were the "my way or the highway" kind of guys, and Hubbard, the outsider, abruptly resigned in 1975. The salacious story inside the department was that Hubbard was surreptitiously caught with a prostitute and Crumby had obtained revealing pictures of the encounter. Hubbard could not afford a scandal of that magnitude nor could he afford to call Crumby's bluff.

Once Hubbard left, Crumby convinced his old school buddy, Mayor Chandler, to appoint him acting police director with the understanding that he would retire in a year. When the year was up, Crumby wanted to stay a little longer serving in the dual role of director and chief. But the mayor and his top people knew that Crumby, the insider, was not the answer to the department's problems.

With Hubbard gone and the department still in turmoil, Chandler's chief administrative officer, Henry Evans, helped convince the mayor to appoint Chapman as police director. Like Hubbard, Chapman had a military background. But the key difference was Chapman was a Memphian. He grew up on a farm in Raleigh, and he basically got along with everybody, blacks and whites. He developed no-nonsense leadership skills and an outsider's perspective on police work while in the military. And he was bold enough to tell Chandler that both the mayor and department desperately needed him.[7]

In September 1976, Chandler summoned Chapman to his office and told him he had the job. "I'm making you director, but you've got to get along with Crumby," the mayor said.[8] That wouldn't be easy, but Chapman wanted the job so much he was willing to try. He demanded, however, that he get the office Crumby was now occupying. Chandler didn't understand the big deal about the office, but he agreed to the move. To Chapman, however, it was symbolic. As long as Crumby was in that office, everyone in the department would consider him the guy in charge.[9]

Chandler versus Higgs

It was not the only seat Chapman took from Crumby. He removed the chief as a member of the Memphis and Shelby County Law Enforcement Coordinating Committee and put himself in that position.[10] Crumby was furious. He had already publicly described Chapman as an amateur and called his appointment as director "a slap in the face to all Memphis police officers and the citizens as well."[11]

As the city council was considering whether to approve the appointment, Crumby threatened to leak embarrassing information about Chapman's finances and his personal life to the newspapers. To this day, Chapman still recalls the encounter: "He said, 'if you don't leave just like Hubbard did, it's all going to the paper.' I said, 'well chief, the best thing I can do is give you a ride to the paper." Crumby followed through and leaked a negative story about Chapman allegedly passing a bogus check. The chief also passed along that and other damaging information about Chandler to City Councilman Bob James.

When Chandler learned about it, he demanded that Crumby, his long-time friend, resign. But Crumby was a civil service employee and Chandler could not legally fire him. Chandler vowed to fire him anyway and appeal any reversals to the local and state courts. The *Commercial Appeal*'s editorial page sided with Chapman who "has the power and Crumby should realize it and take defeat in stride."[12] With public sentiment now running against him and with the prospect of prolonged legal wrangling, Crumby retired on February 2, 1977.

The battle with Crumby wasn't the only headache Chapman faced after taking over the police department. Almost immediately, Chapman learned about the "John Gaston turban." That was the term cops on the street used to describe incidents where they had beaten a suspect—virtually all of them black—severely enough with a nightstick to require a head bandage and a trip to John Gaston Hospital for treatment. Chapman summoned his commanders into his office and told them, "I don't want to hear of that term again."[13] Sporadic beatings continued, but eventually the brutality complaints started to subside.

Just days after taking over as director, Chapman was asked to appear before the Tennessee Advisory Committee of the U.S. Commission on Civil Rights. The committee, headed by local civil rights leader Samuel Billy Kyles, was looking into longstanding complaints of police brutality in Memphis. Mayor Chandler refused to cooperate with the inquiry and described those involved with the Commission on Civil Rights as "a bunch of weirdos."[14] Nevertheless, Chapman addressed the committee and promised to identify and correct past problems with police brutality. He acknowledged "a lack of confidence in police services (that was) not necessarily limited to the black community."[15] With that, Maxine Smith, executive director of the Memphis chapter of the NAACP, said she was encouraged by Chapman's appointment "because he intends to move the police department towards a direction of improving community relations.[16]

About a year later, however, Smith's sentiments were not as glowing. During one NAACP chapter meeting in January 1978, she said the only thing slowing down police brutality complaints was snow.[17] Chapman immediately took strong exception to the remark and urged reporters to go ask everyday African Americans whether police and community relations in Memphis had improved rather than talking to black leaders. "If police arresting punks, thugs and hoodlums who are hanging out on street corners to harass and rob the elderly constitutes police harassment, then you're going to see a lot more of it," he said.[18]

The straight-talking director also made headlines in 1981, when, during an anticrime rally sponsored by the Vollintine-Evergreen Community Association, he called for the castration of rapists and the "sizzling" of murderers.[19] Once the comments were reported, news organizations from around the country flooded Chapman's office with calls seeking interviews. But most Memphians supported the director's unorthodox approach to fighting crime. Two days after his initial comment, Chapman said it should be up to the public to decide if sex offenders should be castrated, but that doing so would eliminate the "recreational rapist."[20]

But that tempest was mild compared to the crisis Chapman, Chandler, and the entire city faced three years earlier when contract negotiations with both the police and fire fighters unions stalled in early 1978. City negotiators offered pay raises totaling almost 17 percent over two years across the board to all city unions. For top-level privates in the fire department, the wage offer took their annual salary from $13,306 to $15,550 the first year.[21] However, Local 1784 of the International Association of Firefighters also demanded pay parity with police officers and extra pay for working nights, among other things. Chandler flatly refused and put a final offer on the table. The firemen unanimously rejected the offer on Friday night, June 30, and voted to go on strike the next day at the start of the morning shift change.

Fire Director Robert Walker called Chandler at 6:00 a.m. and told him firemen were walking out of Station House No. 7 against the orders of supervisors.[22] The mayor immediately called Maj. Gen. Carl Wallace, commander of the Tennessee National Guard, and put him on notice that his troops might be needed to keep order in Memphis. Within hours, fire calls were pouring in to the city. By early Sunday morning, July 2, more than two hundred calls had been reported and most of the fires were the result of arson.

They included several businesses and an apartment complex on Cooper near Union. A vacant house at Vance near Lauderdale was set ablaze, and the fire spread next door and gutted the Vance Avenue branch of the public library. Five schools also were damaged. In Whitehaven, an arsonist torched a newly built eighty-five-thousand-dollar home on Airways Boulevard across the street from McKellar Park. The structure represented the dream home of Howard and Juanita Payne, a black Memphis couple who had planned to move in on August 1.[23]

With portions of the city burning down, Chandler declared a state of emergency and fired local fire union president Kuhron Huddleston along with the union's entire executive committee. The mayor's action, however, merely strengthen the firefighters' resolve. Some even thanked the mayor for actually helping to solidify the union.[24] On Monday afternoon, July 3, city attorneys raced into chancery court seeking a restraining order to end the walkout. But before the hearing started, attorneys for the city and union borrowed a courthouse conference room to try to work out a temporary agreement. About ninety minutes later, they entered Chancellor Robert Hoffmann's courtroom and told the judge the impromptu settlement talks had failed.

City Attorney Cliff Pierce told Hoffmann that the strikers "were preventing adequate fire protection and have brought to a standstill adequate medical attention." With Chandler and his two public safety directors—Chapman and Walker—seated in the courtroom, Pierce made the case that under state law, a municipal union and its members did not have the right to strike.

Allen Blair, the union's attorney, made a counterargument that city leaders had done all they could "to agitate and aggravate the crisis." The strike, he said, was a result of "years of broken promises" to the union. "We submit that we cannot agree to any injunction."

At that point, Hoffmann had heard enough: "No one has asked you to agree. The people, that's the primary concern of this court. All other rights are secondary to the rights of the citizens, as a whole, of Memphis, Tennessee. I gave you an hour and a half to work this out. We're not playing games. We're dealing with people's lives."

"I realize that," Blair responded.

"And it's time everybody realized it," Hoffman continued. "I want to know why you couldn't work it out. What was the impasse?" Without responding further, Blair asked for a moment, then quickly huddled with Pierce, Mayor Chandler, and the assistant city attorney, Art Shea. As a scowling, red-faced Hoffmann waited patiently on the bench, Blair shuttled the short distance in the courtroom between the city officials and Huddleston, the union president. Blair then announced to Chancellor Hoffmann that the union would end the strike and return to work with the condition that two off-duty informational pickets be allowed outside each fire station. Hoffmann approved the agreement, and the striking firefighters returned to duty the following morning, Independence Day. But the dispute was far from over.[25]

Less than two weeks later, negotiations with the police union reached a stalemate after union members rejected a tentative settlement by a nine-to-one margin. Chandler enjoyed a better relationship with rank-and-file police officers than with firefighters. In an extraordinary public relations move, the mayor agreed to a televised debate with police union president David Baker. Both men were acutely aware that the firefighters strike left a bad taste on the mouths of Memphians, and both felt they could sway public opinion their way.

The July 28 debate was moderated by Dr. Richard Ranta, dean of the College of Communication and Fine Arts at Memphis State University, and was broadcast live on WREG-TV and WKNO-TV. Baker argued that because of the tough work police officers are required to do, they should have higher pay. Chandler countered that the increases being offered were generous and that taxpayers could not afford any more.[26]

The impasse dragged on for another two weeks before the city gave the union one last take-it-or-leave-it offer. The union left it. And at 11:00 p.m. on August 10, 1978, Memphis police officers set up picket lines and officially went on strike. Chandler immediately called in the Tennessee National Guard and tried to calm the fears of city residents still jittery from the July firefighters strike. "Everything's covered," police director Chapman told reporters just after midnight. "Cars are on the street. There are no problems whatsoever, to my knowledge."[27]

Baker also offered assurances that the strike would be peaceful. "There will be no violence or problems like that. "We're going to conduct ourselves professionally. Obviously, I can't control 1,100 people, but we're going to put the word out that we don't want violence." Although the spate of arsons did not return, several striking cops were unruly on the picket line. Some were openly drinking beer and other alcohol, and still had their guns strapped to their side. Others shouted obscenities at passing motorists and threatened reporters on the scene.[28]

Again city attorneys marched into chancery court seeking a restraining order to force police officers back to work. The presiding judge this time, however, was Chancellor George T. Lewis, who had to be coaxed into issuing the order. Lewis was a lame-duck jurist. He had lost his judicial seat to Memphis City Court judge D. J. "Tene" Alissandratos in an election a week earlier and appeared to be just going through the motions in his waning days on the bench.

Lewis described the police strike as a "situation of extraordinary emergency" with the potential for "chaos and anarchy" in Memphis. But he waited a full day to hold a hearing and issued a restraining order that did not expressly tell the officers to go back to their jobs. At the hearing the following day, Lewis equivocated again. Ruling from the bench, he said, "This strike is unlawful . . . and this court orders all of the members of the city police association back to work or in the alternative to submit their resignations within a period of a week."

Union attorney Russell X. Thompson called the one-week grace period reasonable, but City Attorney Cliff Pierce was beside himself: "I can't believe even Mr. Thompson would be saying that. Time is of the essence." Lewis then ordered the police officers back to work "with all deliberate speed or as expeditiously as possible." That still did not satisfy Pierce. "Your honor," he said, "I don't want to argue with the court, but unless this court faces a specific hour (to end the strike), it's not going to take place." Only then did Lewis order striking policemen back to work by midnight.[29]

Later that evening, police officers gathered for a massive rally downtown on the Mid-America Mall near city hall. Baker, the union president, told the officer they had to return to work and even read the court order to them. But they refused to budge and showered Baker with boos. Union vice president Chris Cothran then literally pushed Baker aside and told the officers he was now in charge. They would remain on strike, he said, court order or no court order. "We want Chris! We want Chris!" the strikers shouted. Baker left the makeshift stage in disgust.

Two days later, the firefighters joined the police on the picket line. City sanitation workers refused to report to their jobs as well. And for the second time in a month, Memphis faced an all-out public safety crisis. To make matters worse, just past midnight on August 16, 1978, the one-year anniversary of the death of Elvis Presley, the entire city was plunged into darkness. A drunken security guard somehow flipped a switch at a LG&W substation in Cordova, and the city went black for three hours. Except for sporadic looting, Memphis remained relatively calm that night and throughout the second strike. But with national media attention again focused on Memphis, city leaders had to act fast.

Henry Evans, the city's chief administrative officer who by now was Chandler's most trusted adviser, devised a plan to end the strike and still allow the strikers to save face. He called Baker and asked him to meet him at Evans's Germantown home. They met on the back porch, and Evans offered a deal in which the city's last offer would remain but the city would agree to the creation of fact-finding committees to review future contract proposals. Baker rejected the offer and left.[30]

Meanwhile, a group of business and community leaders were recruited to help resolve the crisis. The group was led by Jim McGehee, president of the Memphis Area Chamber of Commerce, and included Dr. Adrian Rogers, pastor of Bellevue Baptist Church. As round-the-clock negotiations resumed, the union heads finally accepted that the city would not budge from its last offer. Evans's proposal of fact-finding committees was their only way to save face. Baker, however, went on television and said the city had agreed to arbitration. When Chandler and Evans heard that, they were livid. Fact finding was not arbitration, and eventually both unions accepted the deal as outlined by Evans. The second strike, which lasted eight days, was mercifully over.[31]

In spite of the turmoil that the strikes caused, Chandler remained a popular figure among white Memphians. He soon announced that he would seek a third term as mayor in 1979. Higgs, who had resumed practicing law after his defeat in 1975, again stepped up to oppose Chandler with a campaign theme of "Yes We Can." The voter registration rolls were slightly more encouraging for Higgs as the black population in Memphis continued to ascend. Plus, Higgs was determined to run a smarter and more broad-based campaign.

He was banking on negative fallout from the strikes eroding some of Chandler's white support. And Higgs was hopeful that City Councilman Pat Halloran's entrance into the race would pull white votes from the incumbent. Higgs, however, was less thrilled when eccentric Memphian Robert "Prince Mongo" Hodges announced his candidacy and began to attract a following among young, antiestablishment voters. These were voters whom Higgs sorely needed in his camp to create a path to victory.

The *Press-Scimitar* again endorsed Chandler, but stunningly, the *Commercial Appeal* did not. In mid-November 1975, Michael Grehl took over as editor of the morning paper, and he immediately brought fresher and more progressive thinking, both to the newsroom and the editorial board. He almost singlehandedly changed the culture of the paper and was determined to rid "Old Reliable" of its racist image. He significantly increased the hiring of black reporters (I was one of them), and he encouraged his senior editors to assign black writers to high-profile stories and beats, such as politics, police, and the courts—all plum assignments that had always gone to white reporters.

With Grehl in charge, the paper's editorial board abandoned Chandler and encouraged voters to support Higgs for mayor in 1979. "The incumbent wants to continue to manage the city his way," the paper's endorsement read. "His strongest challenger wants to lead Memphis with the public's help. The people of this city need that kind of partnership. It's the best hope for a unified Memphis. It's the quickest road to progress. And Otis Higgs has the best chance to put it together."[32] The endorsement stunned and angered conservative white readers and many of them canceled their subscription in protest.

With just weeks before election day, however, Higgs's campaign was stagnant. He still had no outward support from the established black leadership in Memphis, and the AFSCME was not nearly as visible in the campaign as it had been four years earlier. Higgs finally asked Russell Sugarmon Jr. to help him get out the vote. He also practically begged local NAACP leaders Maxine and Vasco Smith and Jesse Turner for support. They finally agreed to help after first telling Higgs they were miffed that he had not asked them sooner. But there was still no involvement by the Ford family. Both Harold and John Ford gave lip service to the Higgs campaign, but the organization concentrated its efforts on getting a fourth brother, James, elected to the city council seat that John was relinquishing to devote all his political energy and muscle to the state Senate.

On election day in October, Chandler again finished first with 74,400 votes, but that was only 2,200 more than Higgs. For the second straight election, the two men were forced into a racially polarizing showdown in a November runoff. Perhaps aided by the *Commercial Appeal*'s endorsement, Higgs did surprisingly well in Midtown and even parts of East Memphis. An analysis by the *Press-Scimitar* showed that Higgs carried every voting precinct where the racial breakdown was about even, meaning Higgs performed far better than Chandler in integrated neighborhoods.[33]

Higgs was ecstatic over the results while Chandler's campaign managers showed signs of worry. They were fearful that the thirty-four hundred people who voted for Hodges would now vote for Higgs—if they bothered to show up at all. And they were unsure where the nine thousand people who voted for City Councilman Pat Halloran would go in the runoff. The *Commercial Appeal* repeated its endorsement of Higgs with an even stronger tone, noting that Higgs "represents the kind of change Memphis needs. For one thing, Memphis has always been or has tried to be a white city. And where has that gotten us? Higgs's color would be an historic change for Memphis, but so would his approach to the mayor's job. There is little doubt that Higgs would attract much favorable national attention to Memphis."[34]

The Chandler camp countered by mounting a more aggressive runoff campaign aimed mostly at middle-age and elderly white female voters. The new message would plant doubts about Higgs's leadership abilities and his character without overtly making any racial insinuations. The Chandler campaign produced an effective television ad featuring an elderly white woman pleading with voters to keep Chandler in office while raising concerns about Higgs's qualifications and his ability to effectively fight crime. "We MUST reelect Mayor Chandler," the woman said. "There is no comparison."[35]

Racial politics seeped into the Chandler campaign in other ways. The mayor attended a White Citizens' Council meeting where he pledged allegiance to the Confederate flag. His campaign also asked the Shelby County Election Commission for a list of "white only" registered voters who had not voted in the October election. Higgs responded by accusing Chandler of running a racist campaign. Chandler disputed the charge and privately confided to one key supporter that he felt he had no choice at the White Citizens' Council meeting but to stand up and mouth the words, since everyone else in the room was reciting the pledge. The advisor responded, "That would be a great answer if you didn't know every word of it."[36]

Then, just two days before the November 15 runoff, Higgs reported that someone burned a cross in his front yard in the middle of the morning. The report brought immediate condemnation from Chandler and most members of the city council. If that incident wasn't bizarre enough, what happened the following day, election eve, was positively surreal. And it doomed Higgs's chances. Police disclosed that a Memphis woman had reported that a smaller makeshift cross had been tossed into her home that morning. What's more, rumors began circulating throughout Memphis that the woman's twenty-one-year-old son was also Higgs's "illegitimate son."

Higgs immediately called a press conference and released an awkwardly worded statement in which he neither confirmed nor denied that he had fathered a child out of wedlock. However, he did acknowledge the existence of paternity records in juvenile court. Plus, he said people often make mistakes early in life that they later regret. The woman told reporters that Higgs was indeed the father of her child and that she had told her son about his father year's earlier. Chandler told reporters that the young man had visited city hall asking to see the mayor's office and saying his father would soon have that office. Chandler told the press that he didn't say anything about that incident because he did not want to make it a campaign issue.[37]

All of this was reported prominently in both the *Commercial Appeal* and *Memphis Press-Scimitar* on the very day that voters were heading to the polls for the runoff. And yet the election results were closer than expected. Chandler won with 120,000 votes to 107,000 for Higgs. The challenger still managed to get 11 percent of the white vote while Chandler once again got less than 2 percent of the black vote. It was never clearly determined if the Chandler campaign was behind the cross-burning incidents, but the events totally derailed Higgs's promising campaign. Calling a press conference the day before the election only to give vague answers about the paternity issue was a disastrous move. An election analysis written by *Commercial Appeal* politics reporter Terry Keeter said Higgs also floundered in other ways.

Keeter noted that Higgs got no help from the Fords but also wrote that Higgs likely scared away white support by calling an earlier press conference with sixteen other elected officials—all of them black—who endorsed his campaign. The event gave Chandler the opening to accuse Higgs of racial polarization. The charge wouldn't have mattered if one of those sixteen people at the press conference had been Harold Ford. An editorial cartoon in the *Commercial Appeal* two days after the election highlighted the fact that the Ford machine did not crank up for Higgs. The cartoon showed a dejected Higgs sitting alone at his campaign headquarters, banners falling to the floor around him, as John and Harold Ford are standing at the door saying, "Hi there, Otis. How'd it go?"[38]

Keeter, in his analysis, also wrote, "In the last days, Higgs continued to maintain a hectic pace of speeches and appearances. Yet he spoke to neither the issues nor the voters. Throughout his campaign Higgs displayed a consistent lack of decisiveness. Many of Higgs's positions on important matters facing the city were 'maybe' or 'I'll have to look into that.'"[39]

Chandler was still no closer to gaining approval from black voters. Yet a group of black ministers urged the mayor to reappoint Chapman as police director, writing in a letter to Chandler that Chapman had "done much to improve the department as well as bring credibility and respect to the department in the community of Memphis." Although he was never accepted by black voters, Chandler gets credit for guiding the city during some of its most troubling times. He was a good steward of the city coffers, and he laid the groundwork for revitalizing downtown. "Time will prove that Wyeth was a good mayor for that time," said Henry Evans.[40]

And despite back-to-back losses, Higgs continued to harbor dreams of someday becoming mayor. He ran a third time in 1983 and almost launched a fourth try before returning to the criminal court bench. He also served briefly as interim sheriff of Shelby County in 1990. Had it not been for black political division and his own campaign gaffes, Higgs very likely would have been the one to break the color barrier in the city mayor's office. But it was not to be—at least not yet.

CHAPTER 12

FLEXING THE FORD MUSCLE

WHEN I ARRIVED in snow-covered Memphis in January 1977 to begin work as a reporter for the *Commercial Appeal*, Harold Ford was entrenched as the most recognizable and revered politician in town. The Ford organization, according to columnist Art Gilliam, had established itself "as the political focal point of the black community."[1] Tennessee's first black congressman was fresh off a reelection victory over City Councilman Andy Alissandratos in which Ford got one hundred thousand votes to sixty-three thousand for the challenger. At the time of the November 1976 election, black voters for the first time held a slight majority in the Eighth Congressional District, which covered most but not all of Memphis. Ford captured 99 percent of the black vote and nearly 20 percent of the white vote in trouncing Alissandratos. The Ford political machine was now in high gear and running smoothly.

But the 1976 election was not all roses for Ford. Allegations of voter intimidation were leveled against the Ford organization. The charges were fueled mostly by what was later described in court as a group of "young ambitious Republicans."[2] The complaints persisted and U.S. Attorney Thomas Turley, a Republican appointee, initiated a grand jury investigation focusing on Lee Edward Branch, a Ford campaign worker. But before the investigation really got started, Democrat Jimmy Carter was sworn in as president and Turley was forced to step down.

In April 1977, Mike Cody, a former campaign manager for Ford, replaced Turley as the chief federal prosecutor for West Tennessee—and inherited the Branch investigation. The case was a ticklish one for Cody. He had been heavily involved in several Democratic campaigns, particularly Carter's and Ford's, during the 1976 election cycle. And local Republicans were watching closely to see if Cody would try to quash the investigation.

Instead, Cody took a completely hands-off approach. He allowed his top assistant, Hickman Ewing Jr., and an outside prosecutor from the Justice Department's Publicity Integrity Section in Washington, D.C., to continue presenting the case to the grand jury. But the investigation lingered for months and the grand jury became inactive.

Ford, meanwhile, was busy cementing his reputation as having the best constituent services of any representative in Washington. As a freshman congressman in 1975, he was named to the prestigious House Ways and Means Committee, and the following year he was appointed to the House Select Committee on Assassinations that investigated the murders of President John F. Kennedy and Dr. Martin Luther King Jr. The dormant grand jury investigation back in Memphis was the farthest thing from Ford's mind as he prepared for reelection in 1978.

John Ford also was enjoying major political strength, having vanquished two well-known black elected officials to win seats in the state senate and on the city council. In the spring of 1978, the Shelby County mayoral election became a free-for-all when incumbent Mayor Roy Nixon announced that he would not seek another term. A mad scramble ensued among several big-name white candidates, all of whom felt they could build enough support to win. What they didn't figure on was competition from the Ford machine. But they got it when John Ford announced on Saturday, April 29—three days before the filing deadline—that he was running for the office. The announcement derailed mayoral plans by Ford's nemesis, J. O. Patterson Jr., and twenty-six-year-old black state representative Dedrick "Teddy" Withers, who had run for the office in 1975 as a twenty-three-year-old.

Both Patterson and Withers stepped aside, and after the filing deadline on May 2, Ford was the only black mayoral candidate against eleven whites, which included former sheriff Bill Morris, County Commissioner John Ford Canale, and city official Wallace Madewell.[3] John Ford's supporters were beside themselves with joy. With no runoff to worry about and with the growing strength of the Ford name, they considered their man a shoo-in to become the first black mayor anywhere in Shelby County. Among the white political establishment, however, there was total angst—similar to 1959,

Flexing the Ford Muscle

when Russell Sugarmon Jr. was the only black candidate in a nonrunoff city commission race against five whites. And just like in 1959, Memphis's mayor intervened to derail the black man's chances.

Mayor Wyeth Chandler arranged a private whites-only meeting at the Coach and Four Motor Lodge on Lamar Avenue ostensibly to voice his support for Madewell. But the meeting quickly shifted to a discussion of uneasiness in the white community over the prospect that John Ford could indeed win the election. Those at the meeting included the current county mayor, Roy Nixon, and state Democratic Party chairman William Farris, who ironically was the winning candidate in the 1959 city commission race against Sugarmon.

When word of the meeting was leaked to the media, Chandler made no apologies. He was convinced that John Ford was unacceptable as county mayor and subtly suggested that some white candidates withdraw—just a Henry Loeb had done in 1959. But Chandler insisted there was no racist intent in calling the meeting. "It amazes me that anyone would make an accusation it was a racist meeting when at least 90 percent of the black population will be voting for a black without regard to the background or experience of any other candidate."[4]

Two days later, several black leaders held a meeting of their own at the home of Vasco and Maxine Smith. But participants later gave completely different accounts of what was said—or who even convened the meeting. Rev. H. Ralph Jackson, a black Methodist minister who attended, said Vasco Smith, Walter Bailey, and Cleo Kirk concluded at the meeting that John Ford could not win the election and that he should get out of the race. The Ford organization supported Jackson's account. Vasco Smith, however, was livid. He insisted that there was nothing but solid support at the meeting for Ford, and they all urged him to stay in the race.

Smith said it was Harold Ford who called him asking to meet at the Smiths's home in South Memphis. When Ford showed up, Jackson was with him. Minutes later, Bailey and Kirk arrived. Smith characterized the gathering as a discussion of the meeting Chandler held at the Coach and Four, and the role William Farris—a Ford ally—had in it.

"There was never any discussion of John Ford getting out of the race," Smith told the *Tri-State Defender* newspaper. "Anyone that said a discussion of that type was in my house is lying."[5] Nevertheless, three minutes before the withdrawal deadline on Tuesday, May 9, Ford showed up at the Shelby County Election Commission office and withdrew from the county mayor's race—leaving no other black candidate in the contest. Black lawyer James Swearengen, who was standing nearby, pounded his fist in disgust on the commission's counter. "Why would he screw up Patterson like this?"[6]

John Ford said he withdrew because he did not want to polarize the community with a racially tinged election. He blamed Chandler for injecting racism into the campaign with his secret meeting, and promised to run against the Memphis mayor in the 1979 election. Other black political leaders were having none of it—particularly Patterson, who called Ford's withdrawal treachery and deceit, and Withers, who said John's decision "has set Memphis back another twenty years."[7]

Patterson was the first to imply that John had cut a deal with white politicians to get out of the race: "John can rant and rave about racial polarization and what white people did to him all that he wants to . . . and I will continue to be unconvinced. The serious question that remains in my mind and which, in my opinion has not been adequately answered by John Ford is, what if anything did the boys in the backroom really do to get him out of the county mayor's race?"

Other black leaders also were convinced that Ford had sold out the black community for selfish gain. "I've got no proof that there was a deal, but he's got a lot of explaining to do," said County Commissioner Minerva Johnican. To which Ford replied, "I'm going to be damned if I'll let them continue to question my integrity."[8] The *Tri-State Defender*'s coverage of the controversy tended to favor the Ford organization's account. The paper quoted Lee Edward Branch, who fashioned himself a Ford campaign operative, as saying that local union leaders wanted John Ford out of the mayor's race.[9] But no one else supported that statement.

The furor over John Ford's withdrawal was just beginning to settle when on May 31 the dormant federal grand jury, out of the blue, reconvened for just that day. The federal building was abuzz as other reporters—including Peggy Burch and Kay Pittman Black with the *Press-Scimitar* and Mike Lawhead with WREG-TV—kept vigil with me just down the hall from the grand jury room. Jurors were in the room for about two hours before they emerged with prosecutor Hickman Ewing Jr. and Justice Department lawyer Craig Donsanto and marched into federal judge Bailey Brown's courtroom. There, they announced a two-count misdemeanor indictment against Lee Edward Branch, a volunteer who was working the polls for Harold Ford on election day in November 1976. The indictment was returned one day before the filing deadline for Ford's Eighth District congressional seat. It accused Branch of threatening and intimidating several Republican poll watchers and one election commission official on election day in 1976.[10]

The congressman's immediate public response was that the charges were no big deal. "We're talking about a misdemeanor. The indictment doesn't bother me," he said.[11] But privately, Ford and fellow Democrats were outraged. Many of them directed their anger at Cody, who despite not being involved in the prosecution, was left to defend the timing of the indictment. Cody said the case had been delayed because it involved violations of election laws and the indictment needed approval from the highest levels of the Justice Department.

"I know from a personal standpoint I urged the department that a prompt decision be made on the merits of the case and without any consideration for the political figures or political parties involved. I believe that was done," Cody told the press.[12] Ford didn't buy Cody's explanation. And yet the timing actually allowed Ford to effectively make his own case that the indictment smacked of partisan politics. It also meant that John Ford's exit from the county mayor's race was no longer the topic du jour in Memphis. There was concern that the charges against Branch would cost Harold Ford valuable support among white Democrats if they believed a bunch of thugs were part of his organization. Mostly though, the indictment without a doubt put a strain on Ford's relationship with Cody, the congressman's former campaign manager.

As for Branch, the indictment transformed him from obscurity to headline news. And he took full advantage of his moment in the media spotlight. "The only thing I'm guilty of is being short, fat and black," he told U.S. Magistrate Aaron Brown at his arraignment, to which Brown jokingly responded, "I don't believe being short, fat and black is a federal crime yet."[13] The exchange was one of several circuslike moments during the bizarre case. But for key prosecution witnesses, including young Republican lawyers Henry Shelton and James W. Pate II, this was no laughing matter. They were determined to press the charge that the Ford organization ruled through intimidation. Branch and his lawyer, Tim Schaeffer, along with Ford were equally determined to take the case to trial in hopes of painting local Republicans as liars and sore losers.

Ford testified as a character witness for Branch, and the trial ended with a hung jury with a vote of eleven to one for acquittal. Prosecutors retried the case several months later, and on October 3, 1979, a second jury made up of eleven blacks and one white found Branch not guilty of all charges. Ford was in the courtroom when the verdict was returned and shook hands with several jurors as they left the federal building. "This was nothing but political harassment by the Justice Department and the Republican Party," Ford told reporters.[14] Decades later, Cody described Branch as "unstable and scary."[15] Ford also distanced himself from Branch, who had a series of legal troubles following his acquittal. He spent six weeks in a mental institution and later blamed Ford for the federal indictment and for refusing to help him recover from financial ruin.

Despite the acquittal, Branch was dropped as a campaign worker, but the Ford organization's legal battles were far from over. Just months after the acquittal, Cody's office opened another grand jury investigation, this time into possible insurance fraud charges against another brother of the congressman, state representative Emmitt Ford. Cody again recused himself from direct involvement in the investigation. He and Emmitt had been co-chairmen of Harold's first congressional campaign in 1974, and Cody considered Emmitt the nicest of all the Fords.[16] Cody, however, did examine some of the evidence compiled against Emmitt and concluded that the government had a solid case. He assigned the investigation to assistant U.S. attorney Dan Clancy, a bulldog of a prosecutor who rarely lost a case in court.

Still, Cody knew he was again in an awkward predicament. Harold Ford's political muscle had helped secure his appointment as U.S. attorney. The Ford organization also delivered 90 percent of the black vote for Cody in his victory over incumbent Jack McNeil for a city council seat in 1975. But Cody, the impartial federal prosecutor, put politics and media hype aside and ran the U.S. Attorney's Office strictly by the book. His two favorite words to reporters were "no comment." And that was particularly true during any political corruption cases his office was conducting, and there were many. The grand jury's insurance fraud investigation, however, continued with vigor, and on March 27, 1980, Emmitt Ford and his wife, Earline Ford, were indicted on charges of staging a phony auto accident in 1977 and then collecting nearly $54,000 from claims to twenty-nine insurance companies.[17]

The indictment outlined a series of incredibly brazen acts by an elected official. For example, Emmitt coaxed the head of the police department's traffic division to change the original accident report—which listed no injuries—to reflect that his wife, Earline, had been seriously hurt. The scheme came to the attention of federal agents after investigators with the J. C. Penney Insurance Company concluded that the auto accident never happened. J. C. Penney refused to pay Ford's $3,450 claim. But he sued the company in Shelby County General Sessions Court and won a judgment for $1,350.[18]

The Ford couple professed their innocence and took the case to trial, but both were convicted in November 1980 of mail fraud and insurance fraud. Emmitt was sentenced to twenty months in prison and was automatically removed from his seat in the Tennessee legislature. Ford's wife got a one-year suspended sentence and twenty months on probation.[19] The case was embarrassing to the Ford political organization, but it did nothing to hurt the other Ford brothers at the polls. Harold was easily reelected in 1980, despite a challenge in the Democratic primary from Minerva Johnican, the first black woman elected to the Shelby County Commission.

Two years later, during the summer campaign of 1982, Johnican got another bitter taste of Ford's political strength. The congressman aggressively supported Julian Bolton, a young political unknown, who challenged Johnican for her county commission seat. Ford and Bolton had met years earlier when, fresh out of Southwestern at Memphis, Bolton was making a name for himself in community theater. He and other young black political enthusiasts joined the Ford organization in 1976 because it represented a new and innovative way of managing election campaigns.

Bolton also brought political spunk to the Ford team that the congressman liked. After the *Commercial Appeal* published a series of articles profiling who the paper believed was the city's black leaders, Bolton led a group that called a press conference to criticize the newspaper articles. In Ford's 1980 race against Johnican, Bolton ran the get-out-the-vote effort in the Klondyke neighborhood and delivered the highest vote total ever for the congressman from that community. Ford was so impressed that he asked Bolton, "What office do you want to run for?" Bolton picked Johnican's commission seat, and it was done.[20]

At first, Johnican dismissed Bolton as an insignificant challenger with no political name recognition. But she soon discovered she was no match for Bolton's hard work and Ford's masterful campaign strategy. Bolton started by spending forty dollars to create about ten thousand wallet-sized campaign cards that identified him and his credentials to prospective voters. He laminated the plain-page cards and passed them out everywhere in the district. He also methodically went door to door with campaign signs for Ford and himself. Before long, he had saturated each neighborhood with neatly aligned yard signs that told voters Ford and Bolton were a team.

Early one Sunday morning, Bolton and a group of campaign workers planted several Bolton-Ford signs illegally along the roadway near Johnican's home. When she left for church, all she could see were campaign signs for her opponent. After she left the neighborhood, Bolton plucked up the signs, satisfied that he had rattled his opponent once again.[21]

Desperate to ignite her struggling campaign, Johnican sought help from other black community leaders and black pastors, who criticized the congressman for playing retaliation politics. Just days before the election, a group led by A. W. Willis and Russell Sugarmon hand-delivered a letter to Ford asking him to reverse course and support Johnican. It was a political stunt designed to generate sympathetic support for Johnican, but Ford was unmoved. He penned a letter of his own harshly criticizing Willis and Sugarmon as being out of touch with the black community.

The congressman then held a press conference in which he cited numerous examples of what he called Johnican's ineffectiveness, from her no votes for the appointment of blacks to county positions to her support for dismantling agencies designed to help the black community. "I am supporting Julian Bolton for one reason and one reason only," he said. "He is a far better candidate than the incumbent. I support him with enthusiasm and with conviction." At the press conference, Ford made a convincing argument that he was not supporting just anyone merely to get rid of a political opponent. Bolton, he said, represented the next generation of Memphis leaders and was eminently qualified for the position.[22]

The *Tri-State Defender*, which carried a weekly column by Ford, helped him make the case that Johnican should be replaced. Ford never directly addressed his opposition to Johnican in his column. But the paper endorsed Bolton early and often. After the polls closed on election day, August 5, 1982, the Johnican-Bolton race was the closest contest in the ballot. Johnican kept a razor thin lead throughout the evening, but the race remained too close to call. Finally, Ford and Bolton drove to the studios of WREG-TV, where Ford declared victory for Bolton live on the air. Ford told viewers that according to his count, Bolton had upset the incumbent by a slim margin. It was a total bluff. Neither of them knew who had won. But the gamble paid off. Shortly after 3:30 the following morning, Bolton, the thirty-two-year-old unknown, was declared the winner by 398 votes out of 18,094 total votes cast. Once the results became official, Ford told Bolton, "Damn Julian, I thought you were going to make a good showing, but you kicked her ass."[23]

Thus, within a four-year span, the Ford organization had successfully weathered two highly publicized federal indictments, John Ford's controversial about-face for county mayor, spirited challenges at the polls from rival black politicians, and assorted other charges of voter intimidation. Through it all, the family's political standing was as strong as ever. Political candidates, black and white, coveted a spot on the influential Ford ballot and paid handsomely for it. With Harold's sky-high approval from voters fueled by his congressional office's superior handling of constituent services, key supporters began to urge him to finally make the black community's long-awaited dream come true by running for city mayor.

The congressman didn't initiate the "Draft Harold for Mayor" talk, but he didn't discourage it either. Speaking to a gathering of the Big Brothers and Big Sisters organizations on August 31, 1981, Ford made his most definitive statement to date about seeking the mayor's office. He said if the Democrats lose control of the House of Representatives in the 1982 midterm election, "I will immediately announce my candidacy for mayor of the city of Memphis."[24]

With congressional Democrats still in charge, Ford stood to move up in rank on the House Ways and Means Committee, which he called the most powerful committee in the world. He was not about to give up that much national prestige for a risky attempt at becoming mayor of Memphis. In May 1982, Ford donned a cap and gown to receive a master's degree in business administration from Howard University in Washington, D.C. And in November, three months after securing an improbable victory for Bolton, his protégé, Ford won reelection to a fifth term without breaking a sweat. In the process, he helped Democrats maintain their majority in the U.S. House.

But Ford's November victory was overshadowed by yet another defining moment in Memphis politics. On September 28, 1982, Wyeth Chandler resigned as mayor to accept an appointment from Governor Lamar Alexander as a circuit court judge. Chandler had mellowed a bit from his years as a rowdy womanizer and two-fisted drinker and made no secret of his desire to be a judge. He toyed earlier with running for a probate court vacancy before opting to remain in the mayor's office. Chandler practically begged

Alexander, telling the governor in one phone call from city hall, "I've got to get out of here."[25] Alexander said OK. And after almost eleven years as mayor and four years as a councilman, Chandler was finally through with local politics.

The council chamber was filled to capacity when Chandler addressed Memphians for the last time as mayor. "I hope that history will be kind to me," he told the council and assembled audience, including several people who wiped away tears. Then, describing himself in third person, Chandler said, "But if it but records that he did his best, that he was honest in his dealings, that he kept his promises, that he helped to restore pride in the city among its citizens and that no one loved his city more, that will be enough."[26]

The timing of Chandler's departure was a godsend for city council chairman J. O. Patterson Jr. Under the city charter, when the mayor leaves office, the council chairman automatically becomes acting mayor for up to twenty days. After that, the council would appoint an interim mayor to, in this case, complete the remaining fifteen months of Chandler's term. Thus, on October 1, 1982, Patterson became the first black mayor in Memphis history. This son of a prominent Church of God in Christ bishop who had followed his father into the ministry now had the authority to conduct the city's business just as all of his predecessors had done, including Boss Crump and the cantankerous Henry Loeb. But there were no festive celebrations in the black community. Patterson indeed made history, but he was merely a short-term placeholder. His official swearing-in by criminal court judge H. T. Lockard was even noteworthy in that the wording in the oath had to be changed from "having been duly elected mayor" to simply "having become mayor."[27] And the rancorous city council would almost certainly appoint a white person as interim mayor once Patterson's twenty days were over.

But just as the council squabbling began, Memphis attorney Dan Norwood—along with co-attorneys Hayden Lait and David Cocke—filed a petition in chancery court demanding a mayoral election that would coincide with the November 2 general election. Patterson was thrilled. He figured his chances of keeping the job were better at the ballot box than in the council chamber. He asked the council to seek immediate approval from the Shelby County Election Commission to hold a special mayoral election. Patterson said council members were too consumed with their own "selfish political aspirations and are ill-equipped to wisely choose an interim mayor."[28]

Council members summarily rejected the request. Councilman James Ford, brother of the congressman, said Patterson was being "plain old silly," adding than an election at this late date "was utterly impossible." Fellow black councilman Michael Hooks said he was adamantly opposed to Patterson's idea, and white councilman Thomas Todd said Patterson was merely showboating for media attention. "This man apparently loves publicity."[29] Patterson also did not help his cause when he announced that he would seek to keep his voting privileges on the council while serving as acting mayor.

As the council squabbling continued, Judge George Lewis, who was back on the chancery court bench after defeating the incumbent judge, Wil Doran, in the August county election, refused to consider Norwood's petition for a mayoral election. Lewis agreed with the council that an election was not only impractical but also illegal. But Norwood and his cohorts refused to give up. They filed an expedited appeal directly to the Tennessee Supreme Court. On October 7, the high court issued a three-to-two decision ordering Chancellor Lewis to call for a special election if he determined that there was enough time to get it onto the ballot. O. C. Pleasant, chairman of the Shelby County Election Commission, was emphatic that there was enough time. Two years earlier, the commission added a Shelby County General Sessions Court race to the general election ballot with just seventeen days to spare.

Lewis quickly scheduled another hearing for the following day. Minutes before it began, however, lawyers for Congressman Harold Ford filed an emergency petition asking the judge to delay the election until December. Ford was not in the courtroom, but he contended later that "three weeks and three days are simply not enough time for candidates to mount an issue-oriented campaign." At the hearing, Chancellor Lewis patiently listened to testimony from Ford's designated witness, Karl Schledwitz, who said a hasty election would be a disservice to voters. Lewis, however, said he had no choice. He ordered the election placed on the November 2 ballot.[30]

Patterson was the first to announce his candidacy, and he used the moment to rip Ford: "I'm just sorry that Congressman Ford sought to block the will of the people. The congressman recognized the fact I stand an excellent chance of winning this election and this was a willful attempt to block me. This is just another step to keep a black man from getting that office other than a Ford."[31]

The acting mayor's harsh words were not far-fetched. Had the congressman been successful in getting the election pushed back to December, he or another Ford—most likely John—almost certainly would have been a candidate. But both of them were busy with their own November reelection campaigns for Congress and the state senate, respectively. Plus, Harold knew the numbers. His congressional district did not cover the entire city, and he was not about to risk losing his safe seat in Washington to chase the mayor's office in a pop-up election. Still, John promised that "there will be a Ford on the ballot. That is a definite. But we have to answer some legal questions before we decide which one of us it will be."[32]

Once those questions were answered, the Fords opted to sit the election out. Patterson then immediately went to work trying to convince the city's black leadership that he could win, possibly without a runoff if black voters turned out for him in heavy numbers and if he could get 10 to 15 percent of the white vote. It was a calculation that Ford knew was unrealistic. But for the sake of appearances within the black community, the congressman agreed to publicly endorse Patterson. Other black leaders in the city, including A. W. Willis, Otis Higgs, A. Maceo Walker, and Jesse Turner announced support for Patterson. And former county commissioner Minerva Johnican, still smarting from her August defeat to Julian Bolton, vowed to get into the mayor's race if a Ford ran. She ended up also supporting Patterson.[33]

On October 26, one week before election day, Detroit mayor Coleman Young flew to Memphis to highlight a rally supporting Patterson at Olivet Baptist Church. More than seven hundred people attended. Harold Ford was among them. When it was his turn to speak, Ford issued a tepid endorsement along with an extraordinary admonishment. "Mayor Patterson, we support you," Ford said. "We wish you well. But if you don't make it we want you to step aside in 1983 because one of the Fords will run."[34]

Meanwhile, most of the top business leaders in town saw the abbreviated election as a chance to elect a progressive mayor who could do a far better job on race relations than Chandler. The group tapped Mike Cody, a liberal former city councilman who had just completed a successful four-year stint as the U.S. attorney. Cody could tout an impressive law and order record as the chief federal prosecutor in West Tennessee. During his tenure, the U.S. attorney's office aggressively pursued local and state corruption and brought numerous indictments, mostly against current and former Shelby County officials—elected and appointed—for extortion and bribery. The investigations had also dipped into city hall with an FBI inquiry into public works construction contracts. That trail of the investigation did not lead to any indictments against city officials, but it was a source of embarrassment for the Chandler administration.

Cody was also portrayed as a mayoral candidate who could appeal to both white and black voters. He had been a co-manager of Harold Ford's first congressional campaign and had received more than 90 percent of the black vote during his own run for the city council in 1975—thanks to the Ford organization. Once the special mayoral election was officially on, Cody met with several heavy hitters in the business community, including Fred Smith, Pitt Hyde, and Ron Terry. Michael Grehl, editor of the *Commercial Appeal*, also attended the meeting. Together they convinced Cody to run. Grehl promised Cody the paper's editorial backing and the businessmen promised to supply enough cash to saturate the local television stations with campaign ads.[35]

But neither Patterson nor Cody saw the mayoral campaign coming from Shelby County Clerk Dick Hackett, a Chandler protégé who had crunched a few numbers of his own. Hackett knew he could count on almost all of Chandler's old supporters, even with Cody in the race. And with the run-off provisions in place, all Hackett needed to do was finish second and he would become mayor.[36] City Councilwoman Pat Vander Schaaf also entered the race and for a time was considered a major candidate. But her cash-starved campaign never got started and she was a nonfactor on election day.

As expected, Cody bombarded the airwaves with commercials. Hackett, however, relied on the same campaign signs that helped him get elected county clerk in 1978 and August 1982. The sign borrowed the image of the Tennessee license plate and they were neatly erected throughout key sections of the city. Hackett had no expectation of getting the endorsement of the *Commercial Appeal*. Nevertheless, he agreed to meet with the paper's editorial board.

During the endorsement interview, Hackett was asked what he intended to do about the racial divide in Memphis and about ensuring that his administration would have a fair representation of the entire community. Hackett looked around the table at the all-white editorial board and responded, "I'll do a hell of a lot better than you're doing. You don't have one (black person) in here. I don't need your endorsement." Hackett then rose from his chair and ended the interview. "Print that," he shouted as he stormed out of the room.[37]

Both the *Commercial Appeal* and *Press-Scimitar* enthusiastically endorsed Cody even as a team of reporters at both papers scrambled to cover the four major candidates equally during the truncated campaign. Hackett's camp set its sights squarely on trying to discredit Cody among conservative white voters. Team Hackett considered Cody the only candidate standing in the way of a second place finish. The Sunday before election day, Hackett's campaign distributed thousands of fliers at major white churches in Memphis—including Bellevue Baptist—attacking Cody:

> **Did you know that Mike Cody**
> - Is a liberal Democrat
> - Was an active member of the American Civil Liberties Union
> - Supports forced busing
> - Was an early supporter of Harold Ford and served on his first campaign staff
> - Has supported liberal causes and candidates for the whole 20 years of his political life
> - Has been married three times
> - Marched with Martin Luther King
>
> These facts were taken from the newspapers, but if you don't believe them, ask Cody or someone at his headquarters. They are really quite proud of their man's record. Although I wouldn't take any of the above facts alone and incriminate a man, I do believe that taken as a whole, they tell us a lot. We really don't need a new Kennedy in the city of Memphis.[38]

Each of the flier's bullet points about Cody was true. And he was proud of his liberal record as an advocate for civil rights and equal justice. Cody's main goal in running for mayor was to be a bridge to the inevitable election of the city's first black mayor. He was warmly received in black churches during the twenty-seven-day campaign. He got encouragement from black political leaders Fred Davis and Michael Hooks and from Apostle G. E. Patterson of the Church of God in Christ. But his split with the Ford organization, mostly over the indictment and conviction of Emmitt Ford, cost him crucial support among black voters, while his liberal record did him in among white voters.

The real killer for Cody occurred when J. O. Patterson's name—and not his—appeared on the all-important Ford ballot. And on election night, Cody—despite raising and spending the most money—finished third. Patterson was first with eighty-eight thousand votes or 40 percent of the total. Hackett was a distant second with sixty-four thousand votes, or 30 percent, and Cody finished with fifty-six thousand votes or 26 percent. Cody had counted on getting at least 10 percent of the black vote. But according to a *Press-Scimitar* analysis, he got only 4 percent compared to 93 percent for Patterson. Only 1 percent of blacks voted for Hackett.

But Hackett's 51 percent showing among white voters was all he needed to get into the runoff where he was certain he could overtake Patterson. Once again, both daily newspapers shunned Hackett's campaign and endorsed Patterson. "For voters who really want a more responsive, representative and aggressive city administration, the Patterson candidacy is their best hope," the *Commercial Appeal* stated in an endorsement editorial that kept lamenting the fact that Cody had been rejected by voters.[39]

The Fords also reiterated their support for Patterson, but their get-out-the-vote effort for him was not robust at all, mainly because Patterson himself ran such a lackluster campaign. The Fords believed in working around the clock, if necessary, to win every vote possible—something Patterson wouldn't do. Hackett knew that, and was confident he would win—so confident that on election day, November 30, Hackett went fishing. That evening as the returns starting to come in, the results weren't even close. Hackett garnered 119,000 votes, more than 54 percent of the total, to Patterson's 100,000 or about 45 percent. The tumultuous 1982 election year was finally over and Hackett had accomplished his goal of becoming mayor a year earlier than expected. Yet he told himself that had he lost the 1982 special election, he would not have run the following year—which would have completely changed the city's political future.[40]

To show appreciation to voters for his improbable victory, Hackett printed scores of Thank You signs and, in an in-your-face gesture, personally planted one on the front lawn of the *Commercial Appeal*.[41] The quiet, unassuming thirty-three-year-old county clerk had claimed the grand prize in city politics, and African Americans once again were shut out of the mayor's office. The Ford organization, however, continued to rule the rest of the city's political roost. It had settled a few political scores and served notice to competing black politicians once and for all that the high-powered Ford machine was on cruise control.

CHAPTER 13

THE HACKETT YEARS

WHEN RICHARD C. HACKETT took office after being elected Shelby County clerk in 1978, he ordered a new license plate for his own vehicle. The personalized plate, 1MM983, stood for Memphis Mayor 1983. Practically from the moment he went to work in the administration of Mayor Wyeth Chandler in 1976, Hackett set his sights on replacing Chandler at city hall.[1]

Chandler had long confided in his young political understudy that he intended to be gone from the mayor's office when the 1983 city election rolled around—if not before. And Hackett intended to be ready when that time came. He had been an energetic worker for Chandler during his successful mayoral campaigns. Hackett was Chandler's sign manager, and he methodically and strategically placed the campaign signs in ways that couldn't help but be noticed by potential voters.

Each yard sign was exactly the same distance in inches and feet from the curb. As a reward, Chandler appointed him as the first director of the Mayor's Action Center, an agency set up to handle all sorts of citizen complaints. In that role, Hackett quickly developed a reputation for prompt response to community problems, large and small. But politically and administratively he wanted more.

When the job of sanitation department director came open in 1978, Hackett, who was twenty-eight at the time, let his bosses know he wanted it. But Henry Evans, the chief administrative officer, said no. Hackett was too young and politically inexperienced for such a demanding and high-profile position. Hackett got up from that meeting with Evans, walked out of city hall, and went straight to the Shelby County Election Commission office, where he picked up a qualifying petition to run for county clerk. Later that day, he told Chandler of his plans, and the mayor instantly pledged his support.

The incumbent county clerk, Robert M. Gray, had already announced that he would not seek reelection after thirteen years in the job. Gray, however, endorsed Patricia Russell, his deputy clerk, for the job. But Hackett had several advantages over Russell and seven other challengers. Outside of Shelby County government buildings, Russell was virtually unknown to voters, while Hackett had strong name recognition from being director of the Mayor's Action Center. He also had seasoned campaign help from Chandler's old political team. Plus, a low-key, grass-roots clerk's race was tailor made for Hackett's emerging political skill set. He created eye-catching campaign signs using the image of a Tennessee license plate bearing the words "Hackett for County Clerk."

The only real issue in the campaign was the unreasonably long wait times for people to purchase automobile tags at the clerk's office. Gray had done a horrible job addressing the long lines, and Hackett promised to open satellite offices and keep them open longer. On election day, Hackett beat Russell by nearly twenty thousand votes, and a political career was born.

His first term was uneventful—and that was just fine with Hackett, because it meant that the office was running smoothly. He managed an efficient and responsive staff, and cruised to reelection in August 1982, getting 74 percent of the countywide vote against just two opponents—one of whom got only two votes. In an obvious attempt to take advantage of Hackett's popularity with voters, a political unknown with the name Daniel Hatchett entered the criminal court clerk's race against longtime incumbent Bubba Blackwell. Hatchett got thirty thousand votes in losing to Blackwell.

As Hackett prepared to be sworn in for a second term, he was aware that Chandler was lobbying Governor Lamar Alexander for a judicial appointment. But when the appointment to the circuit court bench came through and Chandler resigned in late September, Hackett was still thinking about "Memphis Mayor 1983." He, like everyone else, assumed that the city council would appoint an interim mayor who would complete Chandler's term. He did not figure on a legal challenge to the council appointment, which led to the Tennessee Supreme Court ordering a chancery court judge to set a special mayoral election for November 1982.

As the courts were considering the issue, Hackett spent an entire week listening repeatedly to a sermon from Adrian Rogers, pastor of Bellevue

Baptist Church. The line from the sermon that stuck out the most was "The things that you regret in life, a lot of the time will be the things you did not do." Hackett felt those words were speaking directly to him. And they propelled him to run for mayor in the special election.[2]

Hackett ascended to the mayor's office solely on the votes of white conservative Memphians. But he was determined to run his administration vastly differently from Chandler and certainly differently from Loeb. In one of his first mayoral decisions, Hackett replaced police director Buddy Chapman—who had supported Mike Cody for mayor. John. D. Holt, a career Memphis police officer who had risen through the ranks to become deputy director, was Hackett's choice for the top job.

The new mayor was torn, but eventually he became convinced that the department could be effectively managed from within, and Holt was liked well enough by most rank-and-file officers. But it ended up being arguably the biggest appointment blunder of Hackett's mayoral career. The new director had zero rapport in the black community and never took the time to build trust in neighborhoods where his officers spent most of their time making arrests.

It didn't take long for Holt to face his first police crisis. It happened on January 11, 1983—two weeks after Holt became director—at 2239 Shannon Street in North Memphis. Patrolmen Robert. S. Hester and Ray Schwill answered a call at the home, but were attacked by a group of black men immediately after they set foot on the property. Schwill was shot in the face but managed to escape. Hester was not as lucky. He was taken captive and severely beaten by the group, led by Lindberg Sanders, forty-nine, a religious cultlike figure in the neighborhood. Sanders kept younger black men hanging around his house by supplying them with marijuana as they studied the Bible. Sanders also told his young followers that police officers were "agents of the Devil."[3]

Police surrounded the house and tried to convince Sanders and the others to release Hester and surrender, but they refused. Hester could be heard screaming in agony a block away. Specially trained tactical squad officers pressed for permission to storm the house, but Director Holt, with Mayor Hackett's approval, refused to give the go-ahead. Holt later defended the decision not to attempt a rescue by saying he believed that the group was holding Hester at gunpoint and would kill him if officers rushed the house.

Hackett told United Press International that Sanders considered himself a "black Jesus" and was prepared for an apocalyptic showdown with police.

"We knew they had food stored inside. It was there because they expected the world to end and had it for their ritual. You have a man calling himself the black Jesus and the people in the house with him who thought they were his disciples."[4]

The negotiations went nowhere. Finally, at 3:30 a.m. on January 13, about thirty hours after the incident began, officers invaded the darkened three-bedroom house and fatally shot Sanders along with six others, including Sanders's twenty-six-year-old son. Hester was found dead just inside the doorway. He was handcuffed from behind and had been beaten to death. An autopsy revealed that Hester had been dead for several hours—a fact that angered his fellow officers.[5] But the community reaction to Hackett's and Holt's handling of the crisis was generally favorable. Few Memphians, black or white, felt sorry for cop killers.

The incident was similar in many respects to a case two years earlier in the Algiers community of New Orleans. A white police officer, Gregory Neupert, was found bleeding to death from a gunshot wound next to his patrol car near a black housing project. Cops who responded to the shooting killed four black citizens and later brutalized others who were taken into custody for questioning. Three officers were eventually convicted of federal civil rights violations for the beatings—but not for the killings.[6] Around the same time, a plethora of excessive force complaints were also filed against police in other cities from New York to Los Angeles and from Jackson, Mississippi, to Detroit.

In Memphis, no criminal charges resulted from the death of Lindberg Sanders and his followers. But Hester's brutal death shook the police department from top to bottom and upset Hackett's plans to get his administration off to a smooth, uneventful start. The mayor wanted to focus on more upbeat issues such as downtown redevelopment and tourism. He also tackled one of his pet peeves, the escalating and highly profitable topless nightclub industry in the city. Hackett pushed the police department to crack down on prostitution. He then took a bold new antinudity ordinance to the city council and heavily lobbied the members to pass it. The ordinance was patterned after a similar law in Chattanooga, which had been upheld by the Tennessee Supreme Court.

The most contentious portion of the proposed ordinance was this paragraph: "It shall be unlawful for any female to appear in a public place so costumed or dressed that one or both breasts are wholly or substantially exposed to public view, and it shall be unlawful for an owner or operator or manager of premises constituting a public place to knowingly permit or allow any such person to appear on the premises owned or operated by him. 'Wholly or substantially exposed to public view,' as it pertains to breasts, shall mean the showing of the female breast in a public place with less than a fully opaque covering of any portion of the breasts below the top of the nipple."[7]

The ordinance defined public places as including "streets, sidewalks, or highways; transportation facilities; schools; places of amusement; parks; playgrounds; restaurants; nightclubs; cocktail lounges; burlesque houses; bars; cabarets; taverns; taprooms; private fraternal, social, golf or country clubs; or any place that allows the consumption of intoxicating beverages on the premises."

Topless club owners were incensed. The ordinance, if allowed to stand, would all but drive them out of business. The council scheduled a final vote on the proposal for March 29, 1983. That afternoon, scores of topless dancers, other club employees, and their children gathered in the parking lot of Danny's, a topless club owned by Danny Owens. He and another topless bar owner, Steve Cooper, had chartered two buses to take the crowd downtown to the council meeting. They were joined by dozens of other supporters, and the group practically filled the council chamber.

The children carried homemade protest signs that read, "If you take my mommy's job are you going to offer her a new one?" and "At least I'm not on welfare." The protesters vastly outnumbered those in the audience who favored the ordinance and hooted at everyone who spoke in support of the proposal. Council chairman Billy Hyman finally grew impatient with the catcalls. "We're not going to have these outbursts and a competition to see who can squeal the loudest," he said.[8]

During the debate among the council, Jeff Sanford spoke for members who planned to reluctantly vote for the ordinance: "I have serious doubts as to the constitutionality of what we're looking at and if not that, then the ability to enforce it. Having said that, I intend to vote for it and let the courts decide whether it's constitutional."

The council then passed the ordinance by a vote of eleven to zero. Voting in favor were Hyman, Sanford, Bob James, Andy Alissandratos, Oscar Edmonds, James Ford, Ed McBrayer, Glenn Raines, Barbara Sonnenburg, Thomas Todd, and Pat Vander Schaaf. Councilman Michael Hooks was out of the room when the vote was taken, and J. O. Patterson Jr., a chronic no-show at council meetings, was absent. Cooper, as he left the council chamber, called the ordinance ridiculous and promised it would be business as usual at his clubs.

Thirteen days later, on April 11, police made their first arrests under the ordinance during a raid at GiGi's, another topless club operated by Danny Owens. Several club employees were hauled to jail, where they spent hours before being released—even though the ordinance carried only a maximum fifty-dollar fine and no jail time. Cops later arrested topless dancer Phyllis Jones at Club Tiffany, a bar owned by Cooper. Cooper, Jones, and another dancer, Lisa Tolbert, responded by filing suit on May 3 in federal court seeking an injunction against enforcement of the ordinance.

Mayor Hackett and the police were already on shaky legal ground because the ordinance was being selectively applied only to the most notorious topless clubs in Memphis. But it was a Metropolitan Opera Company's performance of the play Macbeth that led to the ordinance's undoing. A scene in the opera featured a witch bearing her breasts. On the night of the performance, two topless dancers were in the audience, and when the witch scene occurred, the dancers stood up and exposed their breasts as well. Police officials had gotten word that the breast-bearing protest was being planned for the Macbeth performance, but Police Director John Holt ordered his officers not to show up and try to arrest the dancers.

During a May 20 hearing on the lawsuit before federal judge Robert McRae Jr., Holt admitted that he did not understand the ordinance and sought advice from the city attorney's office. He said he was told that the breast scene in Macbeth was classified as art and was not a violation of the antinudity ordinance. But Judge McRae ruled that the ordinance was patently unconstitutional and unenforceable. He said the law could apply to a woman breast feeding an infant or posing nude for a painting. In effect, the judge said, the city was attempting "to legislate the morals of persons who patronize topless dance locations and the dancers there."[9]

From a civil liberties standpoint, the showdown over nudity ended up being an embarrassment for the city council and Hackett's administration, which was still in its infancy. After McRae's ruling, council chairman Billy Hyman said he wasn't surprised the ordinance was struck down, but he felt the council politically had no choice. "When it came to us, the momentum was rolling and no one could afford to vote against it," he told a Commercial

Appeal reporter. Hackett was considered a hero among most of his constituents for standing up against debauchery in Memphis. Just by pushing for passage of the ordinance, he had banked a ton of political capital with his white, conservative, churchgoing voters. And as the 1983 city elections approached, the interim mayor was well positioned to win again.

On the other side of town, however, the Ford organization remained determined to make good on its promise to run one of its own against Hackett. But which Ford would it be? Harold, as the head and the brains of the Ford machine, stood the best chance of winning. But his family enjoyed life in D.C., and the congressman was well respected on both sides of the congressional aisle. So when he opted not to pursue the mayor's office, the choice was obvious. It would be older brother John. Despite his perceived double-cross in 1978, when he jumped out of the Shelby County mayor's race literally at the last second, John and the organization were sure that there would be no lingering backlash from black voters. Instead, the pushback came from an old familiar foe—Otis Higgs.

Despite back-to-back mayoral defeats, Higgs wanted another shot. In his mind, he had come so close, particularly in 1979, against a political heavyweight in Chandler. He also thought that the Fords should be magnanimous enough to share political power at the highest level with a black man who carried a different last name. He was wrong. As far as the Ford organization was concerned, Higgs had been a political failure and it was time for him to step aside.

Meanwhile, a coalition of moderate white Memphians renewed efforts to run a white candidate against Hackett—hopefully with backing from the Ford organization. And again, the coalition's top choice was Mike Cody. But Harold Ford rebuffed the idea and called the coalition members hypocritical when they would not agree to support black candidates in two at-large city council races. Cody put the final kibosh on the coalition's plans when he announced he was not interested in another mayoral run. The 1982 special election had convinced Cody that blacks and whites still were not ready to come together politically in Memphis.

"My campaign was based on a hope that I could form a consensus on the issues—mainly economic—and articulate a new sense of community and understanding among blacks and whites and between the business and labor interests," Cody said. "I couldn't put a majority together on that basis. At the present time, I cannot see any change in that situation or foresee any circumstances that would lead me to consider asking the public to support me for mayor a second time. I believe I had my chance."[10]

At the filing deadline, Hackett found himself in the enviable position of being the only major white candidate against three African American challengers: John Ford, Otis Higgs, and attorney D'Army Bailey, who surprised everyone with his entry into the race. Black community leaders were dismayed by the development because they already knew the outcome. Three black candidates would split the black vote and Hackett would waltz back into the mayor's office. The Ford organization tried to convince both Higgs and Bailey that they were unelectable and needed to get out of the race. And the *Tri-State Defender* newspaper called for a consensus black candidate. The paper, however, did not formally endorse any candidate in the race.

Higgs and Bailey refused to knuckle under to the Fords. Deep down, both knew their chances were slim. Higgs had lost most of his support from 1975 and 1979, and Bailey never gained enough traction to be a serious contender. But both men pressed on—especially if it meant damaging John Ford's campaign. Hackett, meanwhile, continued to solidify his base of conservative white voters. He pumped more city dollars into renovation of the Orpheum Theater downtown and the Brooks Museum of Art in Overton Park.[11]

Both the *Commercial Appeal* and the *Press-Scimitar* endorsed Hackett. It was the last political endorsement the *Press-Scimitar* would make. The paper ceased publication on October 31, 1983, marking a somber end to an important news and political voice that had existed in various forms in Memphis since 1906.

In its editorial backing Hackett, the *Commercial Appeal* wrote that the young mayor had improved in the job as he went along: "We like what we see in Hackett far more than what we saw during his campaign for the mayoral vacancy last year and his early performance in office. He has matured as a politician . . . and now he seems best equipped by that experience and his relations with different segments of the community to do what the next mayor must do to help the city make substantial economic and civic progress."[12]

After the votes were counted on election night, Hackett had run away with the race. He amassed nearly 132,000 votes to just 51,000 for John Ford. Higgs got 36,000, and Bailey finished fourth with 7,000. Hackett had predicted that he would get 55 percent of the vote and win without a runoff. He did better than expected, getting 57 percent of the total vote, including about 5 percent of the black vote. About 95 percent of white voters, including moderate and liberal Democrats, went for Hackett. He also was helped by a 63 percent white turnout compared to just 48 percent among black voters—the lowest in years.[13]

In his victory message, Hackett made a convincing case that he now had a mandate to lead and he intended to represent the entire city. "I will no longer be concerned with where my votes came from and who voted against me," he told a cheering crowd.[14] At the Ford campaign headquarters, where I was assigned as a reporter on election night, John Ford was gracious and conciliatory in conceding to Hackett. "We gave our best shot at it," he said. "We didn't do so bad after all. I congratulate him. I'm not a sore loser."

Harold Ford, however, was just the opposite. He lashed out at the Hackett campaign, white voters, and the newspapers. "It's mighty strange when the white community gives us their worst and we give them our best," he told reporters. He accused Hackett of bringing out closet racism on election day. "Dick Hackett and Bill Boyd ran one of the racist campaigns in this city," Ford said, adding that Hackett's campaign workers made more than 135,000 phone calls telling white voters, "Let's stop this nigger." Meanwhile, at Higgs's headquarters, the somberness of losing for a third time changed to cheers throughout the room when supporters learned that John Ford had lost as well.[15]

The election results fueled speculation that the Ford organization was losing some its luster. In reality, Harold Ford remained as strong as ever, but he was simply unable to transfer enough of his political strength to John in order to win a citywide race. It was the organization's first significant campaign defeat, and Harold took it personally.

Hackett, now with a fresh four-year term, pressed forward with an aggressive economic agenda for the city. He pumped money into infrastructure projects, but he also worked to pay down the city's debt and put money into the city schools. Annual budget sessions were rarely contentious, mostly because a majority council members—with Hackett's blessing—ignored the Tennessee Sunshine Law and routinely met privately, often at the Rendezvous restaurant, to work out budget agreements. Hackett considered it his responsibility to shoulder the headaches of the city's financial issues, and he had no qualms hashing out those issues in back rooms because—in his mind—he was doing it in the best interest of the city.[16]

The mayor also took on the Environmental Protection Agency, which threatened to put a freeze on the city's gas-tax revenues because of unacceptable auto emission standards. Hackett persuaded the agency to back off by promising to build more auto inspection stations. He also took on federal highway officials over a plan to expand an interstate along Tom Lee Park and once dropped F-bombs during a heated meeting with a U.S. Corps of Engineers official after hearing that the corps had no plans for a stabilization project on the bluffs overlooking Riverside Drive and Tom Lee Park.

The always mild-mannered mayor went ballistic after the corps official acknowledged there was nothing preventing the building that housed the Holiday Inn Rivermont from sliding on to Riverside Drive and sloughing off into the Mississippi River, potentially costing hundreds of lives. The official left the meeting but later told Hackett the stabilization work would be done.

In addition, the Hackett administration moved forward with annexation plans in Cordova and Hickory Hill—which were designed in part to help boost the city's white voting population. Hackett also was instrumental in keeping St. Jude Children's Research Hospital from leaving Memphis for St. Louis, particularly after an ill-timed series of negative articles in the *Commercial Appeal* in 1985 about the hospital's fund-raising arm, the American Lebanese Syrian Associated Charities, known as ALSAC. The mayor was never a big fan of the newspaper's editorial board. After the articles were published, Hackett happily sat in on an editorial board meeting in which ALSAC's top leadership literally cursed out the newspaper's editors for publishing the series.[17]

On the issue of race, Hackett was committed to bringing more black Memphians into city government in meaningful roles. When he took over as mayor, blacks were practically nonexistent in leadership positions, and Hackett was determined to change that. He appointed the first two assistant city attorneys and oversaw the promotion of other African Americans both at city hall and in the police department. The mayor was determined to do more, but opted to wait until after his reelection campaign in 1987.

Hackett was confident that voters would return him to the mayor's office for a second full term, and it became even more of sure thing when the Ford organization decided not to field a candidate against him. At the filing deadline, two black candidates were in the race—city council member Minerva Johnican and former state representative Dedrick Withers. They were joined by white councilman Bill Gibbons.

The Hackett Years

The incumbent's outreach to the black community paid dividends as two former mayoral candidates, A. W. Willis and D'Army Bailey, signed on with the Hackett campaign. He also received endorsements from Shelby County Mayor Bill Morris and Congressman Don Sundquist. Surprisingly, John Ford announced his support for Gibbons, but that failed to sway black voters, particularly after Harold Ford decided to make no endorsement in the mayor's race.

It was all falling into place for Hackett until the morning of September 24, 1987. That's when police were called to the LeMoyne Gardens public housing complex, across the street from LeMoyne-Owen College in South Memphis. When officers arrived, they encountered a twenty-seven-year-old mentally disturbed black man named Joseph DeWayne Robinson, who was carrying a twelve-inch butcher knife. Robinson had already cut and stabbed himself 120 times—all but one of the wounds were minor—and he refused police orders to put down the weapon.

What happened next remained in dispute for weeks. The police said Robinson approached them with the knife. Witnesses say he made no such moves. At any rate, the officers opened fire and shot Robinson ten times—twice in the head, once in each arm and six times in the torso. He died at the scene. The police account said Robinson was on the ground, but got up and charged after officers. But at least one witness said a plain clothes officer shot Robinson while he was still on the ground.[18]

The fatal shooting came just days after another black man, Hugh Curtis, died while in police custody. Curtis's death was caused by an overdose of cocaine, but witnesses said they saw police beating him while placing him under arrest.

The black community's anger over Robinson's death was fueled further by police director John Holt's hasty pronouncement that the shooting was totally justified. Just one day after the shooting, Holt said the officers "were protecting themselves and all of the other citizens who were present." But Johnican and Withers said the killing was an example of a police department out of control with Holt in charge. "The community demands answers. The community demands justice. The community demands a stop to these senseless killings," Johnican said. "Enough is enough."

Withers went to the scene of the shooting to make the claim that police have declared "open season" on black men in Memphis. "Any black man who gets stopped by the Memphis Police Department, his life is in immediate danger. The bottom line, it was murder. I don't care what they say."[19]

Two days after the killing, Hackett attended a community forum on the LeMoyne-Owen College campus where he promised a thorough and impartial investigation of the incident. Withers was also at the forum, and the two men engaged in a heated exchange in which Withers pointed his finger at the mayor and shouted, "You owe (the public) a response for what's under your leadership. (The police) have done it over and over again. Now what are you going to do about it?" Hackett responded by criticizing Withers for inciting turmoil. "We owe the family, we owe the neighborhood and we owe the city more leadership than that."

Hackett left that meeting determined to do more than just spout words. He and his bodyguard, Bobby Sides, picked up D'Army Bailey and the three of them went to the home of Robinson's mother, Reba Brownlee, so that Hackett could personally express condolences for her son's death. The mayor, as usual, was behind the wheel, Bailey was in the front passenger seat and Sides sat directly behind Hackett. As they slowly entered LeMoyne Gardens, hostile residents greeted the vehicle by rocking it from side to side. "Don't stop the car. Keep going," Sides said, putting his hands on Hackett's shoulder.[20]

Inside the apartment, however, the mayor was greeted warmly. He was careful not to say anything to Brownlee that might put the city and the police in legal jeopardy, but he did express deep sorrow for the incident. And they both agreed that there must be better ways of dealing with people with mental health issues. Robinson, who lived with his mother, sister, and her two children, had been acting strangely for months. A heavy cocaine user, Robinson told his mother he expected to be killed because someone was trying to get him. Just days before the shooting, he told Brownlee not to open a closet door in their apartment because he feared someone was in the closet waiting to attack him.[21]

The mayor's visit lasted about ten minutes. Hackett and Brownleee embraced each other just inside her screen door in full view of the gathering crowd that responded with light applause. Bailey then told Hackett to walk out slowly, keep his head up, and nod respectfully to the bystanders. "Don't look like you're scared," Bailey said. The mayor followed the instructions to the letter, and he drove away without incident.[22]

A *Commercial Appeal* editorial on September 29, five days after the shooting, concluded that police had overreacted and failed to take appropriate action to subdue Robinson without killing him. The editorial also criticized

Holt for insisting that there is no distrust of the police department, adding that the director "doesn't know beans about half the people he's supposed to be serving."

"Memphis should have a first-class police department in every respect. That will take training, the weeding out of ineffective officers, continuing education and programs for better police-community relations. The department's present leadership doesn't appear to be capable of doing that job. It's time for Holt to make way for a new director."[23]

But as election day approached, there were no signs that Johnican or Withers had turned the Robinson shooting into voter animosity against Hackett. Indeed, separate federal and state investigations eventually cleared the officers of any wrongdoing. Frustrated by her sagging campaign, Johnican stopped attacking the mayor and instead went public with racially charged criticism of black community leaders who were supporting either Hackett or Gibbons. "We've got some 'Uncle Toms' in the city of Memphis," she said. "Selfish blacks are selling out our people."[24] Johnican also called for picketing at businesses owned by African Americans who refused to support her in favor of white candidates—which included the Ford family funeral home. No pickets ever materialized.

The *Commercial Appeal* again abandoned Hackett and endorsed Gibbons, saying he would provide the kind of leadership the city needed. The endorsement, however, was of little benefit to the councilman, who finished a distant third with 26,434 votes, just 15 percent of the total. Hackett again won in a landslide, getting 99,000 votes. The incumbent also again avoided a runoff by getting 58 percent of the vote. Johnican finished second, but only managed 38,300 votes or 22 percent of the total. Withers finished a dismal fourth with just 2,700 votes, which amounted to less than 2 percent.

Despite Gibbons's presence in the race and his allegiance with Shelby County Republicans, Hackett got 89 percent of the white vote. Even more impressive was the mayor getting nearly 20 percent of the black vote. Thanks to John Ford's endorsement, Gibbons collected 24 percent of the black vote, but he only received 8 percent among white voters. Johnican, who had gotten 38 percent of the white vote in winning her at-large council seat in 1983, got just 1 percent in the mayor's race.

The results were proof positive that Memphians were more than satisfied with Hackett's performance as mayor. African Americans in huge numbers showed their disapproval of the ongoing squabbling among black politicians by either voting for Hackett or Gibbons—or staying home. Most were satisfied with the mayor's preelection promise to make major changes in his administration, including the top job at the police department. The mayor kept saying that Holt would soon retire.

After being sworn in for his second full term, Hackett made good on the promise. He appointed James Ivy as the city's first black police director replacing Holt. The department also developed the Crisis Intervention Team, a model program to better handle police encounters with mentally disturbed individuals. In addition, Hackett increased black managers and supervisors in city administration from next to nothing to 41 percent. Black city workers overall grew to 43 percent. And in 1991, as the next election loomed, Hackett named Greg Duckett as the first black chief administrative officer, the number two position at city hall. Duckett had served in the administration as public service director and director of Memphis Housing and Community Development. The mayor also appointed Monice Hagler Tate as the first African American and first woman city attorney.

Hackett seemingly was riding a wave of biracial populism, the likes of which had not been seen in Memphis since the Boss Crump era. He had, in many ways, accomplished what Mike Cody had intended with his failed 1982 mayoral campaign—to usher in a more moderate city administration that was at least partly inclusive of the black population. Hackett's utopian goal was to reduce the city debt to zero, win reelection to a third full term, and then run for governor in 1994.

But despite gravitating in unprecedented numbers to Hackett in 1987, a majority of black Memphians still longed for the day when the color barrier would be broken in the mayor's office. Job one was getting the city's black political leadership on the same page. And as the decade of the 1990s approached, there were finally quiet signs that it was about to happen.

CHAPTER 14

"DOC"

WHEN EDWARD H. CRUMP died on October 16, 1954, in his stately home on Peabody Avenue, Willie W. Herenton was fourteen years old and living in a tiny South Memphis apartment surrounded by poverty. The place young Willie called home was on Barton Street, near where it intersects with what was once called Iowa Street but was renamed E. H. Crump Boulevard in honor of Memphis's longtime political boss.

Willie and Boss Crump never met, mainly because the young boy seldom ventured too far away from his own neighborhood. And Crump, who loved to surround himself with Memphians of all ages at public gatherings, rarely included Willie's area of the city on his travel schedule. Segregation was the accepted rule in Memphis. Willie and his friends were forced to play in the streets around their apartment units because blacks were not allowed at nearby John Gaston Park. They weren't even allowed to walk through the park.[1]

Crump's death, then, was no big deal to Willie. He was oblivious to the solemnness that gripped the city. In fact, he couldn't care less about Memphis politics—past, present, or future—and whether the Crump machine would live on or sputter into nonexistence. Willie was too busy just surviving day to day with his mother, stepfather, and sister. About the time Crump died, Willie had landed a job at a small grocery store nearby so he could have pocket money and help with the family's living expenses.

His dream was to become a pro boxer and follow in the footsteps of his prize-fighting idols, Joe Louis and Sugar Ray Robinson. Young Willie was both street smart and book smart, a rare combination in many black neighborhoods. He excelled as a student, first at LaRose Elementary, then Booker T. Washington High and LeMoyne-Owen College, where he earned a bachelor's of science degree in elementary education in 1963.

Boxing by then had taken a back seat to teaching, and Herenton immediately went to work as a fifth-grade teacher at Shannon Elementary. He also enrolled in graduate school at Memphis State University, which was now accepting black students, and earned a master's degree in educational administration in 1966. It was at Memphis State that Herenton, for the first time ever, sat in a classroom with white students.[3]

Two years later, he was named principal of Bethel Grove Elementary. By now, Herenton could clearly see his future, and it was in school administration. But he could not ignore the racism that was interwoven into the Memphis school district. In the fall of 1969, black students, teachers, and community activists launched a one-day-a-week boycott of classes that became known as "Black Mondays."

Up to sixty-three thousand African American students skipped classes for at least five consecutive Mondays to protest the fact that the school board was all white and few black teachers were being hired. Herenton was the only principal who joined in the walkout. He was fully aware that his participation carried risks for his career, but they were risks he was willing to take. The protests ended only when the city council appointed two nonvoting black members to the school board.

In 1971, Herenton earned his PhD in education from Southern Illinois University. His dissertation was titled "A Historical Study of School Desegregation in the Memphis City Schools: 1954–1970." The tall, thin and scrapping young man from South Memphis was now Dr. W. W. Herenton, but his friends and admirers simply called him "Doc."

With his doctoral degree in hand, Herenton was named principal at LaRose Elementary, where he supervised some of the same teachers who had taught him. He was in his early thirties and was determined to do all the things necessary to succeed the right way. That included spending a summer as a visiting professor in curriculum and instruction at Kansas State University in 1972 and participating in the Rockefeller Superintendent Training Program in the Baltimore City Public Schools in 1973 and in the District of Columbia Public Schools in 1974.

The following year, he was put in charge of a school system–wide evaluation program working with Memphis State University and the University of

Tennessee. Then, when veteran superintendent John P. Freeman submitted a staff reorganization plan to the school board, Herenton was listed as the new deputy superintendent for instructional services—thus becoming the highest ranking black public school official in the history of Memphis.

The recommendation left some whites on the school board aghast. At one meeting, board member Neal Small, recalling the Black Monday protests, described Herenton as a "black militant" who did not have enough seniority to be the number two person in the district. Board member Juanita Watkins was no less subtle. She said Herenton's promotion would harm morale, which was code language for the fact that white school administrators would not take kindly to being supervised by Herenton or any black man.

Freeman, however, dismissed the talk as nonsense, while Herenton was more expressive, yet respectful. "I guess in some matters I'm conservative, or liberal, or moderate. But I try never to be extreme," he told a *Press-Scimitar* reporter covering the meeting. "Anyhow, I don't feel the necessity of responding to unjustified remarks."[3]

The board voted six to three to approve Freeman's reorganization plan, which included the appointment of Herenton as deputy superintendent. Suddenly, the black community had a new civic role model and an authentic, homegrown superstar. After a lifetime of being overlooked for important administrative roles in local government, black Memphians now saw Herenton as someone with the intelligence, experience, and credentials that could not be ignored by the white establishment.

Herenton's ascension to deputy superintendent turned heads in the white community, particularly among those still fuming over court-ordered busing to force desegregation of the city schools. White students were already leaving the system by the thousands. A district that was once majority white was now more than 70 percent black. White school board members, along with many others, feared that the flight would only increase with a black person now just one step away from the top job.

What they didn't realize was that Freeman's reorganization plan was really setting the stage for his imminent retirement. And it put Herenton in a position to legitimately compete for the superintendent job. In the minds of most black Memphians, Herenton was the obvious and only choice to succeed Freeman. When Freeman finally announced his retirement in 1978, the school board—made up of six whites and three blacks—decided to conduct a national search using a local citizen's committee to screen the candidates and recommend six finalists. Each finalist was then interviewed by the board in sessions that were open to the public. Herenton, to no surprise, was selected as a finalist and was the fifth person interviewed.

His session, on August 15, 1978, occurred during the middle of a strike by city police. A widespread power blackout hit Memphis later than night. Herenton, however, was not deterred by the distractions of a police walk-out. At his interview, he spoke eloquently and passionately about the time and effort he had put into developing credibility with blacks and whites in Memphis. "I do not consider this as a job in the true sense of the word," he said. "I consider it a noble opportunity to render service to my community. I am an applicant for what I consider to be one of the most crucial positions in public life. If it were not for the opportunities provided me by public education, I would not be here as an applicant today. I would probably still be at Barton and Crump."[4]

Herenton sensed that most white board members wanted someone from outside Memphis, but he was sure he could change their minds. So he addressed the point during his interview: "I do not believe Memphis has the luxury of time in terms of waiting for a person to come from outside to learn the programs and needs of the school system." The system, he said, does not need a "knight in shining armor."[5]

The following day, the board interviewed its last candidate. He was Dr. William Coats, superintendent of the Grosse Pointe, Michigan, public school system in suburban Detroit. Grosse Pointe was one of the wealthiest communities in southeastern Michigan, with an enrollment of about eleven thousand. Its black student population was miniscule. Coats told the board the Memphis job intrigued him, but he was not sure if he would accept the position if offered. He also spoke in unimpressive generalities about the state of large urban school districts such as Memphis.

In a word, Coats's interview was lackluster. Most of those who heard and observed him, particularly black board members and blacks in the audience, came away thinking Coats had no legitimate shot. He had no experience working in a racially diverse school system. The closest thing to it was a four-and-a-half-year stint as superintendent of the Kalamazoo, Michigan, school district, which was 23 percent black. To black Memphians, Herenton had clearly outshined every other candidate. He had done all the things necessary to earn the job. And only an act of pure racism would prevent the homegrown prodigy from getting the appointment.

Herenton had impressed most of the white board members, and yet they could not bring themselves to vote for him. On Sunday afternoon,

August 20, board member James Blackburn invited three of his white colleagues—Barbara Sonnenburg, Frances Coe, and Mal Mauney—to his home to informally discuss the appointment. Also present, according to later accounts from Blackburn and school board attorney Ernest Kelly, were officials from Memphis State University and LeMoyne-Owen College. Blackburn and Kelly said the college leaders were there to make the case to board members that a superintendent from outside of Memphis was preferable because city school students were unprepared for college study.[6]

After their secret meeting, Blackburn, Coe, Mauney, and Sonnenburg felt they had the necessary cover story for their vote against Herenton. Later that evening, Coe phoned black school board member George H. Brown and let it slip that she had met with three other white members. During the rest of the conversation, Brown treated the slip as if it never happened. But disappointment and anger were already building up inside.

The board's vote was set for the following evening, August 21. Earlier that day, Coe also called Herenton and asked to meet with him alone in his office. If Herenton had any chance of getting the appointment, he knew he needed the support of Coe, who was considered a liberal by most standards. Herenton instantly got an ominous feeling about the meeting. When Coe arrived, there was no small talk. "Willie, I think you have done an outstanding job, and in time you will ascend to be the superintendent. But now I think we need an outside perspective," she told him, frequently looking away as Herenton stared straight at her.

Her words cut Herenton like a knife, but he felt he had to "man-up" to Coe. Which meant he had to take the bad news without visible anger but with his chin up and with a poker face. "Mrs. Coe," Herenton said calmly, "I respect whatever decision you have to make." She dropped her head again, and he rose from his seat and escorted her to the door without another word being said.

Doc left the building immediately and drove directly to the only real safe haven that he knew—his old South Memphis neighborhood to see his grandmother and his mother. "I didn't get the job," he told them the moment he walked through the door. His grandmother, without changing her expression, said, "Willie, if God is for you, you'll get that job."[7]

Despite her comforting words, Herenton was crushed. In his mind, even the most liberal white Memphians were perfectly fine with denying a top position in the community to a black man based solely on his race. White board members had looked at Coats—young, handsome, and blue-eyed, then looked at Herenton—tall, black, and imposing—and made their decision on skin color alone.

As the board meeting started that evening, it was obvious how the votes would shake out. Once they were recorded, Coats was the winner by a 5-3-1 vote. Five of the six white board members voted for him. They were James Blackburn, Frances Coe, Mal Mauney, William Ray Ingram, and Barbara Sonnenburg. The sixth white member, Juanita Watkins, cast her vote for Dr. William Payne, an assistant superintendent in the city school system who was an underling to Herenton.

The three black board members, George H. Brown, Carl Johnson, and Maxine Smith, voted for Herenton and were incensed at the outcome. "I think racism has prevailed," said Smith, who was shaking and near tears. "I thought we had taken a turn for the better, but we have not. Racism is still America's number one problem. It definitely is around this table. Hopefully everybody, the people in the community, including the patrons in the school system, will rebel against this. If they choose to do it, I will join that rebellion."

Brown, visibly angry, called the board meeting "a damn farce." He then went public with criticism of the white board members for holding the private meeting the night before at Blackburn's home. Brown said white members had even agreed ahead of time on an annual salary for Coats of $53,000, plus fringe benefits, which would make the total yearly compensation $60,000. Freeman, the retiring superintendent, was being paid $45,516.

"At least four of the votes (Coats) received voted against the frontrunner because of racism," Brown said. "The biggest difficulty Dr. Herenton had is that he stayed in the oven too long and had a permanent tan."[8] Johnson also chimed in with heavy criticism of the vote: "I have talked to people in the community, both black and white and they advocated for Dr. Herenton. I can't see what the reason is that precipitated five votes for Coats."[9]

White board members, now on the defensive, sought to justify their vote by saying the system needed fresh thinking from the outside. Coe even said there had been too much "inbreeding" within the system: "At this stage in the Memphis City Schools, we need someone to get us on a path of management by objectives, someone to set rigorous goals and make us work very hard. We need someone who is able to assess the weaknesses both in instruction and in other areas. We need someone who is forceful, persuasive and articulate to give us leadership."[10]

Coe's words only angered the black board members and blacks in the audience even more. Every attribute she described could be found in Herenton—but racism prevented the white members from seeing that. The protests against Coats's hiring started the moment the meeting ended. Annie Green, leader of a group known as Title 1 Parents who took part in a federal program to aid low-achieving and low-income students, immediately organized a protest rally for the following evening at Lincoln Park. "We will pull our children out of schools," she told a reporter. "We are going to try to get the board to rescind this."[11]

White board members left the meeting with little to say about the private gathering at Blackburn's home. When asked about it, Sonnenburg admitted to attending but called it a "meeting of community people at which the needs of the city and needs of the system were discussed. I'm not going to say anymore."

In the days that followed, black board members, particularly Brown, continued to stoke the flames of anger against the board's decision. "I am as bitter about this as anything that has happened," he told the *Commercial Appeal*. "I don't think the board members who voted for Dr. Coats have been honest with the community as to their reasons. I believe some of them figure they are getting a white knight on a white horse in shining armor galloping through this community, and that suddenly confidence in the school system is going to be restored and white children are going to return."[12]

Several other black community leaders added their voices to the protest. Samuel Billy Kyles, head of the Memphis chapter of Operation PUSH, spoke the sentiment of virtually the entire black population: "We have been hearing all through the 50s and 60s that black people ought to get themselves qualified, and who was more qualified than Dr. Herenton, a native son having gone through the school system? Now all of a sudden we need new blood infused from the outside. Once again they allowed the trauma of race to stymie the progress that Memphis so badly needs."[13]

Kyles's organization also held a community rally in support of Herenton, during which Maxine Smith repeated the racism charge. "I support Willie Herenton with every fiber of my being," she told the pumped-up audience. "I don't care how much I am charged with always talking about racism. Racism is the thing that holds the tightest grip on America today and until it releases us, none of us will be free. And racism is the only reason Willie Herenton is not city superintendent."

Under persistent criticism about the private meeting, Blackburn finally addressed the issue and insisted there was nothing sinister about the gathering. He said he wanted to vote for Herenton but was convinced otherwise after a lot of soul searching. His vote for Coats was his attempt to get the school system "out of the ditch."

Surprisingly, the *Commercial Appeal* opted not to publish an editorial position on the public rancor over the selection of Coats. The *Press-Scimitar*, however, addressed the controversy in an editorial that chastised the black board members for making ill-founded charges of racism. "It is regrettable that the board's black minority attacked the election of Dr. Coats as an act of racism by the majority," the paper stated. "This simply is untrue. . . . To charge that choice of a superintendent was made solely on the basis of color rejects the idea that legitimate and good faith arguments could be made in behalf of Dr. Coats. The *Press-Scimitar* believes the board has made a good choice and we hope that Dr. Coats accepts the challenge that could lead to a fruitful career in Memphis."[14]

On Friday, August 25, Coats, his wife, and his five daughters flew to Memphis for a weekend visit that included house hunting. They were met immediately after exiting their Delta Airlines flight by a group of city school parents who respectfully, but emphatically, let Coats know he was not wanted in Memphis. Later, during a press conference at the Board of Education, city school parent Vivian Bell interrupted the questioning to speak directly to the superintendent-elect: "Are you aware we are going to pull our children out (of the school system)? The day you take office, we are pulling our children out of schools."[15]

During the visit, Coats also met with Herenton and Superintendent Freeman, both of whom were gracious and welcoming. He also met separately with Maxine Smith and George Brown, who told him, "Because of the circumstances, I would not be able to pledge my support. The issue here is broader and bigger than William Coats, and this is where I have to take my stand."[16]

Coats left town on Sunday with a weighty decision to make. On Monday, August 28, he rejected the board's offer in a written statement: "If I am going to be superintendent of a majority black school system, I've got to have support from the start from black board members. It was not there. I think it's important for the board to go back to the drawing tables to have a free and open discussion of candidates. I am not able to accept the offer under the conditions under which it was made."[17]

At the school board meeting that evening, four hundred more people showed up to protest the rejection of Herenton. Board members, however, tried to strike a more cordial tone, promising to hold a special retreat the following weekend to air their differences and try to improve communication. Coe ended up saying she had made a "major mistake" by attending the private meeting at Blackburn's home. Meanwhile, Sonnenburg, the board president, had gotten word of Coats's decision before the board meeting started, but she did not announce it. Reporters and others in the audience learned of it after the meeting ended.[18]

In its Tuesday, August 29, edition, the *Commercial Appeal* finally addressed the firestorm on its editorial pages, expressing strong criticism of white board members for meeting in secret. "How could they have been so blind to the potential repercussions of that meeting?" the editorial stated. "Black leaders, some of whom may have objected to Coats's selection under any circumstances, were given perfect justification for protest."

But the editorial also criticized those same black leaders for pushing Herenton's candidacy at any cost, thereby risking the continued loss of white students from the school system. "The search has been marked by hostility, secrecy and reckless charges that can only do harm to the schools and to the city." Accompanying the editorial was a drawing by cartoonist Bill Garner showing Maxine Smith standing in front of the school system's doors blocking Coats from entering.

A *Press-Scimitar* editorial on August 30 also took the school board to task for its handling of the entire matter: "The stakes are too high for the selection process to be reduced to a black vs. white power struggle which the selection process heretofore has given the appearance of being," the paper stated. "We doubt that any member of the board meant it to take that turn. But the private meeting of four white board members invited suspicion among black Memphians that it had. That's why open meetings are important to constructive conduct of the public's business. They dispel mistrust and build understanding of the basic issues involved. The issue is who's the best man—whether he's black or white—for the big job of improving, restoring confidence in, and rebuilding public support for public education in Memphis. That's more important than skin color."[19]

The startling developments threw the entire selection process into chaos. And the weekend retreat did little to calm board tensions. Coe acknowledged the anger in the black community over the naming of a white person over Herenton, but she candidly said the selection of Herenton would lead to a loss of support in the white community, including financial support. The statement further angered black board members. "If that is saying that if Dr. Herenton gets the slot the white community will withdraw its support from the Memphis City School system, if that is in fact the case, this community is in a much worse situation than I thought," Johnson said. "It says to me we are in sad straits."[20]

Some white board members, however, remained insistent that Coats should get the job. Mal Mauney, the most conservative member, accused blacks on the board and others in the community of bullying tactics to overturn the decision. "How long are we going to keep this Mickey Mouse game up?" he said. Nevertheless, on September 11, the board voted 7-0-2 to rescind the offer to Coats and postpone the selection of a superintendent until the group could agree on a new set of criteria for the job. William Ray Ingram and Mal Mauney opted not to cast votes.

The board's decision came after Coats had his secretary to send another message saying, without equivocation, that he was rejecting the offer. "I remain greatly honored to have been selected by the board majority," it read, "but concerned for Memphis in the lack of reasonable and responsible compromise on the part of the board as a whole. It is imperative that your next superintendent have support and cooperation from all members of the board of education."[21]

With that, Coats gracefully and emphatically bowed out of a place where he clearly was not wanted and where he could never be effective. But the situation left Herenton torn. He made no public statements during the crisis, but he was upset at how he was treated by white board members. Freeman agreed to stay on as superintendent until the end of the year, but the issue remained unsettled for weeks. During a later meeting, Coe again summed up the dilemma the board faced: "Blacks feel that because the system is 73 percent black, a qualified black should be the superintendent and that in rejecting the black deputy superintendent, we would be giving further proof to young blacks that a black cannot win a top position in our society.

"Whites feel that choosing the deputy over an outside white candidate who had received a majority vote would signal that the system will have an increasing black majority, that adequate funding from local political bodies will be even more difficult in the future and that needed improvements will not be made. There is also a growing feeling among whites that the system is being controlled by the NAACP and recent events have strengthen that feeling."[22]

Several weeks later, Coe announced that she was switching her vote to Herenton. Blackburn then followed suit and became the swing vote that gave Herenton the appointment. In announcing his change of heart in writing, Blackburn said, "Dr. Herenton has many desirable attributes. He is intelligent, listens well, and has patience, integrity and a desire to succeed, both for himself and the system as a whole. I sense that he will make us proud and will carry on the fine tradition of service and leadership. If we have learned one thing, it is the need to communicate in an environment of trust and openness. We have been through a great deal the last few months and matured as a group considerably."[23]

An angry Mal Mauney took issue with Blackburn's letter, saying, "Is maturity the willingness to give in to intimidation? To cave in to the bitter opposition and the inflammatory statements made by black board members and other so-called black leaders? To subvert the will of the majority of the board?"[24] Mauney's rant, however, proved to be nothing more than sour grapes. The real question was would the thirty-eight-year-old Herenton swallow his pride and accept the job? The answer came swiftly and emphatically. He would take it if offered. But the entire episode changed his perspective on race in Memphis. "I went through such humiliation," he recalled years later. "The racism on the part of some school board members was so blatant it was disgusting. I sat there and suffered and never for one minute did they discuss my qualifications."[25]

On December 6, 1978, more than three months after the debacle over the hiring of William Coats, the board voted 6-2 to name Herenton the first black city school superintendent in the system's history. Voting for Herenton were James Blackburn, George H. Brown Jr., Frances Coe, Carl Johnson, Maxine Smith, and Barbara Sonnenburg—three blacks and three whites. William Ray Ingram and Juanita Watkins voted for William Payne, and Mal Mauney declined to vote. "I refuse to lend my vote to this orchestrated farce," he said.

Mauney continued to insist that an outside person was needed. "Nothing has changed that except infantile actions, demonstrations, caving in and being intimidated," he said. "I think this is more nails in the coffin of public education in the city of Memphis."[26]

The following Sunday, December 10, the *Commercial Appeal* again addressed the controversy with a lengthy editorial praising Herenton: "He has demonstrated a concern for the schools that crosses racial lines with perhaps more insight and sensitivity than any of the other candidates showed.

There should be no confusion in the public's mind on this point. Herenton was a first-class candidate in his own right, no matter what other issues may have entered into the search or how the final choice was made."[27]

Where the newspaper failed, however, was in providing editorial leadership earlier that possibly could have helped ease the tensions roiling in the community. Whites in Memphis were still seething over court-ordered busing. With Herenton now in the top job, the white exodus to the private schools and to Shelby County schools continued, which helped reduce the white voting population inside the city limits.

Herenton, however, got high marks for his performance as superintendent, even though student scores on standardized tests either remained stagnant or went down. He broadened the district's optional school program as a way to retain white students. He was successful in creating a new teacher evaluation process because he involved teachers in developing the model. And Herenton would go anywhere and everywhere in the community to spread the message about the school system's goals and initiatives.

Doc was without question the most popular nonelected public official in Memphis. He was intelligent, forceful, and decisive. Plus, he was not reluctant to stand up to powerful white folks. In essence, Herenton was someone the black community could be proud of and respect, no matter what.

The superintendent pressed city and county elected officials to increase funding to the city schools and publicly chastised them when he thought they were failing in that effort. During one public spat in 1980, Herenton criticized the city council for not increasing its annual share of the school budget beyond $30 million. He called the council members irresponsible and said they were serving as puppets to Mayor Wyeth Chandler. Once he learned of the comment, Chandler was furious and insisted that Herenton publicly apologize, which the superintendent never did.[28]

Instead, Herenton continued to express disdain for politicians and the racism that was holding Memphis back. The more he spoke out, the more black Memphians loved it, and some started to propose out loud that Herenton run for mayor. He eventually addressed the issue by saying he was intrigued by the idea of seeking the mayor's office in the 1983 city election. "Memphis is a city that I love, and I would like to see this city thrive and become prosperous," he said. "I would like to think I could be a part of that. I don't intend to retire as a superintendent. I intend to move on to something else. I'm not ruling out a bid for elective office."[29]

The statement delighted many in the black community. But Mayor Wyeth Chandler's resignation in September 1982, which created a court-ordered mayoral election, ended—for the moment—thoughts Herenton had of seeking the office. But it did not curtail his outspokenness about the issues that plagued Memphis or the prospects that an African American would one day become mayor.

In a question-and-answer session with the *Commercial Appeal* in March 1984, Herenton was asked about the importance of a black mayor in the future. "I really think that the progress of this city to a great extent will be predicated on the community's ability to deal forthrightly with the question of race," he replied. "I don't know about many other Memphians, but I am tired of fighting the Civil War in Memphis. I'm growing weary of the residue from the civil rights movement. I'm growing weary of what I call the plantation-type attitude. And Memphis is an urban plantation.

"By and large, black Memphians have been excluded from the arenas of power, authority and wealth in this community. Memphis needs a face-lifting in the sense that we need to convince ourselves that we have the ability to move beyond the question of race when it comes to providing leadership, when it comes to making decisions about what's good for Memphis. I have been disenchanted with the quality, commitment and dedication of the vast majority of people who serve on political bodies in this city. Somehow or other we seem to attract people to political offices, elective and appointive, with the exception of a few, who do not reflect the best that we have to offer. . . . We seem to attract a lot of these people with ego needs that supersede their concern about Memphis."[30]

In another interview five years later, Herenton returned to the theme of racism and his dislike for self-serving politicians: "Memphis has resisted change in the sense of accepting the eventuality that blacks are going to be in the majority and that there should be greater participation on the part of blacks in the political and economic life. I just deeply believe that the biggest problem we have in this city is race, and there are many people who exploit this. . . . We have bigoted politicians in political offices, and we also have blacks in political offices who seek self-aggrandizement and do not serve their constituents fully."[31]

The talk of Herenton becoming mayor persisted throughout the black community even as he poured himself into the job of superintendent with all of its frustrations. And Herenton was getting plenty of notice beyond the Memphis city limits. Just days after Ned McWherter was elected governor in 1986, he asked Herenton to become the state commissioner of education. "I'm very interested in his him," McWherter told reporters. "He is a top quality man of proven ability who is recognized in the Memphis community, the state and the nation as a leader in education. I want him because I want Tennessee to have the best."[32]

Herenton was surprised and elated by McWherter's offer, but he turned it down because he was committed to staying in Memphis. A year later, the Atlanta Public Schools came calling with an offer for Herenton to become superintendent there. The offer caught Herenton at a vulnerable time, when he was convinced that Memphis would remained stagnant and unwilling to change. During a school board meeting on October 12, 1987, a tearful Herenton announced that he was resigning as superintendent to take the Atlanta job.

Mal Mauney, who had become board president, attempted to restrain his joy that Herenton—a person he never wanted as superintendent—would soon be gone: "I think the board has a mixture of feelings—one of congratulations and happiness for you that you have been selected to another system, a system like the Atlanta system. I think also that we feel a moment of sadness as well."[33]

The black community's response to the news was one of shock and profound sadness. Several white business leaders also were despondent over Herenton's resignation. For the next two days, everywhere he went, people asked him not to leave Memphis. They included school kids at his alma mater, Booker T. Washington High, and even a drunkard on the street. Corporate heads and ministers, including his own pastor, begged him to stay.[34]

Finally, three days after announcing his resignation, Herenton held a press conference at the Memphis Cook Convention Center to say he had changed his mind. His heart and soul was in Memphis and he intended to remain city school superintendent. A huge crowd of school employees and city residents who attended the press conference erupted with applause. Herenton was overcome by the elation. "I walk these streets, and a lot of people who are poor, who have no hope, no aspiration for their futures, they feel good by virtue of my achievement," he told the assembled crowd. "My thrust in going to Atlanta was out of a growing frustration about the lack of progress in Memphis, and that hasn't changed. But what has changed is my perception of my value to this community, and especially the role I serve as a black role model."[35]

His critics considered the comments overly boastful, but they were also completely accurate. With Harold Ford content to remain in Congress and his brother John firmly planted in the state senate, black Memphians viewed Herenton as the city leader they had spent decades longing for. And like George W. Lee nearly forty years earlier, they were not about to lose Herenton to Atlanta either. To many, Doc could do no wrong, even when his judgment calls were questionable.

He did his best to maintain a school administration that was free of mismanagement and abuse of the rules. When he learned that illegal practices were being used to recruit high school athletes at certain schools and keep them eligible, Herenton went public with the issue and vowed to end it. As a former athlete who was also an exceptional scholar, Herenton had little tolerance for allowing ball players to skirt transfer rules and then skate by in the classroom.

His efforts to reform the system and also lift academic performance across the board won him genuine praise, and again supporters urged him to run for mayor in 1987. But again, Doc said no. He preferred to remain with the school system, mostly because every recent mayoral election had exposed a lack of unity among black voters in rallying behind a consensus candidate. To win the mayor's office, Herenton knew he needed help from virtually every black politician in town, and he had few nice things to say about any of them.

"There is no unity or sense of direction among black politicians in Memphis," he told the *Tri-State Defender*. "I see black politicians with strong ego needs and the desire to fatten their own pockets and improve their personal status, while neglecting to serve our people." Herenton did not identify anyone in particular, but the comment was an obvious reference to the Ford organization.[36]

With Herenton and the Fords on the sidelines, Mayor Dick Hackett easily won reelection in 1987. Doc, however, continued to win friends and influence people from his perch running city schools. But in the spring of 1989, ten years into the job, Herenton faced his first and biggest crisis as superintendent. It came in the form of a circuit court lawsuit filed by fifth-grade teacher Mahnaz Bahrmand. The suit, filed on May 2, 1989, asked for $3 million in damages. It accused Herenton of initiating a two-year affair during which he promised Bahrmand job promotions and promised to marry her. Other salacious charges in the suit included the fact that during the affair, Bahrmand had two abortions and one miscarriage.

The explosive allegations were the talk of Memphis, and opinions naturally were split along racial lines. Many white Memphians believed the charges were proof that Herenton was using the school district as his own personal playground and was unfit to be superintendent. Almost all of black Memphis felt that this was just another attempt to destroy a credible and strong-willed black man. The fact that Bahrmand was Iranian and not a "sister" also factored into the black community's belief that Herenton was the real victim.

At a school board meeting on May 15, 1989, Herenton acknowledged having a personal relationship with Bahrmand. But he strongly denied that he promised to advance her career in exchange for sex or that he promised to marry her. The meeting room was packed with Herenton supporters who cheered wildly when the superintendent said he had no intentions of stepping down. "Come hell or high water, I am hanging in here," he told the board.[37] After the board meeting, he and his attorneys—A C Wharton and Richard Fields—held a brief press conference. Herenton then went to a rally on his behalf at New Salem Baptist Church in South Memphis, where several hundred supporters showered him with applause and cheered his every word. Lawsuit or no lawsuit, Doc was as strong as ever.

When Bahrmand's lawyers later dropped the suit only to refile it with different allegations, Herenton's supporters were convinced even more that the charges were baseless. White Memphians believed just the opposite. And the lawsuit gave Shelby County Commissioner Pete Sisson, long a critic of how Herenton was running city schools, the perfect avenue to try to remove him from the job. As chairman of the commission's education committee, Sisson felt it was his duty to look into the charges being leveled against Herenton. He also was acting as the self-appointed spokesman for all of Herenton's critics among white residents.

Sisson had been in local politics for more than twenty-five years and was a throwback to the days when blacks were virtually excluded from top government jobs—elected or appointed—in Memphis. He was first elected in 1963 to the old city commission in charge of public works. The position meant that Sisson oversaw the Sanitation Department, where almost all black city employees worked. Sisson was staunchly antiunion and refused to recognize Local 1733 of AFSCME, the union that represented black sanitation workers.

And while Sisson was no longer in office when the sanitation strike occurred in 1968, blacks blamed him for helping to create the horrible environment under which black garbage workers had to work. The fact that he was now attacking Herenton's character and honesty only served to bolster black solidarity around the superintendent.

Two weeks after Herenton admitted to having a personal relationship with Bahrmand, Sisson demanded that the school board replace Herenton because he could no longer be effective in the job. Sisson also launched a personal investigation into sexual harassment allegations against Herenton. "We're trying to teach these girls out there not to get pregnant, not to do certain things. And then we're out there doing it. That's not right."[38]

Black political leaders—including state lawmakers Lois DeBerry, Ulysses Jones, and Roscoe Dixon—took turns denouncing Sisson for trying to smear Herenton. They were among some twenty-six people who attended a June 5 school board meeting urging that the superintendent be left alone. "This community is upset," said James Smith, executive director of AFSCME, who threatened job action if Herenton was removed. "This community is concerned and Dr. Herenton means too much to us. All 7,000 members of AFSCME will be where we have to be if Dr. Herenton is not where he should be."[39] Even the *Commercial Appeal* chastised Sisson for leaping into the Herenton controversy "far ahead of the facts." The paper's editorial compared Sisson to a juror making a hangman's noose while the trial was still in progress.

The school board responded to the crisis by hiring an independent consultant to look into the school system's hiring and promotion practices. In mid-September, Bahrmand's lawsuit was dismissed after she and Herenton reached an out-of-court settlement, the details of which were not disclosed. For black Memphians, the matter was now closed. But not for Sisson or the school board.

Two weeks later, Sisson convened a group of reporters for a press conference and showed them grainy photographs supposedly of Herenton in the Los Angeles airport with Joyce Kelly, who had become principal of Corry Junior High School. Sisson said Herenton and Kelly were on their way to Hawaii together and the pictures helped prove that Herenton was trading promotions for sex. Sisson again demanded Herenton's resignation or his firing.

Herenton responded angrily, insisting that Kelly had gotten her promotion on merit alone. "We have bigots hiding behind elected office," he told the media. Neither he nor Kelly, however, would address their personal relationship which was an open secret in the community.

But the superintendent could not ignore the stinging consultant's report which said the school administration was in disarray and plagued by morale problems. The report urged the school board to look further into uncorroborated complaints of favoritism and mismanagement.

White board members knew the community would not stand for the removal of Herenton, who was now divorced, over personal issues. And despite the consultant's report, there was still no concrete proof that he was guilty of a fireable offense. Instead, board member Tom Stern proposed that an ombudsman be hired to oversee school operations independently of Herenton and report directly to the board. Another proposal was floated to hire three additional administrators to basically do the superintendent's job.

At a November 27 board meeting, three hundred people showed up, most of them Herenton supporters who complained that the board was trying to strip the superintendent of his authority and force him to resign. In the face of the angry crowd, Stern backed down and withdrew his proposals. The board then voted unanimously to simply create three committees made of board members to monitor the district's financial and personnel practices—something the board was supposed to do anyway.

Again, Mal Mauney walked away disgusted that the board had given in to intimidation and threats from what he called a "mindless mob" of black Memphians.[40] It was the most tumultuous year of Herenton's professional career, but he emerged from the controversy unscathed. The insults from Mauney served only to further convince blacks that racism alone was at the core of the attacks against their superintendent. The black community stood united and perhaps was finally ready to carry out its most ambitious undertaking ever—the election of a black mayor.

CHAPTER 15

THE PEOPLE'S CONVENTION

ICK HACKETT'S OVERWHELMING reelection victory in 1987—aided by nearly 20 percent of the black vote—had most people in Memphis, black and white, thinking that he was invincible. No successful mayoral candidate had gotten that much black support since William B. Ingram in 1963. Back then, black voters were merely searching for the best white candidate possible, someone who would pay at least some attention to the needs of the African American community. Now they wanted much more. And the numbers were about to tell them they could have it.

Results of the 1990 census showed that for the first time in Memphis's history, blacks were the majority population with 54 percent compared to 44 percent for whites. What's more, by late 1990, blacks accounted for 48.2 percent of registered voters in Memphis while whites made up 45.9 percent. And with a vigorous voter registration push, the percentage of potential black voters would go even higher.

The *Commercial Appeal* used the new voting numbers as basis for a series of articles on America's black mayors and the prospect that Memphis would have one before the decade of the 1990s was over. "Whoever that may be will celebrate on election night, and then wake up the next morning to face the double whammy familiar to many of the nation's pioneering black mayors," the paper said. "Not only do they have to manage vast social and economic problems, they must do so amid a climate of unwarranted fears and unreal expectations that usually follow their elections. How that Memphis mayor copes with the challenge—and how the city responds—will go far to define this city's future."[1]

An accompanying editorial concluded that despite the new census and voter registration numbers, Mayor Hackett was in a strong position to win reelection in 1991, "but four or eight years from now the situation is likely to be much different. It doesn't have to be divisive. To the contrary, the election and administration of a black mayor could be the most unifying thing that ever happened in Memphis—a living testimonial to the ideals of the man who died in Memphis for the sake of black and white cooperation, Dr. Martin Luther King Jr."[2]

Months before the series was published in the *Commercial Appeal,* a trio of black thirty-something political enthusiasts started meeting secretly at various coffee shops around town to talk about the need to find a consensus black candidate to run for mayor. The three were Shep Wilbun, Dedrick "Teddy" Withers, and Vernon E. Ash. Wilbun and Withers were buddies from childhood. Wilbun's father, S. A. Wilbun, had a law office in a building on Beale Street and Withers's father, Ernest Withers, had a photography studio in the same building.

Teddy wanted one more shot at the mayor's office after his poor showing in 1987, but he was willing to step aside if a stronger consensus candidate, particularly his boyhood friend, Shep, could emerge. Shep felt the same way about Teddy. Either way, both men knew the quest for a black mayor would never work unless there was one black candidate. They also knew the idea needed buy-in from the city's two most acclaimed black leaders—Harold Ford and Willie Herenton.[3]

Wilbun's motivation was fueled by living a year in Atlanta in the mid-1970s right after the mayoral election of Maynard Jackson. Wilbun witnessed firsthand the vibrancy that became readily apparent in Atlanta, and how Memphis had fallen far behind economically and socially. When he returned to Memphis, Wilbun was intent on building a successful career in real estate development, architecture, and city planning. He wanted to be "the black Henry Turley," a nod to arguably the most successful white real estate developer in the city.[4]

But politics was in Shep's blood. His father was the first African American circuit court judge in Shelby County, and many of his closest friends—including Withers and state representative Ulysses Jones Jr.—were political pros. In 1987, Wilbun signed on as campaign statistician for winning city council candidate Rickey Peete. But in 1989, Peete was forced to resign after his conviction in a bribery scandal. Shep's friends talked him into seeking the appointment as Peete's replacement.

Wilbun got the appointment with help from Mayor Hackett, Councilman Jack Sammons, and other white council members. The two remaining black councilmen, Kenneth Whalum and James Ford, voted against Wilbun. They supported Velma Lois Jones, who had finished second to Peete in the 1987 election. In 1990, Wilbun ran unopposed for the council seat in a special election.

Now, as his coffee-shop meetings with Withers and Ash continued and as the voter registration numbers started to swing in favor of African Americans, the Ivy League graduate began to think seriously about one day occupying the mayor's office. The trio kept their planning quiet, fearing that black politicians would undermine it and white politicians would destroy it.

Meanwhile, Willie Herenton also was keenly aware of the voting numbers and began to consider his next challenge. He was ready to leave the superintendent's office, and a run for mayor would bring out the fighter in him and make history in the process. There was just one problem. Herenton was a frequent critic of politicians, and vowed he would never become one. And yet he was about to pull off the shrewdest political move since the days of Boss Crump. It started on Monday, January 21, 1991, at Clayborn-Ball Temple AME Church on the outskirts of downtown Memphis. Herenton was the keynote speaker for an event marking the sixth national holiday celebration of Martin Luther King's birthday.

The superintendent was about ten minutes into his prepared speech when Harold Ford entered the sanctuary and quietly took a seat on a back row. But Herenton spotted him immediately and called for the congressman to come up front. Herenton then digressed from the speech and challenged Ford to take on the responsibility of holding a black summit meeting in Memphis to find a consensus black candidate to challenge Mayor Hackett: "Harold Ford, in my opinion, has been a great congressman, and Harold, I want to challenge you publicly, because you are very distinguished and I consider you to be the most powerful political leader in the black community. . . . I know he might have a problem with me putting him on the spot like this. But he has been our leader and I think he has the responsibility to bring us all together."

Minutes later, Ford stepped to the microphone. "I gladly accept that challenge from Dr. Herenton today. The time is here and the time is right now," he said as the crowd rose to its feet in thunderous applause. "And I want everybody to know, public officials and all, don't be misled about the newspapers and television stations and everybody talking about it's Harold Ford. It doesn't have to be a Ford. It can be a Chevrolet. It can be anybody, but we have to unite this community in October of 1991."[5]

The King event received scant coverage in the *Commercial Appeal*, which made no mention of Herenton's challenge to Ford. The *Tri-State Defender*, however, reported it in detail, and by the time the *Commercial Appeal* picked up the story days later, the buzz about a consensus black mayoral candidate was rippling through the black community.

With his challenge, Herenton put Ford in a political vise and the congressman had no choice but to say yes. Ford was savvy enough to know that, next to himself, Herenton had the biggest following among the black electorate in Memphis, and the congressman had to treat the challenge with more than lip service. He announced a series of meetings aimed at holding what he called a leadership summit. But Wilbun and his small group did not think the choice of a unity candidate should be left to a handful of black community leaders. Wilbun believed Ford's summit would include only Ford's people who would only select Ford's candidate. It was now time to make his private plans public.

On February 7, Wilbun called a press conference to announce a different proposal—a "People's Convention" in which all black registered voters in Memphis would be permitted to vote for a consensus mayoral nominee. Wilbun said his idea would eliminate the perception that the black candidate of choice was selected "behind closed doors in smoked-filled rooms. That process ought to be open. It ought to be public and we ought to be involved in it, especially since it is going to be the people who mobilize, galvanize and get energized to make this victory possible."[6]

Wilbun also went on black radio talk shows to tout his proposal. He said people who were not a registered voter could still attend the convention, register on site, and participate in the selection process. Under his plan, all potential mayoral candidates would be required to sign an agreement to abide by the decision made at the convention.

Both Herenton and Ford were lukewarm at best to Wilbun's proposal but were careful not to slam it outright. The attempt at black political unity in

Memphis was still in a fragile state, and neither of them wanted to be seen as perpetuating more political division among black Memphians. Ford told the media his leadership summit would be about more than just picking a mayoral candidate. It would also define the critical issues facing the black community over the next decade.

Mayor Hackett said nothing about either proposal. His political philosophy was to never talk publicly about what other potential opponents were doing. Instead, he left town to attend the funeral of entertainer Danny Thomas, founder of St. Jude Children's Research Hospital, in Beverly Hills. The *Commercial Appeal*'s editorial writers also offered no opinion on the budding controversy and were dubious that either event would ever take place. Privately, though, Hackett was perturbed that Wilbun, the man he helped to get a seat on the city council, was now plotting his defeat.

But others had plenty to say publicly. Pat Vander Schaaf, one of Wilbun's colleagues on the city council, and former council member Minerva Johnican blasted the People's Convention idea. Both of them had been mayoral candidates before and they called Wilbun's proposal self-serving and racially divisive. "I think the idea is sick and serves as an insult to blacks and whites," Vander Schaaf told the *Commercial Appeal*. "What do you think would happen if I called for a white conference or convention? You know what. I'd be burned alive."[7]

Others in the white community also harshly criticized both Wilbun's idea of a convention and Ford's plan for a summit, saying they were too polarizing at a time when blacks and whites were trying to bridge the racial divide that had always been a way of life in Memphis. Herenton, however, called the criticism paranoia. He said his initial call for a summit was intended to unite the community rather than divide it, and he had no intention at the time of being the consensus mayoral candidate. But Herenton cared little about what some in the white community thought, harkening back to their racially based opposition to his 1978 candidacy for superintendent.

Despite the criticism, the planning and strategizing continued, mostly by Wilbun, Withers, and Ash, along with others who favored his idea of a more inclusive People's Convention. The group expanded from the initial three to ten and then to twenty. It included political operative Del Gill, who set up the convention process, Alma Morris, head of the Kennedy Democratic Club, and Barbara Cooper, who later became a state representative. On March 3, about seventy-five people, including local Teamsters and leaders of the health-care employees union, met to officially proclaim that the convention would be held as soon as organizers could book a suitable location.

That same day, the *Commercial Appeal* published results of a random telephone survey of ninety-one black voters asking them to rank their preferences among seven potential mayoral challengers. Harold Ford was their first choice with twenty-two votes, followed by Benjamin Hooks with seventeen and Herenton with ten.[8] The survey results did nothing to deter Wilbun and his convention organizers. But they needed a big name to attract a sizable crowd. So they worked on coaxing Herenton into participating.

Eventually, Herenton started to see value in a broader People's Convention as Ford continued to hold small unity meetings but kept delaying plans for a leadership summit. Herenton also started to listen to the voices of those who were telling him he's the one to run for mayor. When reporters called, he chose his words carefully: "I am concerned that the convention be orderly, fair and open to a wide variety of people. Once there are some final plans, then Willie Herenton will decide whether to participate as a citizen or a candidate," Herenton told the *Commercial Appeal*.[9]

As talk of a black unity candidate gained steam, Otis Higgs, despite three mayoral defeats, went public with his desire to give it one more shot. "I believe my time has come. I have paid my dues in years of service to this community," he told a reporter.[10] At his home, Higgs kept a pillow on his sofa with the word "Mayor" written on it. He desperately wanted to be the candidate of choice, either through the convention or Ford's planned summit. He didn't care which one.

With Herenton on board, Withers and his co-planners rented the twelve-thousand-seat Mid-South Coliseum—despite efforts by Councilwoman Vander Schaaf to block the use of the arena—and set the convention date for Saturday, April 27. The group drew up detailed ground rules for the nomination process in which each nominee who attended would be given five minutes to address the crowd, which was expected to number about ten thousand. A candidate needed 70 percent of the vote to be declared the consensus winner.

During the event, six people were nominated—Willie Herenton, Otis Higgs, Shep Wilbun, Dr. Talib-Karim Muhammad, Isaac Richmond, and A. C. Wharton. Once the first-ballot votes were counted, Herenton was the clear choice. He says he got more than the 70 percent of the votes cast. According to Wilbun, Herenton got 67 percent and he got about 20 percent. But Wilbun conceded after the first ballot at the urging of talk radio host Rev. Bill Adkins, who convinced him he had no chance of overtaking Herenton in subsequent voting.

The convention's attendance, however, did not meet earlier expectations. But Wilbun was far from disappointed. He said the turnout was about three thousand, which he considered extraordinary given that there was heavy rain and thunder storms in Memphis that morning. The *Commercial Appeal* reported the attendance at about eighteen hundred and attributed that figure to Beth Wade, the coliseum's manager.

The dispute over attendance only added to the resentment that many black political leaders had of the *Commercial Appeal*. One of three resolutions approved by a voice vote of convention participants was a call for blacks to cancel their subscriptions to the newspaper. On April 30, the *Commercial Appeal* published an editorial sharply critical of the convention and its overall purpose. "One problem with the People's Convention may have been that it seemed to have an excessively narrow focus of race-based politics," the paper said. "The low turnout . . . may indicate that there's less black anger toward whites in Memphis than the convention's organizers thought—or perhaps hoped."[11]

For his part, Ford did not believe that the People's Convention had produced a consensus candidate, and he renewed his promise to find one. But Herenton grew tired of waiting and decided to make another strategic political move. On May 24, the superintendent announced that he would accept the convention's endorsement and enter the mayor's race. "We do not have the luxury of waiting anymore," Herenton said. "We have given Congressman Ford ample time . . . to be forthright with the summit. We are obligated to launch a campaign, with no disrespect for him."[12]

Exactly two weeks later, on June 7, Herenton officially stepped down as city schools superintendent, and later that day he filed his qualifying papers to run for mayor. Other black mayoral hopefuls, including Wilbun and Muhammad, deferred to the more electable Herenton. But not Higgs, whose only hope now was to court Harold Ford—the one person he never thought he would need in order to become mayor.

Herenton's announcement put pressure on Ford to put up or shut up. Ford was acutely aware of the now-former superintendent's popularity among black Memphians. But he also relished his role as the city's political kingpin, and the only person in town who could make the dream of electing a black mayor come true. Ford's pledge to hold a leadership summit finally resolved itself during a chance encounter with Rev. Ralph White at a Union Avenue video store.

White approached Ford inside the store and offered the congressman the use of his church, Bloomfield Baptist Church in South Parkway, as a venue for the summit. The men agreed to it on the spot, and the meeting was set for Saturday, June 15.[13] When Herenton got word of the plans, his campaign secured a personal invitation from White—and decided to pack the church with Herenton supporters.

On the morning of the summit, people with Herenton campaign signs filled the church sanctuary, covered the front grounds, and stretched down the street to the corner of South Parkway and Florida—directly in front of the N. J. Ford and Sons Funeral Home.

Harold Ford arrived at the church with Otis Higgs, a clear signal that the congressman intended to tap Higgs as his consensus candidate. But the support for Herenton was too overwhelming to ignore. It included several prominent black pastors, other black elected officials—including Julian Bolton, Lois DeBerry, Ulysses Jones Jr., and John Ford—and grassroots voters, virtually all of whom had been loyal supporters of the Ford organization for years.

Shelby County Election Commission chairman O. C. Pleasant also was there as a nonpartisan observer. He was seated in the section reserved for the choir behind the pulpit and had a clear view of a sea of red Herenton signs throughout the sanctuary. The meeting began with several preliminary speeches. One of them was given by Hattie Jackson, an ardent Ford supporter for years. She ended her remarks by saying, "We're going to support Dr. Herenton, aren't we congressman?"[14]

By now, Ford realized he had to alter his plans. He, Herenton, and Higgs then retreated up a stairway to Pastor White's private study to try to settle the issue once and for all. It was a final political showdown that Herenton now calls "the meeting in the Upper Room."[15] It lasted almost an hour, as Higgs forcefully argued that he had support in both the white and black communities and that Ford needed to endorse him. "I can win this thing," he said.

Herenton immediately shot back, "Otis, that's the very reason we can't let you run. You believe that white folks are going to vote for you. First of all, black folks are not in love with you. And the white folks you think are going to vote for you, ain't going to vote for you. You are a loser."

Herenton then turned to Ford. "Harold, that's the very reason we can't let him run." The room fell deathly silent for several seconds before Ford finally responded. "Otis, I think Doc is right. I've got to go with Doc." The Upper Room meeting was over and Higgs was livid. He stormed out shouting, "It ain't right. It ain't fair." As he left the room, Rev. Bill Adkins appeared in the doorway. "Harold, these people are restless," he said. "You've got to come out with a decision."[16]

Higgs left the church through a side door as Herenton and Congressman Ford walked back into the sanctuary together. Ford stood front and center and launched into fiery oratory criticizing the Hackett administration, the *Commercial Appeal*, and white political dominance in Memphis—which needed to end with the election of a black mayor. As the crowd hung on his every word, Ford then announced that Herenton was "the unanimous choice" as the consensus candidate. No votes were taken, but no one cared. The audience erupted in thunderous applause. And at that moment in the crowd's mind, Harold Ford and Willie Herenton became a political dream team—the two most powerful black political figures in Memphis and an unbeatable combination.

To assembled reporters, Ford said the summit "worked out like I said it would. There wasn't a vote because we didn't need a vote. The right candidate emerged and it was obvious."[17] Higgs, however, spent the rest of the weekend stewing over the turn of events. He felt betrayed and abandoned, but he was determined to remain in the race—a move that every other black elected official in Memphis called foolhardy. Doing so would only make Higgs a spoiler and the black community would never forgive him for it.

By Monday, Higgs had come to his senses. "I have decided to withdraw my candidacy for mayor," he said in a written statement to the press. "It is our assessment that my candidacy would create a division within the African-American community and substantially diminish the prospect of a true consensus victory."[18]

The withdrawal was a bitter pill for Higgs and ended a sixteen-year quest to become mayor. But in stepping aside in 1991, Higgs ingratiated himself to the black community even though he never officially endorsed Herenton's campaign. He accepted the fact that his legacy of public service would not be fulfilled at city hall but in the halls of justice. In 1998, countywide voters returned him to the criminal court bench, where he remained until his death in February 2013.

Few doubted that Higgs could have been a competent mayor. He was honest and sincere and likely would have won over white Memphians who repeatedly rejected him as a viable leader. In politics, however, timing is everything. And in 1991, with the numbers just barely on their side, black voters in Memphis were determined to make their stand—and they wanted to make it with Willie Herenton. The reality was, even with Herenton the fighter and newfound black unity, the odds against winning were still tremendous. It would take the equivalent of a miracle to pull it off. But the black community of Memphis was ready for one.

CHAPTER 16

THE ELECTION

O N NOVEMBER 26, 1990, nearly a year ahead of the next city election in Memphis, the *Commercial Appeal* published the results of a poll of 584 registered voters who were questioned about possible mayoral matchups in the 1991 election. The aim was to gauge how incumbent mayor Dick Hackett would fare against seven possible opponents. In each scenario, Hackett was the heavy favorite, particularly if the potential challenger was African American.

For example, the poll found that in a race between Hackett and Harold Ford, Hackett was favored 57 to 25 percent, with the rest undecided. Against Willie Herenton, Hackett was favored 61 to 23 percent; against Otis Higgs, the incumbent was favored 55 to 23 percent; and against A. C. Wharton, Hackett was favored 58 to 19 percent. The white mayor of Shelby County, Bill Morris, scored better than any potential challenger in the newspaper's poll, but Hackett still beat him 50 to 27 percent.[1]

Black political leaders looked at the poll results and called them laughable. With the city's changing racial demographics, there was no way that Hackett retained such a firm grip on the mayor's office. Most African Americans viewed the poll as yet another example of the *Commercial Appeal's* racial bias, particularly under its newest editor, Lionel Linder. A transplant from the *Detroit News*, Linder was named editor in March 1988 after a major shakeup in leadership at Memphis's only daily newspaper. Less than three years into the job, Linder was regarded by most black Memphians as probusiness, pro-Republican, and, if not anti-black, certainly indifferent to many minority concerns.

In 1989, President George H. W. Bush came to Memphis and gave the *Commercial Appeal* the first Point of Light Award from Bush's Thousand Points of Light Foundation, recognizing the newspaper for spotlighting volunteerism throughout Greater Memphis. The *Commercial Appeal* historically had a solid record of promoting education, community service, and agriculture throughout the mid-South. But when it came to politics, the paper left a lot to be desired in the black community, dating to the days of managing editor C. P. J. Mooney in the early twentieth century. It was only during the tenure of Michael Grehl, who served as editor from the mid-1970s to the mid-1980s, that the paper was viewed as supportive editorially of black political candidates.

As the pivotal 1991 mayoral election approached, black political leaders and their constituency were sure that they would find no allies on the *Commercial Appeal*'s editorial board—which meant they were distrustful of the paper's news coverage as well. Despite thorough and balanced political reporting—mostly by staff writers Charles Bernsen and Michael Kelley—black politicians, particularly Harold Ford, slammed the newspaper at every opportunity. Herenton, however, was singularly focused on winning. He officially kicked off his campaign on July 3 at the Peabody with black city council members Shep Wilbun and Kenneth Whalum at his side and a raucous audience of about one thousand supporters. "I want to make it emphatically clear that the time is not four years from now. The time is now," Herenton said.

The crowd was almost all black, but Herenton tried to reach out to white voters. "We're saying to white Memphis to join hands with black Memphis. I firmly believe we are on our way. City hall, city hall, city hall." Whalum, however, took a cheap shot at Mayor Hackett, making note of the fact that Herenton had earned a doctoral degree and Hackett never finished college. Whalum told the crowd that Hackett had ignored education, saying, "Even if he doesn't have any, it's still his responsibility." [2]

Hackett refused to respond publicly to the criticism. Instead, he took to the stage behind U.S. Education Secretary Lamar Alexander during a press conference announcing that Memphis was the first city in the nation to enroll in President George H. W. Bush's America 2000 education reform plan. [3]

Still, the early momentum was clearly with Herenton. His campaign kickoff at the Peabody also benefited from the simultaneous weeklong dedication of the $9.2 million National Civil Rights Museum at the Lorraine

Motel, where Martin Luther King Jr. was assassinated in 1968. Museum founder D'Army Bailey claimed the spotlight the entire week hosting nationally known civil rights leaders and celebrities at events that reminded black Memphians of the long and arduous struggle to attain equal rights and voting rights. The attendees included Rosa Parks, Coretta Scott King, Jesse Jackson, Joseph Lowery, and Julian Bond. The list of entertainers included singer Pete Seeger and actors Morgan Freeman, Blair Underwood, and native Memphian Cybil Shepherd.[4] The theme for the series of events was "A Celebration of Hope," which could have easily been Herenton's campaign theme as well.

Hackett remained mostly out of sight during the week of festivities, allowing Herenton's campaign to piggyback on to the museum dedication and its star-studded lineup of civil rights icons. But that was just the beginning of the troubles ahead for Hackett. The mayor had been anxiously awaiting a federal court decision on lawsuits challenging runoffs in city elections. The first suit was filed in 1988 by community activist Talib-Karim Muhammad, founder and director of the Islamic Center of Memphis. The complaint alleged that runoffs were discriminatory and deprived blacks of winning a citywide office.

A second suit containing similar allegations was filed by Rev. Leo LaSimba Gray and others. Finally, the Justice Department joined in with a companion suit in February 1991, claiming that at-large elections, runoffs, and the city's annexation policies discriminate against black Memphians. With Republican President Bush's Justice Department now a plaintiff in the dispute, city officials could no longer stonewall the case. Editorials in the *Commercial Appeal* urged city leaders to seek a settlement by compromising on the runoff issue. The paper took issue with the overall claim that runoffs discriminate against blacks. But the editorials suggested that instead of requiring candidates to win 50 percent or more of the vote, a lesser percentage could be used to avoid runoffs.

In a July 10 editorial, the paper said, "Runoffs were not adopted 'in order to prevent the possibility that black candidates would win election by plurality vote,' as the lawsuit claimed, but to help guard against the accidental election of candidates with a tiny percentage of the vote in a widely split race."[5]

However, the editorial ignored history. During the 1959 city elections, in which there were no runoff provisions, incoming mayor Henry Loeb tried to force white candidates to drop out of a city commission race to prevent the election of Russell Sugarmon Jr., the only black candidate in that race. Seven years later, in 1966, Memphis voters passed a referendum instituting runoffs. Had there been no runoff in the 1982 special election, Hackett would not have won. Instead, J. O. Patterson Jr. would have been elected the city's first black mayor.

After nine years in office, Hackett now was more than a little nervous about the prospect that runoffs would disappear from city elections. As the legal dispute dragged on, the Justice Department upped the ante by filing a motion in mid-July asking federal judge Jerome Turner to cancel all citywide elections scheduled for October 3. That included elections for mayor, city clerk, city court judge positions and at-large seats for the city council and Memphis school board. Hackett and all ten white city council members objected and asked the judge to allow the October elections to proceed under the current system.

Black political leaders, who welcomed the Justice Department's involvement in the federal case, nevertheless fretted that delaying the election would create a loss of momentum, which had been building for months in the black community for Herenton's campaign. Leo LaSimba Gray was among those expressing concern. "I am not in favor of perpetuating an illegal system, but I don't want to rain on the parade of the African-Americans," he said.[6]

Judge Turner set a hearing for July 26. Most Memphians thought he would only rule on whether to delay the election. But when the hearing concluded, Turner issued a bombshell decision. He banned runoffs in all citywide elections—obviously including the election of mayor. "Race has been the reason for the runoff provision," Turner said. "The evidence was almost overwhelming that the process was put on the ballot to make sure whites retain power to elect their candidates. It cannot be denied that blacks have been precluded because of racially polarized voting."[7]

Turner's stunning ruling angered most of white Memphis and was an election game changer. With eccentric candidate Prince Mongo Hodges also on the mayoral ballot, Hackett could no longer be content with merely coming in second—as he did in 1982—and forcing a runoff. He had to win the election outright. The emphasis immediately shifted to voter registration. Both Hackett and Herenton launched massive registration drives. Herenton was helped by the fact that the People's Convention in April included on-site voter registration at the Mid-South Coliseum.

At the registration deadline on September 3, Hackett's campaign turned in 25,000 registration forms. Many of them, however, were for people already registered. Once the final numbers were compiled, the total registration stood at 380,000, the highest ever. Black voters for the first time outnumbered whites by about 16,000.[8] But about 29,000 registrants listed their race as "other," and election commission officials believed most of them were white.

With one month remaining before election day, the campaign strategies became clear. Herenton repeatedly stressed the need for new and different leadership while Hackett emphasized his experience as an administrator and a prudent manager of the city's finances. Herenton spent practically every Sunday leading up to the election visiting black churches, attacking Hackett at every stop. He blamed the mayor when Sidney Shlenker, who was hired to develop the Pyramid, failed to get the financing to complete the arena and then filed for bankruptcy. Herenton also criticized Hackett for not seeking millions of dollars in federal block grant money for economic development initiatives in poor neighborhoods. And he blamed the incumbent for Holiday Inn moving its headquarters out of Memphis.

Herenton promised that, if elected, he would build more single-family housing in Memphis and add more police officers who would walk the streets in various neighborhoods. He also promised to create tax incentives for minority businesses and put more money into city schools—all issues that resonated with black voters.

Hackett repeatedly refused to respond to the attacks, and he rejected an invitation by the League of Women Voters to participate in a televised debate with Herenton. In fact, Hackett shunned campaign appearances before large crowds. Instead, he attended more than two hundred backyard receptions, virtually all of them at the homes of white supporters. At one such gathering, he reminded the audience that Herenton's entire campaign was racially motivated and the mayor would have no part of it. "I don't have any response to the summit candidate's comments," he said without mentioning Herenton by name.[9]

The mayor eventually realized, however, that he had to appeal more to black voters who had supported him in impressive numbers four years earlier. In his few appearances before black audiences, he touted the fact that he had appointed blacks to high-ranking city positions, including police director, city attorney, and chief administrative officer. His campaign co-chairman was George Jones, a black restaurant owner, and he had a close relationship with Louis H. Ford, the presiding bishop of the Church of God in Christ, which held its annual convocation in Memphis.

About a month before the election, Bishop Ford sent a highly publicized letter to local church leaders asking them to pray for Hackett's success because "I feel he will do what is best for the total city and the church." In addition, state representative Alvin King, the longest serving black legislator, sided with Hackett and accused Herenton of running a racist campaign. Herenton dismissed Hackett's black support, insisting it was coming from people with little or no standing with the majority of black voters. At one campaign stop, Herenton said blacks who were supporting Hackett reminded him of a plantation society where oppressed people sold their brothers out "for a few pieces of silver."

But it was another remark that landed Herenton in a bit of hot water. It came during a campaign speech at Mt. Olive CME Church. "Memphis is a mean-spirited city," he said. "A city that does not care about its poor people black or white. It's a city that puts more emphasis on downtown development and expanding East Memphis than on human beings."[10] After getting heated criticism, Herenton clarified the comment during an appearance at LeMoyne-Owen College: "The people of Memphis are great people. My reference to mean-spiritedness deals directly with the leadership. The leadership has failed to assume responsibility to look after all its citizens."[11]

Most black voters were not offended by Herenton's original comment, and his clarification did nothing to improve his standing with most white voters. Still, Herenton did what he could to attract white support by speaking at Kiwanis clubs, B'nai B'rith, and a few Republican organizations. But for the most part, whites stayed away from Herenton's events.

Hackett, meanwhile, picked up endorsements from two black political groups, the Shelby County Democratic Club and the Independent Political Action Council. At a campaign stop in predominantly black North Memphis two weeks before the election, the mayor said, "I don't believe in this divide-and-conquer approach to politics and I don't believe in the divide-and-conquer approach to administering city government. We feel like we have been a major factor in contributing to the unity of the community."[12]

Despite Hackett's late attempts to sway black voters, Herenton was brimming with confidence based on his voter registration drive. He also was determined to pull off the win without much help for Harold Ford. About a week before the election, however, Ford contacted Herenton's campaign manager, Charles Carpenter, and asked what he could do to help. Herenton initially rejected the overture. "I don't want Harold near us," he told Carpenter. "We've gotten it to this point. Harold has never been for us in this movement. He's a bandwagon guy."[13]

Carpenter, however, pressed Herenton to reconsider. Ford was a superior campaigner and master strategist, and Carpenter knew the campaign needed the congressman's help to bring out the vote on election day. Herenton reluctantly agreed, and the three of them met at the Spaghetti Warehouse downtown to discuss Ford's involvement. Herenton still only wanted Ford to bring national speakers to Memphis to appear at a series of rallies the week of the election. But Ford was genuinely eager to do more. The congressman knew that Herenton was different from all the other black mayoral candidates in the past. He had proven himself as a strong leader and had solid backing from virtually the entire black community. Ford also strongly believed Herenton could win, and he wanted to help make it happen.

On Sunday, September 29, four days before the election, the *Commercial Appeal* published a lengthy editorial endorsing Hackett for reelection. The newspaper said the most important issues facing Memphis were economic development, planning, bringing people together, and effective communication: "If voters measure the candidates by these criteria, we believe they should return Mayor Dick Hackett to office. The challenger, Willie Herenton, has not shown that he would be the leader that Memphis needs at this time."[14]

The paper added that Hackett "has a record of steady, sober accomplishment which has been marked at times by surprising imagination and initiative. He has made a historical change in the racial makeup of city government and he has provided pathways for future black leaders."[15]

Throughout his political career, Hackett had a seesaw relationship with the *Commercial Appeal*'s editorial board. But the mayor found an ally in new editor Lionel Linder, who took over the paper after Hackett's 1987 reelection. The endorsement, along with Hackett's own voter registration drive, stoked the belief that the incumbent would again be the victor. On October 1, two days before the election, a confident Hackett agreed to appear with Herenton in a forty-five-minute televised forum before the Memphis Rotary

Club. The forum attracted some seven hundred people, including other candidates and elected officials. Harold Ford was there, and he seized the opportunity to tell the television audience that he was strongly committed to Herenton.[16]

The event marked the only joint appearance by the candidates and it helped Herenton far more than Hackett. It allowed Herenton to show a predominantly white audience that he had the smarts and the temperament to be mayor, and that he was not the radical, angry black man that many white Memphians feared.

Also that day, Herenton campaigned with Ford and Jesse Jackson at the Dixie Homes public housing project and at an evening really before about twenty-five hundred supporters at Mississippi Boulevard Christian Church. The next day, election eve, Jackson and Herenton campaigned together at several stops, including LeMoyne-Owen College and the Cathedral of Bountiful Blessings Church. Jackson's two-day visit overshadowed Hackett's appearances before much smaller audiences.

Hackett, however, took solace in an article about the mayor's race in the *New York Times* on October 2 in which the paper implied that Herenton's campaign would stumble because it was viewed as antiwhite. The *Times* also noted the racial division that prevented Memphis from joining other cities with sizable black populations—Atlanta, Birmingham, Detroit, Chicago, and Cleveland—in electing black mayors.[17]

Herenton was undeterred. On election day, he and Ford were up and out on the streets early. Ford's well-honed organization was fully mobilized to get voters to polls in every black community in the city. Herenton would say later that Ford worked "like a Trojan horse" to get people to the polls.[18] Hackett's team worked hard as well, mostly to ensure that every white vote available was cast. Ford and his accountants, Frank Banks and Osbie Howard, had already determined that the margin would be razor thin and the race would likely hinge on absentee voting.

Once the polls closed, tenseness gripped the city. Hackett gathered with his supporters at his campaign headquarters in the Poplar Plaza shopping center, while Ford, Herenton, and his supporters practically filled the lobby and meeting rooms at the Peabody downtown. As the evening wore on, the streets around the hotel became jammed with people. Vehicles were double and triple parked along Union Avenue, Second Street, and Third Street.

As the votes were counted, the lead fluctuated between Hackett and Herenton. Once all the precincts reported their results, Herenton held a lead of thirty-six hundred votes. But the eighty-six hundred absentee votes had not been included in the totals, which was unusual because absentee ballots were normally tabulated first. Ford and his political team knew that the majority of absentee votes would go to Hackett—and that is where the election would be decided.

Throughout the early evening, Ford made repeated phone calls to O. C. Pleasant, chairman of the election commission, asking about results from absentee ballots, and repeatedly Pleasant told him the numbers were not tabulated. Tired of the incessant calls, Pleasant invited Ford to come to the commission's office.

The congressman and several others immediately left the Peabody and rushed several blocks up the street to the election commission. Pleasant was giving an interview to television reporters as Ford came through the door. "O. C., what the hell is going on?" Ford asked. The TV cameras instantly shifted from Pleasant and on to Ford, who had a look of indignation.[19] The confrontation did not rankle Pleasant, who was used to election night haranguing from candidates or their supporters over vote totals. He had been a member of the Shelby County Election Commission since 1979 and its chairman since 1985.

As a black teenager, Pleasant had walked the streets of his native of Montgomery, Alabama, rather than use public transportation during the Montgomery bus boycott in 1955 and 1956. The experience gave him a strong sense of racial justice and fairness—qualities he took with him to the commission job.

Pleasant calmly explained to Ford and the assembled media that the delay in counting the absentee ballots was caused by a contaminated computer disc that contained the tallies. Specifically, a commission employee had mistakenly put the absentee votes on a computer disc with other unrelated material. Once the problem was discovered, technicians had to painstakingly transfer the absentee ballots onto a new disc so it could be loaded into the main computer—a process that required about three hours to complete.

The explanation did not placate Ford, who followed Pleasant into his office demanding to see the actual absentee ballots. Pleasant refused and told the congressman he would have to get a court order to see the ballots. Ford then placed calls to a couple of judges in an unsuccessful effort to get an immediate restraining order to invalidate the election results. He also called U.S. Attorney Ed Bryant asking for an immediate federal investigation of the vote count. Bryant, in turn, called Pleasant, who assured the federal prosecutor that the election commission had the problem under control and that the votes were being counted fairly. "That's basically all I wanted to know," said Bryant, who promptly hung up.[20]

Pleasant was convinced that Ford never really wanted Herenton or any other black candidate to win the mayor's seat. The congressman had told him weeks earlier that the only reason he was actively supporting Herenton was because of heavy pressure in the black community—mostly by black preachers. In Pleasant's mind, Ford's only intent that night was to overturn the election.[21]

As tempers continued to rise, Ford and others with him strongly implied that commission officials were trying to steal the election from Herenton. At one point, someone in Ford's entourage shouted at Pleasant, calling him an "Uncle Tom." Unfazed, Pleasant watched as the transfer of absentee votes to a new disc continued. Everyone in the building knew that the final count would be close. Finally, Pleasant was able to project the election outcome based on projections from the absentee vote, the election day votes that had already been counted, and the total number of votes cast from seven boxes that came in late.

Four of those late boxes were from predominantly black precincts, two were from predominantly white precincts, and one was from a racially mixed precinct. Pleasant made the correct assumption that black voters had voted for Herenton and most white voters had cast their ballot for Hackett. Once he finished putting pen to paper, Pleasant looked up and made the historic announcement. "We've got a new mayor tonight."[22]

Other election commissioners and campaign operatives who heard the proclamation scurried to nearby phones to report the stunning news. Minutes later, when the computer tally was complete, it showed that Hackett indeed had won the absentee vote, but the margin was not enough to overcome the election day numbers for Herenton. The unofficial total gave Herenton 122,285 votes, Hackett 122,113 votes, and Prince Mongo Hodges 2,921 votes. Herenton was declared the winner by a scant margin of 172 votes.

The result was greeted at the Peabody with jubilation. In the excitement, Herenton's mother fainted just as Herenton was about to make his victory speech. Someone reported to him that she had suffered a heart attack, but immediately another person told Herenton that his mother was fine.[23] After checking on her, Herenton addressed the standing-room-only crowd as the mayor-elect of Memphis. "This victory tonight represents a new beginning for Memphis," he said. "A new beginning that will move this city toward unprecedented unity and prosperity for all of our city. I want to say this to all of the white citizens of Memphis that I pledge to be the mayor of all the people."[24]

Across town at Hackett's headquarters, the cheers and laughter that had filled the room earlier in the evening, were replaced by tears and stunned expressions. "Isn't that something, electing a man like that," Bill Boyd, Hackett's campaign coordinator, said in disgust. "Memphis will not be portrayed well to the nation." Another Hackett supporter, Willis Ayers, seventy-three, who had spent the day driving voters to the polls, refused to believe the final numbers. "If Herenton wins, there will be an exodus from Memphis," he said. "So for the good of the city, Hackett better win."[25] Some in the room blamed Hodges and his twenty-nine hundred voters for allowing Herenton to squeak to victory. Others put the blame on the ruling by Judge Jerome Turner banning a runoff.

Regardless, Herenton had accomplished the impossible. He collected 98 percent of the black vote and about 10 percent of the white vote in pulling the upset. In addition, three more African Americans—Janet Hooks, Myron Lowery, and Jerome Rubin—were elected to the city council, bringing the total number of black council members to six, the highest ever. The election also created a historic change on the city's board of education. Black candidates TaJuan Stout Mitchell and Sara Lewis won seats, joining Maxine Smith, Carl Johnson, and Hubon Sandridge to become the first majority black school board.

As stunned white Memphians tried to come to grips with the outcome, Herenton again offered assurances that they had nothing to fear: "I think the citizens of Memphis are sensible people. I think they will give me an opportunity to demonstrate what leadership I can bring to this city. We are going to grow together, we are going to live together and we're going to prosper."[26]

A group of white pastors—including Rev. Adrian Rogers at Bellevue Baptist Church, Dr. Maxie Dunnam of Christ United Methodist Church, Rev. Jimmy Latimer at Central Church, and Bishop Daniel Buechlein of the Catholic Diocese of Memphis—also tried to ease concerns among whites. They purchased a quarter-page ad in a Sunday edition of the *Commercial Appeal* calling for unity and support for Mayor-elect Herenton.[27]

The election commission met on Monday, October 14, and certified the final results, which reduced Herenton's margin by 30 votes but still gave him the win by 142 votes. It was the closest mayoral election in Memphis since Boss Crump's first victory by 79 votes in 1909. The final tally was Herenton, 122,596, Hackett, 122,454. Three hours after the election commission finished its work, Hackett announced that he would not contest the results or ask for a recount. More than twenty advisors had urged the mayor to contest the results, but Hackett issued a brief statement to the press saying a challenge "would not be appropriate despite irregularities in the vote."[28]

It was a magnanimous gesture. But Hackett also knew that a legal challenge would have exposed the fact that about five thousand or more votes were cast for him by people who were ineligible. Those voters had long ago moved out of Memphis to suburban cities in eastern Shelby County and across the state line in Mississippi—but still took part in the city election to help Hackett win. Hackett's illegal votes far outnumbered any that Herenton received.[29]

The *Commercial Appeal* also graciously accepted the outcome with an editorial saying, "Herenton has the opportunity to become one of the great mayors of Memphis and a prominent figure in metropolitan government."[30]

Black Memphians reveled in the election outcome—at churches, barber and beauty shops, grocery stores, malls, playgrounds, and schools—right up to and beyond Herenton's swearing-in on January 1, 1992. Memphis had finally joined other major cities—including Detroit, Chicago, Cleveland, Washington, D.C., Los Angeles, and Atlanta—that had already elected black mayors.

A long-awaited sense of euphoria and pride replaced generations of dejection and despair among African Americans in Memphis. What had been unthinkable before, during, and after the reign of Boss E. H. Crump had now become a reality. An African American duly elected by the people would be running the city of Memphis. And in the black community, at least, there was finally political unity, which was expressed best by L. LaSimba Gray on that historic election night, October 3, 1991.

"Brothers and sisters, it's healing time," he told the festive crowd at the Peabody. "A city that was once divided will now be brought together."[31]

2009
1902
107 yrs
of mphs
political
history

EPILOGUE

MY MEMPHIS

T HE IMPROBABLE ELECTION of Dr. Willie W. Herenton as mayor was a crowning achievement—particularly for African Americans in Memphis. It ended decades of political frustration in which black residents desperately sought to have a voice in local government—only to be told repeatedly no or to wait. Of course, Herenton's victory was not a cure-all for race relations and other city ills. Crime continued to plague Memphis, public schools continued to lose ground academically, and whites continued to flee by the thousands. In those respects, what occurred in Memphis was no different from other major cities after electing their first African American mayor.

Herenton, however, became the most popular mayor since Boss Crump. He was reelected easily in 1995, 1999, 2003, and 2007 before voluntarily leaving office in 2009. Thus, he became the longest serving mayor in the history of Memphis. Along the way, though, Herenton made political enemies—black and white—who tried to get him out of office, sometimes by devious means. Mike Fleming, a former sports writer for the *Commercial Appeal* who later became a conservative radio talk show host, was one of Herenton's chief critics. Fleming, who died in 2016, is credited with creating the nickname "King Willie" to describe Herenton's heavy-handed political grip on Memphis.

But the fact remains that Herenton, who grew up in poverty-stricken south Memphis, rightfully earned his place in the annals of Memphis politics alongside Edward H. "Boss" Crump, who grew up in post–Civil War

Mississippi and moved to Memphis alone and practically penniless as a teenager. The two of them are, in my view, the most significant political figures in Memphis history, and this book represents my attempt to capture their respective rise to political dominance thanks to enduring loyalty and trust, mostly from black Memphians.

Neither man was perfect by any means. Crump was stubborn, overly defensive, and vindictive. He insisted that everything be done his way or not at all, and he made no attempts to ensure that his political machine would survive after his death. But Crump was the first white political leader in Memphis who believed that black citizens at least deserved to be heard by local government.

Make no mistake, Crump was a staunch segregationist and felt that blacks could not be put into positions of authority over whites. But he and his hand-picked candidates repeatedly earned the votes of black citizens because he was willing to listen to their concerns and provide public amenities, such as parks, schools, and playgrounds, exclusively for them.

With Crump in charge, black Memphians, particularly those of financial means, believed they had a voice—albeit small—in the operation of government. And over time, that voice grew louder and more influential. It is why Memphis became a destination point for blacks escaping the oppression of plantation life in Mississippi, Arkansas, and Tennessee.

Like Crump, Herenton has his own streak of stubbornness, and as mayor, he routinely bristled at criticism. He also squandered opportunities to forge coalitions with suburban political leaders in Shelby County that would have benefited Memphis. But much of the intense and long-lasting criticism of Herenton by white suburbanites was rooted in racism. For all of his faults, Herenton was a strong mayor—he once famously said, "there isn't a punk bone in my body"—who believed in Memphis and its residents.

Herenton also had a soft spot in his heart for young, wayward African American children, because in them he saw himself. Once during a visit to the detention area at Shelby County Juvenile Court, Herenton started to cry as he talked to a black teenager who was locked up for a senseless petty crime. Those feelings are what propelled Herenton—in his 70s at that time—to return to education after leaving the mayor's office by opening several charter schools.

Between Crump's death in 1954 and Herenton's election in 1991, Memphis struggled mightily to define itself. As the black population grew, whites abandoned the city and the city schools. The tax base suffered and race relations grew more strained. Politicians, black and white, added to the strain with uncompromising rhetoric and regressive public policies.

My goal in writing this book was not to further divide the city that I love, but to help Memphians understand themselves and to learn the lessons of history. In my research and the numerous interviews I conducted, I developed a deeper appreciation for Memphis and its rich cultural diversity—Beale Street on a Saturday night, Bellevue Baptist Church on a Sunday morning, a Memphis Grizzlies crowd on game night, and Graceland mansion in mid-August.

After most interviews or a full day of research, I often retreated to one of my favorite places in the entire city—Audubon Park—to think through what I had just learned and how it fit into my narrative. Despite the bustling, big-city traffic along Park or Goodlett avenues, Audubon Park, located in the heart of the city, is a place of serenity. People of all races go there to walk, jog, play golf, picnic, or to take a short breather from life itself just sitting in their vehicles or under a shaded tree. Racial segregation that was once enforced there and virtually every other public place in Memphis is now a distant memory.

As this book hopefully explains, Memphis has persevered through race riots, lynch mobs, sit-ins, municipal strikes, a history-altering assassination, and other assorted uprisings and racial strife. Through it all, Memphis still retains its southern charm as a welcoming and soulful city on the banks of the Mississippi River.

There is no longer an appetite to return to the days of machine politics as practiced by Boss Crump and Harold Ford. Yet interest in politics and the election process is at an all-time low. Voter turnout for local elections seldom rise above 35 percent. And after Herenton left the mayor's office in 2009, voter interest dipped to unprecedented lows as A. C. Wharton, who is also African-American, was elected mayor in a special election in 2009 and reelected in 2011.

By 2015, however, voters had grown tired of Wharton, and replaced him with Memphis city councilman Jim Strickland, who became the first white candidate elected mayor since Dick Hackett's reelection in 1987. Strickland also made history by receiving more of a percentage of the black vote than any winning white mayoral candidate since William Ingram in 1963. That tells me that African Americans in Memphis, after more than a century, have finally made their point. They no longer feel compelled in citywide elections to vote strictly along racial lines to ensure that their voices are heard. They started making that point in 2006 when black voters overwhelmingly supported Steve Cohen, who is Jewish, for the congressional seat once held by Harold Ford, followed by his son, Harold Ford Jr.

But despite Memphis's political evolution, the Bluff City continues to suffer from the same nagging problems of poverty, violent crime, and racial strife. And yet, I still believe in the potential greatness of Memphis. This city's history has shown quite clearly that we can rise above despair and division. All we need are the main ingredients of strong, decisive, credible, and forward-thinking leadership along with an engaged and united citizenry.

The unmistakable fact, however, is that race changed Memphis politics. The ongoing mission now is for Memphis to evolve still further—for the better.

NOTES

Chapter 1

1. *Commercial Appeal*, Oct. 17, 1954.
2. Ibid., Oct. 19, 1952.
3. Ibid.
4. Ibid., Oct. 17, 1954.
5. Ask Vance Lauderdale column, *Memphis Magazine*, Sept. 2009.
6. Ibid.
7. *Commercial Appeal*, Oct. 17, 1954.
8. William D. Miller, *Mr. Crump of Memphis* (Baton Rouge: Louisiana State Univ. Press, 1964), 15.
9. *Commercial Appeal*, Oct. 18, 1954.
10. Miller, *Mr. Crump of Memphis*, 19.
11. *Commercial Appeal*, Oct. 18, 1954.
12. Ibid., Jan. 23, 1902.
13. Ibid.
14. Ibid., Oct. 18, 1954.
15. House Select Committee on the Memphis Riots, 39th Cong., 1st sess., *Memphis Riots and Massacres*, July 25, 1866 (Washington, D.C.: Government Printing Office, 1866), 5.
16. Ibid.
17. Ibid.
18. Ibid.
19. Bureau of the Census, data on population growth of African Americans in major cities, 1910–40.

20. Elizabeth Gritter, *River of Hope: Black Politics and the Memphis Freedom Movement, 1865–1954* (Lexington: Univ. Press of Kentucky, 2014), 18.

21. Ibid.

22. David M. Tucker, *Memphis Since Crump: Bossism, Blacks and Civic Reformers, 1948–1968* (Knoxville: Univ. of Tennessee Press, 1980), 16.

Chapter 2

1. Miller, *Mr. Crump of Memphis*, 58.

2. G. Wayne Dowdy, *Crusades for Freedom: Memphis and the Political Transformation of the American South* (Jackson: Univ. Press of Mississippi, 2010), 4.

3. *Memphis News-Scimitar*, Nov. 3, 1909, and *Commercial Appeal*, Nov. 3, 1909.

4. Miller, *Mr. Crump of Memphis*, 74.

5. *Commercial Appeal*, Oct. 17, 1954.

6. Miller, *Mr. Crump of Memphis*, 76.

7. *Commercial Appeal*, Jan. 12, 1910.

8. Miller, *Mr. Crump of Memphis*, 79.

9. Ibid., 81.

10. From various accounts in Miller's *Mr. Crump of Memphis* and contemporary newspaper articles.

11. *St. Louis Post-Dispatch*, July 3, 1938.

12. *Commercial Appeal*, Apr. 20, 1910.

13. Ibid., Feb. 14, 1911.

14. E. H. Crump letter, Feb. 22, 1911, Edward H. Crump Papers, Benjamin L. Hooks Central Library, Memphis (hereafter cited as Crump Papers).

15. *Commercial Appeal*, July 12, 1914.

16. Tucker, *Memphis Since Crump*, 7–8.

17. Ibid., 9.

18. Ibid.

19. Ibid.

20. Tucker, *Memphis Since Crump*, 19.

21. *St. Louis Post-Dispatch*, July 3, 1938.

22. G. Wayne Dowdy, *Mayor Crump Don't Like It: Machine Politics in Memphis* (Jackson: Univ. Press of Mississippi, 2006), 21.

23. *Commercial Appeal*, Aug. 5, 1914.

24. *Memphis News-Scimitar*, Aug. 5, 1914.

25. *Commercial Appeal*, Aug. 8, 1914.

26. Ibid.

27. Dowdy, *Mayor Crump Don't Like It*, 23.

28. Ibid., 24.

29. *Commercial Appeal*, Feb. 23, 1916.

30. Miller, *Mr. Crump of Memphis*, 104.
31. *Commercial Appeal*, Oct. 18, 1954.
32. Ibid., Oct. 15, 1974.
33. Blair T. Hunt to Walter Chandler, Nov. 4, 1940, Walter Chandler Papers, Benjamin L. Hooks Central Library, Memphis (hereafter cited as Chandler Papers).
34. Arthur T. Womack to Walter Chandler, Nov. 7, 1940, Chandler Papers.
35. Blair T. Hunt to Walter Chandler, July 17, 1940, Chandler Papers.
36. *Memphis Press-Scimitar*, Feb. 4, 1956.
37. Walter Chandler to E. H. Crump, Dec. 7, 1940, Chandler Papers.
38. Miller, *Mr. Crump of Memphis*, 205.
39. Tucker, *Memphis Since Crump*, 19–20.
40. *Commercial Appeal*, July 9, 2004.
41. Miller, *Mr. Crump of Memphis*, 196.
42. Dowdy, *Crusades for Freedom*, 23.
43. Gritter, *River of Hope*, 38.
44. Tucker, *Memphis Since Crump*, 57.

Chapter 3

1. *Memphis Press-Scimitar*, Oct. 16, 1954.
2. *Commercial Appeal*, Oct. 16, 1954.
3. *Memphis Press-Scimitar*, Oct. 16, 1954, Extra edition, Ned McWherter Library, University of Memphis.
4. Ibid.
5. Ibid.
6. Jackson Baker, in person and telephone interview with the author, May 2014.
7. *Commercial Appeal*, Oct. 17, 1954.
8. *Memphis Press-Scimitar*, Oct. 18, 1954.
9. Miller, *Mr. Crump of Memphis*, 52.
10. *Commercial Appeal*, Aug. 5, 1914.
11. Ibid., Aug. 6, 1914.
12. Ibid., Aug. 5, 1914.
13. Ibid., Aug. 7, 1914.
14. Ibid., Nov. 23, 1926.
15. *Columbia Daily Spectator*, May 15, 1923, Columbia Spectator Archive, http://spectatorarchive.library.columbia.edu.
16. *Commercial Appeal*, Nov. 23, 1926.
17. Ibid., Nov. 24, 1926.
18. Ibid., Nov. 25, 1926.

19. Edward J. Meeman, *The Editorial We: A Posthumous Autobiography*, compiled, edited, and with an introduction and afterword by Edwin Howard (Memphis: Memphis State Univ. Printing Services, 1976), 55.

20. Ibid., 62.

21. *Evening Appeal*, June 30, 1930.

22. *Memphis Press-Scimitar*, Nov. 10, 1930, and *Commercial Appeal*, Nov. 10, 1930.

23. Meeman, *Editorial We*, 81.

24. Ibid.

25. *Memphis Press-Scimitar*, 1932.

26. Meeman, *Editorial We*, 87.

27. E. H. Crump to Edward Meeman, Dec. 10, 1943, Crump Papers.

28. Tucker, *Memphis Since Crump*, 36–37.

29. Ibid.

30. Ibid.

31. Dowdy, *Mayor Crump Don't Like It*, 90.

32. Ibid.

33. Ibid., 91.

34. Ibid., 99.

35. Ibid., 100.

36. *Commercial Appeal*, Oct. 24, 1939.

37. *Memphis Press-Scimitar*, Oct. 23, 1939.

38. *Commercial Appeal*, Oct. 24 1939.

39. Ibid., Nov. 9, 1939.

40. Ibid., Nov. 10, 1939.

41. *Commercial Appeal*, Dec. 17, 1939.

42. *Memphis Press-Scimitar*, Dec. 18, 1939.

43. W. J. Michael Cody, interviews with author, Feb. 2014.

44. From an article by Greg Tucker, president of the Rutherford County Tennessee Historical Society, published in the *Daily News Journal* of Murfreesboro, Tennessee, May 1, 2011; a similar account is in James Summerville, *The Carmack-Cooper Shooting: Tennessee Politics Turns Violent, November 9, 1908* (Jefferson, N.C.: McFarland, 1994).

45. Cody interviews.

46. Ibid.

47. Various stories in Tennessee newspapers, fall of 1948.

Chapter 4

1. *Commercial Appeal*, Oct. 26, 1950.

2. *Commercial Appeal*, Sept. 12, 1955.

3. Ibid., Mar. 2, 1953.

4. *Memphis Press-Scimitar*, Sept. 12, 1955.

5. *Commercial Appeal*, Sept. 12, 1955.

6. Dowdy, *Crusades for Freedom*, 37–38.

7. Ibid.

8. Ibid.

9. Ibid., 41.

10. Ibid., 42.

11. *Memphis Press-Scimitar*, Sept. 12, 1955.

12. *Commercial Appeal*, Sept. 12, 1955.

13. Ibid., Sept. 13, 1955.

14. Ibid., Nov. 10, 1955.

15. Dowdy, *Crusades for Freedom*.

16. Ibid.

17. Ibid.

18. Ibid.

19. *Commercial Appeal*, Nov. 30, 1955.

20. Ibid.

21. Ibid.

22. *Memphis Press-Scimitar*, Nov. 30, 1955.

23. *Commercial Appeal*, Nov. 30, 1955.

24. Ibid.

25. Ibid.

26. Ibid., June 19, 1952.

27. Excerpts from a nine-point program proposed in June 1952 to Memphis city leaders by the Bluff City and Shelby County Council of Civic Clubs; *Commercial Appeal*, June 19, 1952.

28. *Commercial Appeal*, June 20, 1952.

29. Ibid., Dec. 6, 1955.

30. Ibid., Feb. 8, 1956.

31. Ibid., Feb. 10, 1956.

32. *Memphis Press-Scimitar*, Feb. 14, 1956.

33. Ibid., Feb. 15, 1956.

34. Ibid.

35. *Commercial Appeal*, Feb. 15, 1956.

36. *Memphis Press-Scimitar*, Feb. 15, 1956.

Chapter 5

1. James L. Dickerson, *Dixie's Dirty Secret: How the Government, The Media and the Mob Reshaped the Modern Republican Party into the Image of the Old Confederacy* (Jackson: Sartoris Literary Group) 1998, 2016.

2. Ibid, 11.

3. Ibid, 10

4. *Commercial Appeal,* Feb. 8, 1956.

5. Tucker, *Memphis Since Crump,* 84.

6. Ibid., 85.

7. *Commercial Appeal,* Feb. 24, 1956.

8. Ibid.

9. Various newspaper accounts of the Mississippi legislature's action in February 1956.

10. Tucker, *Memphis Since Crump,* 86.

11. *Commercial Appeal,* May 23, 1940.

12. Ibid., Apr. 25, 1948.

13. *Memphis Press-Scimitar,* June 25, 1957.

14. Carroll Reece to George W. Lee, George W. Lee Papers, Benjamin L. Hooks Central Library, Memphis.

15. Ibid.

16. Ibid.

17. George W. Lee to E. H. Crump, July 9, 1941, Crump Papers.

18. *Memphis Press-Scimitar,* June 27, 1941.

19. *Commercial Appeal,* Oct. 15, 1974.

20. Dowdy, *Crusades for Freedom,* 56.

21. Ibid., 58.

22. *Commercial Appeal,* Apr. 3, 1957.

23. Ibid.

24. *Memphis Press-Scimitar,* Apr. 20, 1957.

25. Ibid.

26. *Commercial Appeal,* Apr. 3, 1958.

27. *Memphis Press-Scimitar,* Aug. 8, 1958.

28. Tucker, *Memphis Since Crump,* 88.

29. Ibid., 120.

30. Laurie B. Green, *Battling the Plantation Mentality: Memphis and the Black Freedom Struggle* (Raleigh: Univ. of North Carolina Press, 2007), 254; Tucker, *Memphis Since Crump,* 133.

31. *Memphis Press-Scimitar,* July 14, 1959.

32. *Tri-State Defender,* July 25, 1959.

33. Ibid., Aug. 1, 1959.

34. Russell Sugarmon, interview with author, Mar. 11, 2015.

35. Ibid., June 27, 1959.

36. *Commercial Appeal,* Aug. 2, 1959.

37. Ibid.

38. Ibid.

39. Ibid., Aug. 17, 1959.

40. *Tri-State Defender*, Aug. 15, 1959.

41. *Commercial Appeal*, Aug. 21, 1959.

42. Ibid., Aug. 22, 1959.

Chapter 6

1. Fred Davis, interview with author, May 17, 2016.

2. Green, *Battling the Plantation Mentality*, 233.

3. Ibid.

4. Written press release from City Commissioner Claude Armour, *Commercial Appeal*, Mar. 19, 1960.

5. Ibid.

6. Green, *Battling the Plantation Mentality*, 233.

7. *Commercial Appeal*, Mar. 21, 1960.

8. Green, *Battling the Plantation Mentality*, 239.

9. *Commercial Appeal*, Mar. 22, 1960.

10. Ibid.

11. Ibid., Mar. 23, 1960.

12. *Memphis Press-Scimitar*, Mar. 22, 1960.

13. Green, *Battling the Plantation Mentality*, 239.

14. *Commercial Appeal*, Aug. 2, 1961.

15. Ibid.

16. *Memphis Press-Scimitar*, Aug. 4, 1961.

17. *Commercial Appeal*, Oct. 4, 1961.

18. *Memphis Press-Scimitar*, Nov. 8, 1963.

19. *Commercial Appeal*, Feb. 27, 1979.

20. Ibid., July 4, 1964.

21. Ibid., July 7, 1964.

22. Lewis R. Donelson III, *Lewie* (Memphis: Rhodes College, 2012), 162.

23. Ibid., 162.

24. Ibid., 169.

25. *Commercial Appeal*, July 11, 1964.

26. *New York Times*, July 14, 1964.

27. *Commercial Appeal*, July 14, 1964.

28. Judge Harry W. Wellford (retired), interview with the author, Mar. 13, 2015.

29. *Commercial Appeal*, July 8, 1964.

30. Ibid., Nov. 5, 1964.

31. Ibid., Nov. 8, 1964.

32. Ibid.

33. Ibid.
34. Ibid.
35. Ibid., Nov. 7, 1964.
36. Ibid., Nov. 9, 1964.
37. Donelson, *Lewie*, 167.

Chapter 7

1. *Commercial Appeal*, Nov. 6, 1966.
2. Leaflet, Program for Progress File, Benjamin L. Hooks Central Library, Memphis.
3. Document, Program for Progress File, Benjamin L. Hooks Central Library, Memphis.
4. *Commercial Appeal*, Nov. 9, 1966.
5. *Memphis Press-Scimitar*, Nov. 9, 1966.
6. Papers on the Program for Progress file, Benjamin L. Hooks Central Library, Memphis.
7. *Commercial Appeal*, July 18, 1967.
8. *Commercial Appeal*, July 30, 1961.
9. Ibid.
10. Ibid.
11. Ibid.
12. Flyer, A. W. Willis Jr. Collection, Memphis and Shelby County Room, Benjamin L. Hooks Central Library, Memphis.
13. *Memphis Press-Scimitar* and *Commercial Appeal*, Oct. 4, 1967.
14. *Jet Magazine*, Sept. 28, 1967.
15. *New York Times*, Sept. 29, 1967.
16. Ibid.
17. *Memphis Press-Scimitar*, Oct. 2 1967.
18. *Commercial Appeal*, Oct. 1, 1967.
19. Miriam DeCosta Willis, interviews with author, Mar. 2015.
20. *Commercial Appeal*, Oct. 7, 1967.
21. *Memphis Press-Scimitar*, Nov. 1, 1967.
22. *Commercial Appeal*, Nov. 1, 1967.
23. Ibid., Nov. 3, 1967.

Chapter 8

1. Tucker, *Memphis Since Crump*, 153.
2. *Commercial Appeal*, Feb 12, 1968, and *Memphis Press-Scimitar*, Feb. 12, 1968.

3. *Commercial Appeal*, Feb. 14, 1968.

4. Ibid.

5. Ibid., Feb. 15, 1968.

6. Tucker, *Memphis Since Crump*, 158.

7. *Memphis Press-Scimitar*, Feb. 23, 1968.

8. *Commercial Appeal*, Feb. 23, 1968.

9. *Tri-State Defender*, Mar. 1, 1968.

10. *Memphis Press-Scimitar*, Feb. 24, 1968.

11. *Commercial Appeal*, Mar. 15, 1968.

12. National Advisory Commission on Civil Disorders (Kerner Commission), *Report of the National Advisory Commission on Civil Disorders* (Kerner Report) (Washington, D.C.: Government Printing Office, February 29, 1968), Benjamin L. Hooks Central Library, Memphis.

13. *Commercial Appeal*, Mar. 15, 1968.

14. From various print and broadcast accounts of Martin Luther King Jr.'s appearance in Memphis on March 18, 1968.

15. *New York Times*, Mar. 29, 1968.

16. *Commercial Appeal*, Mar. 30, 1968.

17. W. J. Michael Cody, interviews with the author, Feb. 2014, and Cody's written account, "King at the Mountaintop: The Representation of Dr. Martin Luther King, Jr., Memphis, April 3–4, 1968," W. J. Michael Cody papers, University of Memphis.

18. Excerpt from King's "Mountaintop" speech, recorded at Mason Temple, Apr. 3, 1968.

19. From a report by the Associated Press published on the front page of the *Commercial Appeal*, Apr. 6, 1968.

20. *Commercial Appeal*, Apr. 10, 1968.

21. Ibid., Apr. 8, 1968.

22. Speech by John T. Fisher at the Memphis Rotary Club, reported by the *Commercial Appeal*, Apr. 10, 1968.

23. *Commercial Appeal*, Apr. 9, 1968.

24. Ibid., May 1, 1968.

25. J. Edwin Stanfield, *In Memphis: More than a Garbage Strike* (Atlanta: Southern Regional Council, Mar. 22, 1968).

Chapter 9

1. *Commercial Appeal*, Aug. 27, 1958.

2. Henry Loeb on WHBQ-TV's public affairs show *Press Conference*; *Commercial Appeal*, Jan. 29, 1962.

3. Robert M. McRae Jr., *Oral History of the Desegregation of Memphis City Schools, 1954–1974* (Memphis: Univ. of Memphis Oral History Research Office, 1997); *Commercial Appeal*, Jan. 2, 1998.

4. *Memphis Press-Scimitar*, Sept. 6, 1958.

5. Bobby Lovett, *The Civil Rights Movement in Tennessee: A Narrative History* (Knoxville: Univ. of Tennessee Press, 2005), 188.

6. *Chicago Tribune*, Apr. 6, 1961.

7. *Memphis Press-Scimitar*, Mar. 23, 1962.

8. From various sources, including Kira Virginia Duke, "To Disturb the People as Little as Possible: The Desegregation of Memphis City Schools" (master's thesis, Univ. of Tennessee, Knoxville, 2005), 24.

9. Ibid.

10. *Commercial Appeal*, Dec. 11, 1971.

11. Ibid.

12. Ibid., Nov. 18, 1971.

13. *Memphis Press-Scimitar*, June 7, 1971.

14. Ibid., Apr. 25, 1972.

15. Ibid., May 17, 1972.

16. *Commercial Appeal*, Nov. 28, 1972.

17. Based on the author's interviews with Judge McRae in 1983 for an article published in the *Commercial Appeal*'s Sunday *Mid-South Magazine*, Apr. 8, 1984.

18. Ronald P. Formisano, *Boston Against Busing: Race, Class and Ethnicity in the 1960s and 1970s* (Raleigh: Univ. of North Carolina Press, 1991), 20.

19. Ibid., 1.

20. Ibid.

21. Bureau of the Census, census figures for Memphis, 1960, 1970, and 1980.

22. *Commercial Appeal*, Jan. 2, 1998.

23. McRae, *Oral History*.

24. *Commercial Appeal*, Jan. 2, 1998.

Chapter 10

1. *Commercial Appeal*, Nov. 7, 1974.

2. *Commercial Appeal*, July 1, 1990.

3. *Jet Magazine*, Aug. 29, 1968.

4. *Commercial Appeal*, Oct. 9, 1971.

5. *Commercial Appeal*, Nov. 5, 1971.

6. *Memphis Press-Scimitar*, Feb. 7, 1973, and the *Commercial Appeal*, Feb. 7, 1973.

7. Ibid.

8. *Memphis Press-Scimitar*, Feb. 14, 1973.

9. Cody interviews.

10. Ibid.

11. *Commercial Appeal*, Aug. 2, 1974.

12. *Memphis Press-Scimitar*, Aug. 2, 1974.

13. *Memphis Press-Scimitar*, Oct. 31, 1974.

14. Willis interviews.

15. *Commercial Appeal*, Nov. 18, 1974.

16. Cody interviews.

17. *Commercial Appeal*, Nov. 6, 1974.

18. Ibid.

19. Ibid.

20. Ibid.

21. Ibid., Nov. 7, 1974.

22. Ibid.

23. Ibid., Jan. 1, 1975.

Chapter 11

1. Henry Evans, interview with the author, June 15, 2015.

2. *Commercial Appeal*, Mar. 10, 1975.

3. Evans interview.

4. E. Winslow "Buddy" Chapman, interview with the author, June 11, 2015; *Commercial Appeal*, Nov. 12, 2004.

5. *Memphis Press-Scimitar*, Sept. 30, 1975.

6. *Commercial Appeal*, Oct. 16, 1975.

7. Chapman interview.

8. Ibid.

9. Ibid.

10. *Commercial Appeal*, Dec. 15, 1976.

11. Ibid., Sept. 14, 1976.

12. Ibid., Dec. 24, 1976.

13. Chapman interview.

14. *Commercial Appeal*, Oct. 9, 1976.

15. Ibid.

16. Ibid., Dec. 20, 1976.

17. Ibid., Jan. 25, 1978.

18. Ibid.

19. Ibid., Feb. 2, 1981.

20. *Memphis Press-Scimitar*, Feb. 3, 1981.

21. *Commercial Appeal*, June 29, 1978.

22. *Commercial Appeal*, July 2, 1978.

23. Ibid., July 3, 1978.

24. Ibid.

25. Ibid., July 4, 1978.

26. *Memphis Press-Scimitar*, July 29, 1978, and *Commercial Appeal*, July 29, 1978.

27. *Commercial Appeal*, Aug. 11, 1978.

28. Ibid.

29. Ibid., Aug., 13, 1978.

30. Evans interview.

31. Ibid.

32. *Commercial Appeal*, Sept. 30, 1979.

33. *Memphis Press-Scimitar*, Oct. 13, 1979.

34. *Commercial Appeal*, Nov. 11, 1979.

35. Television ads for Chandler for Mayor campaign, 1979.

36. Richard Hackett, interview with author, June 18, 2015.

37. *Commercial Appeal*, Nov. 15, 1979, and *Memphis Press-Scimitar*, Nov. 15, 1979.

38. *Commercial Appeal*, Nov. 17, 1979.

39. Ibid.

40. Evans interview.

Chapter 12

1. Art Gilliam's column, *Commercial Appeal*, Nov. 18, 1974.

2. Opening statement of defense attorney James F. "Tim" Schaeffer during the trial of Lee Edward Branch, U.S. District Court in Memphis, 1979.

3. *Commercial Appeal*, May 3, 1978, and *Memphis Press-Scimitar*, May 3, 1978.

4. *Commercial Appeal*, May 9, 1978.

5. *Tri-State Defender*, May 13, 1978.

6. *Commercial Appeal*, May 10, 1978.

7. Ibid.

8. *Tri-State Defender*, May 13, 1978.

9. Ibid.

10. *Commercial Appeal*, June 1, 1978.

11. Ibid.

12. Ibid.

13. *Memphis Press-Scimitar*, June 9, 1978.

14. *Memphis Press-Scimitar*, Oct. 3, 1979.

15. Cody interviews.

16. Ibid.

17. *Commercial Appeal*, Mar. 28, 1980.
18. Ibid.
19. Ibid., Jan. 15, 1981.
20. Julian Bolton, interview with author, June 17, 2015.
21. Ibid.
22. *Tri-State Defender*, Aug. 3, 1982.
23. Bolton interview.
24. *Commercial Appeal*, Sept. 1, 1981.
25. Hackett interview, June 18, 2015.
26. *Commercial Appeal*, Sept. 29, 1982.
27. Ibid., Oct. 2, 1982.
28. Ibid., Oct. 7, 1982.
29. Ibid.
30. *Commercial Appeal*, Oct. 9, 1982.
31. Ibid.
32. Ibid.
33. Ibid., Oct. 12, 1982.
34. Ibid., Oct. 27, 1982.
35. Cody interviews.
36. Hackett interview, June 18, 2015.
37. Ibid.
38. Flyer in the possession of W. J. Michael Cody, Feb. 2014.
39. *Commercial Appeal*, Nov. 28, 1982.
40. Richard Hackett, interview with the author, Mar. 29, 2016.
41. Hackett interview, June 18, 2015.

Chapter 13

1. Hackett interview, June 18, 2015.
2. Ibid.
3. United Press International, *New York Times*, Jan. 14, 1983.
4. Ibid.
5. *Commercial Appeal*, Jan. 14, 1983, and *New York Times*, Jan. 14, 1983.
6. *New Orleans Times-Picayune*, Nov. 7, 2010; *New York Times*, July 9, 1981.
7. City of Memphis antinudity ordinance, enacted by the city council, Mar. 29, 1983.
8. *Commercial Appeal*, Mar. 30, 1983.
9. Ibid., May 28, 1983.
10. Ibid., Apr. 3, 1983.
11. Ibid., Aug. 2, 1983.

12. Ibid., Oct. 5, 1983.
13. Ibid., Oct. 8, 1983.
14. Ibid., Oct. 7, 1983.
15. Ibid.
16. Hackett interview, June 18, 2015.
17. Ibid.
18. *Commercial Appeal*, Sept. 25, 1987.
19. Ibid., Sept. 26, 1987.
20. Richard Hackett, interview with the author, Aug. 12, 2015.
21. *Commercial Appeal*, June 5, 1988.
22. Hackett interview, Aug. 12, 2015.
23. *Commercial Appeal*, Sept. 29, 1987.
24. Ibid., Sept. 30, 1987.

Chapter 14

1. Willie W. Herenton, interview with the author, Dec. 23, 2014.
2. Ibid.
3. *Memphis Press-Scimitar*, Sept. 11, 1975.
4. *Commercial Appeal*, Aug. 16, 1978.
5. Ibid.
6. Ibid., Aug. 30, 1978.
7. Herenton interview.
8. *Commercial Appeal*, Aug. 22, 1978.
9. Ibid.
10. Ibid.
11. Ibid.
12. Ibid., Aug. 23, 1978.
13. Ibid., Aug. 24, 1978.
14. *Memphis Press-Scimitar*, Aug. 23, 1978.
15. *Commercial Appeal*, Aug. 26, 1978.
16. George H. Brown, interview with the author, July 2015.
17. *Commercial Appeal*, Aug. 29, 1978, and *Memphis Press-Scimitar*, Aug. 29, 1978.
18. Ibid.
19. *Memphis Press-Scimitar*, Aug. 30, 1978.
20. *Commercial Appeal*, Sept. 3, 1978.
21. Ibid., Sept. 11, 1978.
22. Ibid.
23. James Blackburn to Memphis City Schools Board of Education, *Commercial Appeal*, Dec. 5, 1978.

24. *Commercial Appeal*, Dec. 5, 1978.
25. Herenton interview.
26. *Commercial Appeal*, Dec. 7, 1978.
27. *Commercial Appeal*, Dec. 10, 1978.
28. *Memphis Press-Scimitar*, June 17, 1980.
29. Ibid., Aug. 5, 1981.
30. *Commercial Appeal*, Mar. 22, 1984.
31. Ibid., Oct. 15, 1989.
32. Ibid., Nov., 10, 1986.
33. Ibid., Oct. 13, 1987.
34. Herenton interview.
35. *Commercial Appeal*, Oct. 16, 1987.
36. *Tri-State Defender*, Dec. 20, 1986.
37. *Commercial Appeal*, May 16, 1989.
38. Ibid., May 31, 1989.
39. Ibid., June 6, 1989.
40. Ibid., Nov. 29, 1989.

Chapter 15

1. *Commercial Appeal*, Jan. 20, 1991.
2. Ibid., Jan. 22, 1991.
3. Shep Wilbun, interview with the author, Aug. 6, 2015.
4. Ibid.
5. *Tri-State Defender*, Jan. 25, 1991; Herenton interview.
6. *Commercial Appeal*, Feb. 8, 1991; Wilbun interview.
7. *Commercial Appeal*, Feb. 10, 1991.
8. Ibid., Mar. 3, 1991.
9. Ibid., Mar. 6, 1991.
10. Ibid., Feb. 13, 1991.
11. Ibid., Apr. 30, 1991.
12. Ibid., May 25, 1991.
13. Rev. Ralph White, interviews with the author, July 2015.
14. O. C. Pleasant, interview with the author, Aug. 6, 2015.
15. Herenton interview.
16. Ibid.
17. *Commercial Appeal*, June 16, 1991.
18. *Commercial Appeal*, June 18, 1991.

Chapter 16

1. *Commercial Appeal*, Nov. 26, 1990.
2. Ibid., July 4, 1991.
3. Ibid., July 24, 1997.
4. Ibid.
5. Ibid., July 10, 1991.
6. Ibid., July 26, 1991.
7. From Judge Jerome Turner's ruling, *United States v. City of Memphis*, July 26, 1991; *Commercial Appeal*, July 27, 1991.
8. *Commercial Appeal*, Sept. 4, 1991.
9. *Commercial Appeal*, Sept. 7, 1991.
10. Ibid., July 29, 1991.
11. Ibid., Sept., 19, 1991.
12. Ibid., Sept. 21, 1991.
13. Herenton interview.
14. *Commercial Appeal*, Sept. 29, 1991.
15. Ibid.
16. Ibid., Oct. 2, 1991.
17. *New York Times*, Oct. 2, 1991.
18. Herenton interview.
19. Pleasant interview.
20. Ibid.
21. Ibid.
22. Ibid.
23. Herenton interview.
24. *Commercial Appeal*, Oct. 4, 1991; Herenton interview.
25. *Commercial Appeal*, Oct. 4, 1991.
26. Ibid., Oct. 5, 1991.
27. Ibid., Oct. 11 and 13, 1991.
28. Ibid., Oct. 15, 1991.
29. Hackett interview, June 18, 2015.
30. *Commercial Appeal*, Oct. 6, 1991.
31. Ibid., Oct. 5, 1991.

Bibliography

Books

Dickerson, James L. *Dixie's Dirty Secret: How the Government, the Media, and the Mob Reshaped the Modern Republican Party into the Image of the Old Confederacy*. Jackson, MS: Sartoris Literary Group, 1998, 2016.

Donelson, Lewis R, III. *Lewie*. Memphis: Rhodes College, 2012.

Dowdy, Wayne G. *A Brief History of Memphis*. Charleston, S.C.: History Press, 2011.

———. *Crusades for Freedom: Memphis and the Political Transformation of the American South*. Jackson: Univ. Press of Mississippi, 2010.

———. *Mayor Crump Don't Like It: Machine Politics in Memphis*. Jackson: Univ. Press of Mississippi, 2006.

Eaton, Susan E. *The Other Boston Busing Story: What's Won and Lost across the Boundary Line*. Princeton, N.J.: Yale Univ. Press, 2001.

Formisano, Ronald P. *Boston Against Busing: Race Class and Ethnicity in the 1960s and 1970s*. Raleigh: Univ. of North Carolina Press, 1991.

Green, Laurie B. *Battling the Plantation Mentality: Memphis and the Black Freedom Struggle*. Raleigh: Univ. of North Carolina Press, 2007.

Gritter, Elizabeth. *River of Hope: Black Politics and the Memphis Freedom Movement, 1865–1954*. Lexington: Univ. Press of Kentucky, 2014.

Lovett, Bobby. *The Civil Rights Movement in Tennessee: A Narrative History*. Knoxville: Univ. of Tennessee Press, 2005.

McRae, Robert M., Jr. *Oral History of the Desegregation of Memphis City Schools, 1954–1974*. Memphis: Univ. of Memphis Oral History Research Office, 1997.

Meeman, Edward J. *The Editorial We: A Posthumous Autobiography*. Compiled, edited, and with an introduction and afterword by Edwin Howard. Memphis: Memphis State Univ. Printing Services, 1976.

Miller, William D. *Mr. Crump of Memphis.* Baton Rouge: Louisiana State Univ. Press, 1964.

Pohlmann, Marcus D. *Opportunity Lost: Race and Poverty in the Memphis City Schools.* Knoxville: Univ. of Tennessee Press, 2009.

Tucker, David M. *Memphis Since Crump: Bossism, Blacks and Civic Reformers, 1948–1968.* Knoxville: Univ. of Tennessee Press, 1980.

Court Cases

Deborah A. Northcross et al. v. The Board of Education of the Memphis City Schools et. al. 341 F. Supp. 583 (W.D. Tenn. 1972). U.S. district court ruling.

Tolbert v. City of Memphis. 568 F. Supp. 1285 (W.D. Tenn. 1983). U.S. district court ruling granting an injunction against enforcement of a city antinudity ordinance.

Government Documents

City of Memphis. Performances, Lewd and Indecent Acts and Conduct. Code of Ordinances, City of Memphis, Tennessee (1983). Antinudity ordinance passed the City of Memphis on March 20, 1983.

National Advisory Commission on Civil Disorders. *Report of the National Advisory Commission on Civil Disorders.* Washington, D.C.: Government Printing Office, February 29, 1968. Benjamin L. Hooks Central Library, Memphis.

U.S. Bureau of the Census. Data on the population of Memphis, 1910–90.

U.S. Congress. House Select Committee on the Memphis Riots. *Memphis Riots and Massacres.* Washington, D.C.: Government Printing Office, July 25, 1866.

Personal Interviews

Bailey, Walter. July 2015

Baker, Jackson. July 2014.

Bolton, Julian. June 17, 2015.

Brown, George W. July 2015.

Chapman, E. Winslow "Buddy." June 11, 2015.

Cody, W. J. Michael. Feb. 2014.

Evans, Henry. June 15, 2015.

Hackett, Richard. June 18, 2015, Aug. 12, 2015, and Mar. 29, 2016.

Herenton, Dr. Willie W. Dec. 23, 2014.

Pleasant, O. C. Aug. 6, 2015.

Sugarmon, Russell B. Mar. 11, 2005.
Wellford, Judge Harry W. (retired). Mar. 13, 2005.
White, Ralph. July 2015.
Wilbun, Shep. Aug. 6, 2015.
Willis, Miriam DeCosta. Mar. 2015.

Newspapers and Periodicals

Chattanooga Times
Chicago Tribune
The Economist
Jackson Clarion-Ledger
Jackson Daily News
Jet Magazine
Memphis Commercial Appeal
Memphis Evening Appeal
Memphis Magazine
Memphis News-Scimitar
Memphis Press
Memphis Press-Scimitar
Nashville Banner
New York Times
St. Louis Post-Dispatch
The Tennessean
Tri-State Defender

Personal Papers

Chandler, Walter. Papers. Benjamin L. Hooks Central Library, Memphis.
Cody, W. J. Michael personal papers., University of Memphis.
Crump, Edward H. Papers. Benjamin L. Hooks Central Library, Memphis.
Lee, George W. Papers. Benjamin L. Hooks Central Library, Memphis.
Willis, A. W. Collection. Memphis and Shelby County Room. Benjamin L. Hooks
    Central Library, Memphis.

Index

Index